LAUREL and HARDY
The British Tours

Part 2 — 1951-1954

The Last Stage

by

"A.J" Marriot

Marriot Publishing

LAUREL and HARDY – The British Tours
Part 2 — 1952-54

ISBN 978-0-9521308-9-5
First Edition published November 1993
This Revised Second Edition November 2019
Marriot Publishing
Ciudad Quesada, Alicante, Spain
Text Copyright © by "A.J" Marriot 2019
Printed by "LULU"

Written, compiled and designed by "A.J" Marriot. Layout by "A.J" Marriot
COVER DESIGN by "A.J" Marriot
Cover artwork by Paul Wood (TT Litho, Rochester, Kent. ME1 1NN. – www.ttlitho.co.uk)

All rights reserved

"A.J" Marriot is hereby identified as author of this work in accordance with Section 77 of the Copyright, Designs and Patent Act 1988

o-o-0-o-o

This book is sold subject to the condition that it shall not, by way of trade or otherwise, be lent, resold, hired out or otherwise circulated without the publisher's prior consent in any form of binding cover other than that in which it is published and without a similar condition – this condition being imposed on the subsequent purchaser.

o-o-0-o-o

FOREWORD (2019 Edition)

STEVE COOGAN – (Stan Laurel in — "*Stan & Ollie*")

The pressure to play the man who is your comedy hero, and to do him justice, can be totally overwhelming, so I was lucky to have A.J Marriot's book to hand. "*The British Tours*" was a very special resource, and it offered an essential insight into Stans partnership with Oliver Hardy; their dedication to their craft; and the personal significance - especially for Stan - of touring the UK.

A.J Marriot analyses Stans sketches beautifully, and reveals the perfectionism that drove his work. The book also contains rare behind-the-scenes photographs and personal testimonies that capture the joyous spirit of these tours for the audiences who had the chance to see their legends spring to life, as well as for Stan and Ollie themselves."

Steve Coogan

-----0-----

GEOFF POPE – (Screenplay writer — "*Stan & Ollie*")

When I had the idea of writing a screenplay about my comedy heroes, Laurel & Hardy, I took inspiration from this wonderful compendium of the Boys' British tours.

A.J. Marriot, a lifelong fan, and comedian of some repute himself, has assiduously, meticulously and skilfully gathered together every priceless scrap of information about those British jaunts that Stan & Ollie so enjoyed. Starting with the triumphal procession of their first British tour in the thirties, when they were at the peak of their fame, through to the last, poignant tours of the fifties, when Laurel and Hardy were struggling with the physical demands of the constant travelling and performing.

'A.J' provides us with a glimpse into the lives of the men behind those inimitable movie characters. He goes under the Bowlers to show them as they were, all their struggles and frustrations off stage, and their brilliance once the curtain lifted.

He put together this record of their tours because he felt that what had happened should be recorded for posterity. For this we should all be eternally grateful.

Jeff Pope

-----0-----

PREFACE (from 1993)

In the mid- to late-eighties, when my good friend Roy Sims – expert on Laurel and Hardy memorabilia – started to turn up ephemera which showed the two comedians to have made stage appearances in Britain, I began to ask questions which neither he nor any other Laurel and Hardy scholars could answer. Turning to the authoritative biographical works on the comedy duo, I was further frustrated by their lack of coverage on these tours.

Determined to seek out exactly when and where Laurel and Hardy had played their theatre engagements, I began to do research. The deeper I went, the bigger the mystery became. Why had Laurel and Hardy's tours not been documented by their biographers? Why didnt people want to talk about the tours? Was something being hidden? Had Laurel and Hardy wanted to forget about the tours?

Bit by bit, I began to piece together their movements here in Britain and over in Ireland, and contacted several acts who had worked with them. A handful were helpful in the extreme, but the majority of enquiries were disappointing: a few didnt wish to help; some were able to remember nothing; and others related only nonsense.

Four people who could have solved the great untold mysteries of the British tours – Stan and Ida Laurel, and Oliver and Lucille Hardy – were sadly departed from this world, long before my research began. It was then that newspapers became a great source of information — providing reliable dates, along with interesting comments and reviews from the time. Like "Chinese whispers," personal accounts often become distorted and/or embellished over the years, whereas the contemporary viewpoints in newspapers remain unaltered – hence the prominence of quotations from this medium, within this book.

In most cases, those articles thought to contain inaccuracies or fabrication have been commented upon and corrected, where possible. Many others were treated as garbage, and dumped.

This book, as a story, is not complete, and never could be – not even if the original manuscript, which was twice as long as this book, had been published. It is meant only to supply details of the theatres at which Laurel and Hardy played; the hotels at which they stayed; the acts with whom they worked; some of the people they met; the functions they attended; their modes of transport; and the impact they made on the British public, both off-stage and on, during the British tours. Plus, of course, I aim to present you with the best picture possible of the real men behind the screen and stage characters.

After hearing many myths and rumours, and very little else about Laurel and Hardys British tours, readers will, I trust, find the information they are looking for within these pages.

I hope you get as much fun out of reading it, as I got out of researching it.

"A.J" Marriot

1993

o-o-0-o-o

As the above was written for the 1993 book, I have done a second Preface for this edition.

PREFACE (2019)

In 1987, when I first began research for the first edition of this book, technology was somewhat limited. The computer I worked on was an Amstrad PCW 8256; which was basically a typewriter – with a screen. I often chuckle at the specification: "now with 250kb of memory" – which is about one saved page of text. I am not, however, knocking the Amstrad. It made the chore of re-editing and re-typing twelve drafts oh so much easier.

What was missing in those days, which we now take for granted, was the Internet. Much of my source material came from around THREE HUNDRED people, with whom I had to correspond by letters – that's mail sent by post, and NOT email. Take into consideration that the minimum number of letters to any one person or company was usually four or five, with some up to twenty, and you can see that the total number of letters I mailed was over two thousand.

Photographs of Laurel and Hardy in Britain were particularly hard to obtain. These days you can go on the Internet, do a Google search for "Laurel and Hardy," and thousands of images will instantaneously appear. Back during my research years though (1987-1993) you had to contact the agencies which held the original photographs, borrow them, send them off to a processing laboratory, and have prints made, which was all very laborious and expensive. The alternative was to copy photos using a photocopying machine, the results for which, in those early days, were comparable to charcoal sketches.

To find information on Laurel and Hardy's tours was also very laborious. The second way, after collating the accounts of people who were there at the time, was to search out contemporary write-ups from the newspapers printed in the towns and cities where Stan and Ollie did their shows. However, at that time, no-one knew where and when they had appeared, and it was a full two years of researching before I had the complete schedule for the 1932, 1947, 1952, and 1953-54 tours.

These contemporary newspapers were a valuable source of dates, venues, and reviews of the stage shows Laurel and Hardy did, not only in Britain, but also in Europe, and the USA; plus Chaplin's pre-film stage years. The major problem, then, was that I had to go through actual "hard" copies of the newspapers in the hope of finding the required information. In total, I spent over one hundred and fifty days in the British Newspaper Library (which was then in London) — skimming through newspapers from early morning, until they kicked me out at closing time.

I also did my own "British Tours" when visiting other libraries — namely ones in North Shields, Blackpool, Liverpool, Birmingham, and Northampton. Plus, I visited many towns and cities to interview people who were a part of the story, and also do reconnaissance on the locations of hotels, theatres, houses, and venues Laurel and Hardy had visited. These included: Ulverston (3 times), Glasgow (twice), Rutherglen, Edinburgh (twice), North Shields (twice), Tynemouth (twice), Newcastle (twice), Blyth (twice), York, Leeds, Bradford (twice), Todmorden (twice), Bolton, Morecambe (twice), Blackpool (3 times), Southport, Liverpool, Rhyl, Hanley (twice), Stoke, Barkston, Bottesford, Butlins Skegness (twice), Peterborough (twice), Coventry, Birmingham (twice), Northampton, Cardiff, Bristol, London (165 times), Willesden, Ealing, Brixton, Lewisham, Finsbury Park, Camberwell (3 times), Lambeth, Southend (3 times), Margate (twice), Romney Hythe & Dymchurch Railway (3 times), Brighton, and Southsea. What a busy day that was.

The rest of the newspaper cuttings were obtained by a constant stream of begging letters to the actual newspaper companies, and libraries. [See Acknowledgements!]

Take all that into account and then consider that, these thirty-plus years later, most people think that "doing research" is going on-line and doing a Google search. I actually had one Laurel and Hardy fan who wrote on a Facebook site: "We don't need authorities or books on Laurel and Hardy, as all the information is on the Internet," which is comparable to saying: "We don't need archaeologists digging up sites of historic interest, as all the artefacts are to be found in museums. I hold nothing but disbelief for such a misguided mentality.

In the first edition of this book the early chapters detailed Stan Laurel's life: from birth — right through to his teaming with Hardy in 1927. In this edition, however, the early years have been omitted, and we come in at the point of the story where both Hardy and Laurel are working at the Hal Roach Studios, in California. However, fear not, for you can read the definitive account of Laurel's stage appearances, pre-Hardy, in my book: "*LAUREL – Stage by Stage*," which takes in ALL known stage appearances Stan made, on both sides of the Atlantic, before going full-time into films. [You can also read a similar treatment I did on Charlie Chaplin, by purchasing the book "*CHAPLIN – Stage by Stage*."]

Leaving out Laurel's solo stage career has not, however, led to a smaller page count, as several stories and events which have come to light since publication of the first edition have been added. Plus, there is a vastly increased number of illustrations — mainly contemporary photographs which were not available, or even known about, first time around. The text is also expanded by the inclusion of extracts from scores of letters written by Stan Laurel for which my thanks go to Bernie Hogya for an exchange arrangement.

Obviously, I sought to correct any mistakes and omissions I made in the first edition but, as usual, will accept bouquets and brickbats for this one. However, if all you have to offer is one spelling mistake, or even one mising hypen, please keep it to yourself. This is no time for levity.

"A.J" Marriot

-----0-----

B.S. I deliberately misspelt "missing hyphen" just to test your reaction.

o-o-0-o-o

KEY

Laurel **&** Hardy = on-screen – Laurel **and** Hardy = off-screen

(*ibid.*) = previously mentioned

(*circa*) = around this time

(*sic*) = copied correctly from original

[Square brackets] = author's comments.

[FILM] = refer to Film Footage and TV Broadcasts. (P159-162)

All grammatical errors and mis-spellings in the "Laurel Letters" have been left in.

Stan used the abbreviation 'bus' for different meanings. 1) for "show business" 2) when referring to the number of theatregoers. eg. "bus' was bad." 3) meaning the visual comedy in their act, which is too lengthy to write out a description for. eg. "bus' with swapping hats."

Any other mistakes are attributable to the author.

-----0-----

CONTENTS

Chapter 1	Where Has All the Slapstick Gone?	(1952 Tour pt1)	1
Chapter 2	A Spot of Trouble	(1952 sketch)	11
Chapter 3	A Posh Do	(1952 Tour pt2)	21
Chapter 4	Stan Meets Jefferson	(1952 Tour pt3)	27
Chapter 5	Highlands and Midlands	(1952 Tour pt4)	39
Chapter 6	Dublin Up	(1952 Tour pt5)	47
Chapter 7	Southend, Southport, South Wales	(1952 Tour pt6)	57
Chapter 8	The Last Legs	(1952 Tour pt7)	69
Chapter 9	One in a Hundred	(1953–54 Tour pt1)	79
Chapter 10	The Bells Are Ringing	(1953–54 Tour pt2)	85
Chapter 11	Pigeon English	(1953–54 Tour pt3)	95
Chapter 12	Dumb and Dummy	(1953–54 Tour pt4)	103
Chapter 13	Santa and Holly	(1953–54 Tour pt5)	113
Chapter 14	Sunderland Ain't No Wonderland	(1953–54 Tour pt6)	123
Chapter 15	Keep Right On	(1953–54 Tour pt7)	131
Chapter 16	Marathon Man	(1953–54 Tour pt8)	137
Chapter 17	Cut Short	(1953–54 Tour pt9)	143
Chapter 18	The Last Farewell	(1954 – Epilogue)	149

THE END

ACKNOWLEDGEMENTS	155
FOOTAGE	159
RADIO, TV, and AUDIO RECORDINGS	162
LOCATIONS	165
TOUR DATES and ACTS 1952	173
TOUR DATES and ACTS 1953-54	179
GALLERY	189
AUTOGRAPHS	196
About the Author	198

o-o-0-o-o

DEDICATION

This book is dedicated to two men, without whom the British stage tours would never have happened: (Lord) Bernard Delfont, and his agency partner for many years – Billy Marsh.

I, the author, was living in Blackpool in Blackpool in 1989, and was privileged to interview Lord Delfont in the Presidential Suite of the Savoy Hotel, when he was on a visit there.

When the interview was over, I told Lord Delfont I was hosting the Stan Laurel Centenary Convention in Blackpool, over the weekend covering 16 June 1990, and asked if he would like to attend. Without skipping a beat, he said: "Yes."

Seven months later, he duly came all the way from London to attend the Banquet, in the Baronial Hall of the Winter Gardens complex — the very room where Laurel and Hardy had been guests at a Banquet in 1932 (see page 37).

BERNARD DELFONT

When I asked Lord Delfont why he had so readily agreed to come he told me that Laurel and Hardy had done him such a big favour in the early days when he was trying to get established, that he wanted to give something back.

-----0-----

When Billy Marsh responded to an appeal I put in the *Stage* newspaper, for information on the British tours, I had no inkling that his help would go far beyond any limits I could have wished for. Firstly came an invite to his London office, for an interview. Next was an exchange of around 15 to 20 letters and several phonecalls in which he gave additional information, or corrections, to what I had written. Later he invited me to his house near Regents Park, where I handed over one of the drafts of the book — the feedback for which ran like this:

Billy: That's a great story, but where's the dirt?

AJM: I'm not putting any dirt in it.

Billy: Well it won't sell.

AJM: OK! if that's the case, it won't sell.

BILLY MARSH

I gave Billy a list of every artiste who had appeared in the Laurel and Hardy shows, and he returned it with a short description of their act. An amazing memory, and such a nice gentleman to boot. He also knew all there was to know about every theatre in the country.

Billy, too, came to our Blackpool Centenary Weekend event. In fact, he stayed for the whole weekend. On the first night I did an hour-long interview with him, in front of all the Conventioneers. He was such a modest man, that when I pushed him to tell us about his managing Morecambe and Wise, Tony Hancock, Bruce Forsyth, Keith Harris, and other big names, he skipped any praise he was due by asking me to move on.

Billy and Lord Delfont hadn't communicated with each other for three years, and so my approach to him was a bit tentative when I had to broach the subject that they would be sharing the top table. I was thrilled therefore when, just before leaving Blackpool, Billy said to me: "Thanks for getting us back together, 'A.J'. We came up in the car together.

How ironic that Lord & Marshy had got Laurel & Hardy back together, and the Laurel & Hardy event had got these two back together.

And so all three of us have now paid back what we owe to Messrs. Stan Laurel and Oliver Hardy. I trust you will enjoy the results.

o-o-0-o-o

Chapter 1

WHERE HAS ALL THE SLAPSTICK GONE?

If Laurel had not yet come to terms with his film career having ended, then the first event he attended – less than two weeks after getting home following a year in France filming *Atoll K* – would almost certainly have brought it home to him:

OLD TIMERS OF SCREEN PAID TRIBUTE

> Film greats of the day-before-yesterday gathered last night [8 May 1951] at a movie paying them tribute. In a ceremony under the auspices of the Hollywood Chamber of Commerce, cinema stars who reigned years ago received homage at the Academy Award Theater.
>
> Jack Benny was master of ceremonies for the salute to the former stars. Among those honoured were Betty Blythe, Francis X. Bushman, Chester Conklin, Heine Conklin, Pauline Garon, Julia Faye, William Farnum, Helen Gibson, Stan Laurel, Elmo Lincoln, Hank Mann, Mae Murray, Eddie Polo, Herbert Rawlinson, and Mack Sennett. John B. Kingsley, president of the Hollywood Chamber, and Ronald Reagan, president of the Screen Actors Guild, also took part in the ceremony.
>
> The movie immortals, who played important parts in the birth and growth of a giant industry, were issued citations "For your help in making Hollywood the film capital of the world."
>
> A greeting committee of today's young stars and starlets, including Julia Adams, Tony Curtis and Piper Laurie, escorted the old timers to the special premiere of the film "Hollywood Story," at the Academy Theater.
>
> *(Associated Press – 9 May 1951)*

[AJM: *Hollywood Story* was a 'Universal-International' fictional feature film, into which a bunch of silent stars had been suckered into appearing. Mercifully, Laurel was not one of them.]

But retirement wasn't on Laurel's mind just yet. Only three weeks later came a report that Laurel and Hardy would be touring again soon.

> Come September, Laurel and Hardy return to Europe to star in a revue that will tour the principal cities of Italy. These zanies are so popular in Italy that their old hit "Fra Diavolo," is in its third month at a movie house in Rome.
>
> *(2 June 1951)*

But, on the same day, an announcement in Boxoffice had them following a road that did not lead to Rome — far from it:

> It is rumoured that Laurel and Hardy may come to Australia soon to make a film. A representative of the comedy team has been in contact with principals here, and the only matter to be finalized is that of finances.

It is hard to believe that Stan and Babe would even want to consider going to make a film in Australia, so soon after the traumatic experience of their year in France. In a letter to Betty Healy, Laurel speaks only of projects a little closer to home:

```
                                          June 20th.'51.
Dear Betty:-
I was in the hospital only a couple of days - just an
examination for something due to my operation in Paris last
year - nothing serious & all is OK. I understand Louella
Parsons true to form, gave me the last Rites over the air.
```

```
          Expect to leave for Italy - France & Spain for a years run
          in a Revue about Sept - if the War business does'nt upset
          our plans.
```

[AJM: I believe that, by the "war business," Laurel is referring to the 'General Strike of 1951,' which started in Barcelona, and then spread to many other parts of Spain. An estimated 300,000 workers were eventually involved, which caused the authorities to mobilise police and Civil Guard units to quell the street riots. Thousands of strikers were imprisoned until the strike was eventually broken.]

But there were also offers of work coming in from different media. Firstly, Stan and Babe went into talks with Hal Roach Jr. about a profit-sharing TV deal; then, according to the *New York Times* (8 July 1951):

> Offers are piling up for this unique and beloved team—offers for TV series, for an Italian stage revue, a Japanese cinema; for their life story in a Billy Wilder movie.
>
> Hollywood or no Hollywood, the world is not likely to let this Silver anniversary pass unnoticed.

Come October, with still no word on the Roach TV deal, in came yet another idea for a film:

> Jerry Wald and Norman Krasna are concluding a deal that will bring Stan Laurel and Oliver Hardy back to the screen after an absence of six years. The picture will be the forthcoming RKO Radio, Technicolor musical, "The Girls Have Landed," which stars Tony Martin.
>
> Veterans of many USO tours, Laurel and Hardy will fit aptly into the cast of "The Girls Have Landed," the story of the USO in World War II.

This was yet one more film which seems never to have got past the planning stage. However, the possibility of doing TV shows was still simmering.

The cause of the sudden upsurge in demand for Laurel and Hardy was that, during the mushrooming-spread of television throughout America, selections from the fifty-two Laurel & Hardy shorts which Hal Roach had sold to the TV network were regularly being screened. Consequently, those TV viewers who had missed the Laurel & Hardy films first time around, on cinema release, were clamouring for more: The Boys' old pal, Hollywood columnist Erskine Johnson, interviewed them on the subject: (16 November 1951) [Abridged]

> For the first time in five years Stan Laurel and Oliver Hardy will be on your neighbourhood theatre screens this winter in a feature comedy, "Atoll K." And they're being deluged with TV offers.
>
> "A whole new generation of kids have discovered us," Hardy beamed.
>
> There are no big casts and no big flossy production numbers in the blueprints for new Laurel and Hardy comedies, whether they are for TV or movie theatres.
>
> "It will be the same situation comedy," Hardy made it clear, "with one set and no more than three other actors in the cast. We have to be together. Split us up and put us with other people and we're gone. Everything that happens to us happens in a little corner."
>
> "Laurel, as usual, will be supervising and helping us write the scripts."
>
> "We've been accused of being temperamental because we want to supervise our own stuff," Hardy let it fly. "Well, that's not true. We know just what's right for us."
>
> "We refused to do a picture for a certain producer at Fox. He called us to his office and said:"
>
> "Sit down, boys, and tell me what you don't like in the script."
>
> "We asked him, 'Have you read it?'"
>
> "He replied:"
>
> "'Well, no, I've been a busy man lately.'"
>
> "That's when we quit. How can you do a movie when the producer hasn't even read the script?"

Where Has All the Slapstick Gone?

In Laurel's next letter to Betty Healy, mention of TV shows was totally absent. Also gone were the plans he had divulged to her in the letter six months previously; re a year's run in Italy, France and Spain. However, there *had been* a positive development:

```
                                            December 6th. '51
Glad to tell you, I never felt better, I now weigh 149 lbs
and look like my old self again & expect to leave for
England in February for personal appearances also
Television shorts over there. Needless to tell you I can't
wait to get back in harness again. To be very frank I never
thought I would, last year at this time I weighed only 110
lbs. I shall know definitely next week re the trip so of
course will let you know.
Well Betty, will close now. Am busy digging up a new act to
take over, know you understand.
```

Eleven days later, Stan did indeed confirm the details to Betty:

```
We are leaving for England end of January, due in London
Feb. 3rd. so as you can imagine I am up to my neck in
preparation, a million & one things to do.
Yes, Babe is going too. Our name L&H is magic over there,
it's amazing after all these years, they don't even want to
remember you over here.
```

It is quite understandable, therefore, why Laurel and Hardy were off to England, to begin a six-month tour of variety theatres. The other one-hundred-and-one offers made to them, in the seven years since they had last made a film in the U.S.A., would have to wait until they got back. (Read "The US Tours" to find out the actual number!)

So it was that, on 19 January 1952, the "Laurel & Hardy Family" boarded a train at Los Angeles Union Station (pictured), and three days later detrained in New York.

After an overnight stay at the Essex House Hotel, Wednesday 23 January, Stan, Babe and, this time, both Mrs. Laurel and Mrs. Hardy set sail from New York Harbor on the *Queen Mary*.

ATLANTIC CROSSING

Left: Just before setting sail from New York, Stan and Babe find a stowaway under the bed. It's none other than Jimmy Murphy – Laurel's former butler – who, having been deported from Britain in 1947, is trying to smuggle himself back in.

Bottom Left: The Laurel and Hardy Family snapped in the dining room of the *Queen Mary*.

Below: Just before disembarking at Southampton, Laurel pinched the deerstalker off the English photographer, exclaiming: "It's bloody cold, isn't it?"

Although the day of arrival, Monday 28 January, was an extremely cold day, it didn't stop local girls Gillian Moore and Barbara Wilding from dressing in Hawaiian costume, and treating the two comedians to a hula-hula dance as they disembarked at Southampton.

This welcome was certainly the most humorous which Stan and Babe had ever been given, but short by several hundred on the numbers which had greeted the two Hollywood legends on previous visits. But at least the press were there in numbers, plus both Movietone and Gaumont recorded the comedy legends' arrival, as they stepped onto "good old terra cotta." **[FILM]**

Where Has All the Slapstick Gone?

In the newsreel footage we see Stan and Babe enter a roped off area on the quayside, where stand-mic's have been set up, and the two girls are acting as 'atmospheric extras.' Step forward the interviewer, Tony Tenser, who tries to extract some information from the two stars, as to what their plans are whilst in Britain. But all they want to do is get away as quickly as they can.

Hardy excuses himself with the comment: "I think I'll take the girls to see *Robinson Crusoeland* this afternoon," and starts to lead the two girls away. To make his exit more plausible he adds that he has to go and see to the baggage. Both men are coaxed back in front of the microphones, but still they have no worthwhile contribution to make. Hardy looks to Laurel for inspiration, and seems to try and prompt him into their doing the "You're standing on my foot routine," but again no comic business is forthcoming. Getting more uncomfortable by the second, Hardy abandons Laurel, leaving him to ad-lib some unfunny business in treating the two girls to sugar lollipops.

Tenser and tenser by the second.

It is thought that Tenser was working as publicity man for Miracle Films. Later, he would go on to become a film producer, best known for the 1960s horror movies made by his company – Tigon Productions.

It is seeing Laurel and Hardy in this type of scenario where I have to question my sanity, and ask if those two men really are the ones we see in those side-splitting comedies on the screen, or if they are just a couple of low-grade impersonators.

The scene is reminiscent of one outside Grauman's Theatre, in Hollywood; wherein the Boys were asked to send an impromptu message to radio listeners tuned in to hear what was going on at the premiere of *Hollywood Revue of 1929*. An article by Eleanor Parker, in the October issue of *Picturegoer*, registered her disappointment at the comedy couple's lack of comedy.

> Two quiet unassuming gentlemen, wearing smart straw hats and their dinner coats correctly tailored, stepped up to the microphone in the lobby of the famous Chinese Theatre in Hollywood. "Now we take pleasure in introducing Mr. Laurel and Mr. Hardy, the screen's funniest clowns. They will say a few words to the listeners of the air who are not with us tonight."
>
> The announcer then turned to the two gentlemen. "Say something funny," he whispered, while the standers-by listened to hear words of mirth and humour from the mouths of the two funny men.

And what did the two comedians say? They looked at each other in bewilderment. The people, seen and unseen, were waiting in silent anticipation of side-splitting comedy. "Good evening, ladies and gentlemen. We are happy to be here to-night." Thus did Stan Laurel answer the call for humor.

"Good evening, ladies and gentlemen. We wish that you could be here with us tonight." These were the words of brilliant wit, uttered in his turn by Oliver Hardy.

"That's the reason we avoid all public appearances," Stan confided as he walked into the theatre. "People expect us to be funny all the time. We are like everyone else, with our regular business. Comedy is our business. We can't go around all the time, doing comedy falls and hitting each other."

"Then, if we did try to be funny, and didn't succeed, people would say, 'Oh, they're not half so good as we thought they were'," Oliver added, "So we refuse all requests to appear in public, and keep our funniness for the screen."

Here in 1952 the interviewer, Tony Tenser, next acts as their guide as they are led out of the port via the dockside offices, past banks of waiting press-men. Whether or not Laurel and Hardy gave a better performance in the Press Room (which can clearly be seen in the footage) cannot be confirmed, but that they did do an interview is quite feasible.

Tenser took on a third role when, later that day, he acted as host at a private screening of *Atoll K* — this British release version being renamed *Robinson Crusoeland* – hence Hardy's earlier reference at the dockside, and why the girls there had appeared in Hawaiian costume.

The Boys were staying at the Washington Hotel, Curzon Street Mayfair, W1. As it is doubtful that the hotel had its own in-house 35mm projector, I would surmise that Stan and Babe were picked up and driven to Old Compton Street, in Soho, to view it in, or near to, the office where Tony worked.

Tony Tenser welcoming the film's stars to the screening.

I heard first-hand from a witness that Laurel swore at the screen throughout the screening. In this later letter, however, he limits his feelings to more acceptable language.

```
Dear Ed [Patterson]-                       February 4th.'53.
Yes, I heard they were running some of our old pictures on
TV. They use them here [in the US] every week, have been
for the last three years. The sad part is we don't get any
revenue from them at all. Anyway, it keeps our name in
front of the public which keeps us from dying out
altogether. Note re "Crusoeland", surprised at the reports,
as it is not a good picture by any means. As far as i am
concerned - it stinks!
```

Back to the forthcoming *stage* tour, one must take into account that Stan and Babe were now entering a different Britain to the one they had experienced in 1947. The biggest change for them would be the decline in popularity of variety shows, with theatres around the UK struggling to fill seats. Laurel and Hardy were still idolised as screen comics but, as it was twelve years since they had made anything resembling a decent film, they had lost a whole generation of prospective new fans. Having their films shown on television would have popularised them with the youngster who had missed the cinema releases; but, in Britain, the purchase of TV sets was limited to the very rich. At £110 a set, it is easy to see why.

Surprisingly, the two film legends *were* scheduled to make a television appearance, but were stymied by a tragic event, when King George VI of Great Britain and Northern Ireland, died in

Where Has All the Slapstick Gone?

his sleep at the royal estate at Sandringham on 6 February. So, we will never know what Stan and Ollie had planned to do on their first-ever TV appearance. If it was as bad as their piece-to-camera at Southampton, then maybe the cancellation was a blessing.

However, as regards their stage shows, every faith remained with Laurel & Hardy's box-office appeal, and Bernard Delfont had booked them back on the No.1 circuit – namely, the Moss Empire theatres at Glasgow, Newcastle, Edinburgh, and Liverpool, with the addition of those at Sunderland, Nottingham, Leeds, Sheffield, and Swansea; plus the Hippodromes at Birmingham, Dudley, Bristol, and Coventry. Out went the seaside resorts of Morecambe, Blackpool, Skegness, and Margate; but in came Brighton, Southend, and Southport.

In the provinces there would be a return to the city of Manchester, but the rest involved first-time visits to Peterborough, Hanley, Shrewsbury, Bradford, Sutton, Southampton, and Portsmouth. Wales was represented with dates in Rhyl, Cardiff, and Swansea; and Northern Ireland and Ireland, with two weeks each in Belfast and Dublin.

There were however no bookings in London theatres, even though Laurel and Hardy had done exceptionally good business in London in 1947. Babe explained this away, to one reporter, as though it had been a matter of personal choice: "*We both like the provincial theatres. It is here where our act is best appreciated – especially by the children.*" But Laurel had a different version of why they weren't about to play London, as outlined in this later letter of 27 March:

```
So far, we are not going to play in London this trip, as
Delfont wants to keep us out of there because he wants us
to do a pantomime this Xmas for him at the Savoy Theatre.
so do'nt know when we shall be back home.
```

On the second evening of their stay at the Washington Hotel, a reception was held where the press, bookers, and show business celebrities where in abundance. A surprise guest was comedian Norman Wisdom. I say "surprise" as he was supposed to be appearing in the pantomime *Cinderella*, at the Grand Theatre, Wolverhampton – some one hundred and forty miles away. But time and distance werent going to keep this fan from a reunion with his comedy heroes.

Bernard Delfont, Norman Wisdom, and Australian comedian Albert Whelan attending the press reception at the Washington Hotel. Hardy is a bit wary of that mad glint in Norman's eye.
29 January 1952

And then, on 31 January, the 'Variety Club' treated both men to a luncheon at the Empress Club, at which boxer Freddie Mills, comedian Charlie Chester, CoCo the Clown, and TV broadcaster Eamonn Andrews were also present. Footage shot of the event shows them trotting out their standard "you're standing on my foot" routine; after which they are interviewed by sports presenter, and TV panel-show host, Eamonn Andrews. **[FILM]**

LAUREL and HARDY – The British Tours

The Boys delighted at being served by two of the pretty dancers, acting as hostesses.

Two brilliant clowns, meet a man in a loud checked suit, and too much make-up.

Next they renewed acquaintances with the 'Grand Order of Water Rats,' and attended lodges on 3 and 17 February. Present on the 3rd was Fred Russell and Talbot O'Farrell, who had first proposed and seconded Laurel as a member back in 1947. Also in attendance was 'King Rat' Charlie Chester, Ben Warriss, Barry Lupino, and Albert Whelan. Others are identified below:

Fred Russell – ventriloquist (and the father of Val Parnell), comedian Charlie Chester, Laurel, Hardy, Will Murray.

GOWR meeting – 3 March 1952 – Eccentric Club, London
L-R: Charles Dudley, Nat Jackley, Johnnie Riscoe, Oliver Hardy, Stan Laurel, Norman Evans, Dennis Lawes, George Elrick, Leonard Jones, Will Murray, Harry Ristori, Hal Swain.

Where Has All the Slapstick Gone?

When possible, Stan and Babe would arrange to have press-calls in isolation, away from fans who could so easily get out of hand. Here, in the kitchens of the Washington Hotel, they ad-lib some comedy business with pancake making — even though Pancake Day was some two weeks away (Tuesday 26 February). Still, it beats trying to ad-lib comedy patter.

Other activities Stan and Babe did during their next nineteen days in London are recorded for us in the letter Stan wrote to good friend and confidante, actor Booth Colman:

```
                                          Feb.12th.'52.
Had quite a hectic time since arrival & busy as hell with
rehearsals etc. owing to opening a week earlier than
expected. We were due to open in Peterborough March 3rd but
after announcement the House was sold out in advance so
they requested us to open a week before (Feb. 25th) & play
there 2 weeks. Hence our mad rush to get prepared. We got
two good straight men, so guess we'll make it OK.
```

```
The passing of the King was very sad, a great shock to all
- it stunned us, being so unexpected.
We had a wonderful reception at the Rats also the Savage
Club. We were made members of the later [sic] for the
period of our stay in Eng. No doubt you know of the Club, I
think there is some connection with "The Lambs" N.Y.
```

[AJM: The Lambs Club is a social club in New York City, the membership of which is comprised loosely of stage actors and others with a theatrical background. It began life in New York city in 1874, making it Americas oldest theatrical organization, but its origins go back to 1868, when it was founded in London. Just a few short years after the New York affiliation, the London branch went out of existence, so maybe the Savage Club is somewhat of a revival.]

> On Monday 17 March the Crazy Gang, were celebrating the 2nd Birthday of their comedy sketch show *Ring Out the Bells*, at the Victoria Theatre; which, during its 2-year run, had been seen by 1.5 million patrons.
>
> However, the biggest celebration was not for the two years, but for having the world's two funniest men in attendance.

These outings were, of course, partly to give the Boys a break from the chore of almost four weeks of rehearsing the show. As Stan said in one interview: "*It is one thing to make an audience laugh at a completed sketch, but it takes a lot of hard work to prepare for those laughs.*"

That they were performing a new sketch added to the necessity for such prolonged rehearsals. Before we see how it translates to the stage, let's see how the sketch reads on paper.

o-o-0-o-o

Chapter 2

A SPOT OF TROUBLE

ORIGINS

There have a been a few claims over the years, as to what happened to the original copies of the sketch *A Spot of Trouble*, which Laurel and Hardy played on the 1952 tour. L&H biographer John McCabe states that Laurel destroyed his copies; reasoning that, in his words: "*It worked for us at the time, but I would not want to be remembered for it.*"

But let me tell you what I know about the original copies of *A Spot of Trouble*. The photo at right, taken in November 1953, shows Stan and Babe looking at Hardy's script book. It contains Laurel's original typed copies of *The Driver's License* (the earliest 2-hander version); FOUR different drafts of *A Spot of Trouble*; a radio sketch which the Boys performed in Dublin in 1953; the script for a 1953 live TV show; and FOUR drafts of *Birds of a Feather* — the sketch from the 1953-54 tour. I know this because, in 1993, I BOUGHT IT.

I sold off the odd few copies over the years, but the rest remained in my possession until October 2017, during which time no-one was given access to them.

So here, I have given an outline, and some of the history, of *A Spot of Trouble*. The plot, which Laurel had been working on since December 1951 or earlier, was basically as follows:

> The Boys arrive separately for a pre-arranged meet at a railway station. They go through the business of walking past one another a few times, without one spotting the other, then do a "take" on making contact. They wish to take a train, but have neither tickets nor money. As the train is delayed because a bridge is down, they have a wait of several hours for the next one, and so decide to get some sleep on the only available bench. Lots of mileage is gained from Hardy's vast bulk taking up almost every inch of the bench, and Laurel constantly swapping ends, and changing position to try and find a bit of space.

[Similar routines can be seen to good effect in the Laurel & Hardy films *Berth Marks* and *Pardon Us*.]

> Scene 2 is where the Boys are forced to burgle the Chief of Police's house. Much of the plot and business for this scene was lifted from the film *Night Owls*:

LAUREL and HARDY – The British Tours

A PLOT OF TROUBLE

Left, is the storyboard for *Night Owls* – and right, for *A Spot of Trouble*.

The cop makes a "Help me, or else" proposition.

Problems gaining entry.

Enough noise to wake the dead.

Bungling burglars.

The thief caught by the chief.

A Spot of Trouble

Note the temporary change in title!

```
              LAUREL    AND    HARDY.
                 "ON   THE   SPOT"
            Comedy sketch in two scenes.
                Locale: A small town in the U.S.A.

                       *******

      Scene One- The waiting room in a railroad
                   station.

      Scene Two- Interior of a living room.

                       *******

                  Cast  of  Characters

         Chief of Police- A firery blustering type.
         Officer-  A small town cop with a mind
                     smaller than the town.

         Two gentlemen en route- Stan Laurel and
                   Oliver Hardy.

                       *******

         Property of LAUREL AND HARDY FEATURE PRODUCTIONS.


         *****        ****        *****           *****
```

In Stan's violin case is a hot-water bottle, a tin cup, a pair of binoculars, and a newspaper. Babe is carrying an umbrella, and a carpet-bag — the contents of which are never revealed.

A Spot of Trouble

While the Boys are waiting for the train, an announcement over the louspeaker informs them that, due to a storm, a bridge has been washed out, and there will be a delay of several hours. Knowing they will have to spend the night on the station, they look for ways to kill time. Laurel opens his violin case, to see if anything in there will help. He selects a pair of binoculars, which he firstly uses to try and read the Timetable, but then Hardy becomes the focus of his attention.

```
STAN:        (crosses back to timetable, business looking through
             binoculars) Oh, dear.... Oh, yes. That's much better.
             What's that on your chin? No, the other one.
```

Stan next brings out a hot water, and ask Ollie if would like a cup of coffee. When Ollie declines, on the grounds that it will be cold by now, Stan replies: "*Funny! They told me it was a hot water bottle.*" With no further distractions to occupy their time, they decide to try and sleep the hours away.
ENTER COP.

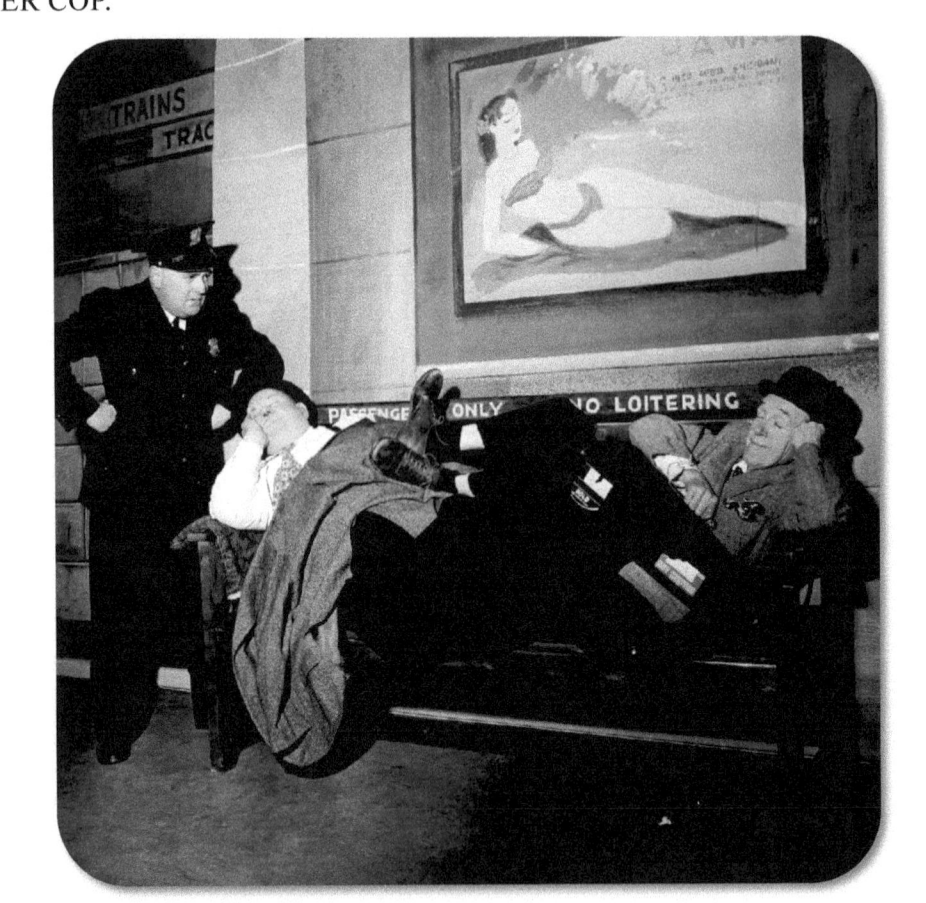

A Spot of Trouble

```
COP:    Hey, you! You can't sleep on there!
BABE:   xxx Pardon us, officer.
COP:    You can't sleep in this station! What are you two
        guys doing here anyway?
STAN:   Well, we're waiting for a train.
COP:    Oh, where's your tickets.
STAN:   We don't need any tickets.
COP:    How do you expect to ride on a train with no tickets?
STAN:   It's simple... We get on a train and they throw us off.
        Then we get on another, and another, and another.
COP:    Oh, yeah? And who said so?
STAN:   He did.
COP:    Is that so?
STAN:   Yes, sir.
COP:    Well, you're under arrest!
BABE:   What for?
COP:    Riding on a train with no tickets. Why you're just a
        couple of low down tramps!
```

Rather than arrest them there and then, for vagrancy, the cop outlines his plan for them to burgle the chief police's house, during which he will catch them in the act, and arrest them. Once he is back in the police chief's good books, for catching the burglars, he says he will let them go.

17

Unwisely accepting the offer, off they go to the chief's house, with the cop keeping an eye on them at a distance.

While Ollie is struggling to climb in through the window, Stan tries the door, and finds it unlocked. Entering the house, he unlatches the window, and gestures for Ollie to climb through.

With neither of them catching on that Ollie, too, could use the door, he is hauled inside, during which he pulls down the curtains.

Further struggles ensue, during their efforts to re-hang the curtain pole, and while making enough noise to wake the dead.

A Spot of Trouble

A similar scene then occurs to the one in the 1947 *Driver's Licence* sketch, in which they consumed the contents of the cop's lunch tin. This time, they again help themselves to cigars, while the cop pours out glasses of whisky for them all.

Stan offers a cigar to the police chief, who has sneaked in, un-noticed, and is standing behind him. A few blank stares later, it dawns on Stan who the guy is, at which he tries to warn Ollie.

But Ollie is preoccupied with listening to the cop bad-mouthing the police chief, and how the Mayor will make *him* the new chief.

```
hief:            ( Steps between cop and Babe, as all are about to drink.)
                 Is that so ? you'll never live that long.

tan, Babe & Cop: ( spit out drinks.)
```

```
op:        Now wait a minute Chief, I can explain everything.

hief:      ( Grabs cops truncheon as cop backs away in half circle.)

UND:       TRAIN WHISTLE.

abe:       Come on Stanley there's our train. ( Stan and Babe start
           for the door as chief goes after cop making swings at him
           with the truncheon. Babe and Stan exit thru door then
           appear at outside of window.)

tan:       Good bye.( Exits.)

abe:       ( To cop.) Dont forget to duck. ( Picks up pants, looks
           after Stan . ) Hey you forgot your pants. ( holds pants
           up and exits.)

                              CURTAIN.
```

[NOTE that this ending was changed to the chief firing a gun at them as they flee the scene.]

The clips from the scripts used in this chapter are from the four different drafts I have copies of. The full script is deliberately not presented, but just enough to reveal the premise of the sketch.

In the first draft, the title is *A Spot of Trouble*; but then, for the other three, it becomes *On the Spot*. However, throughout the theatre tour it was billed as *A Spot of Trouble*.

Draft 4 is dated 14 February 1952, thirteen days before the tour commenced in Peterborough, when both stars were in London. Laurel must have continued to amend the script on tour, as other bits of business are revealed in the text and reviews to follow — which are not in these early drafts.

o-o-0-o-o

[Photo illustrations licensed by Getty]

Chapter 3

A POSH DO

For the start of the tour, Stan and Babe travelled by train to Peterborough where, at the North Station, a crowd of about seven hundred gave them such an enthusiastic welcome that the police had to be called in as crowd-controllers. Admittedly, this was nowhere near the size of the crowds which had greeted them on earlier tours, but the number was highly encouraging.

As it was five years since the comedians had last been in the country, and as they were performing a sketch of unknown strength, Delfont took out "insurance" by assembling a first-class supporting bill from amongst some of the best dance acts, jugglers, cartoonist, ventriloquists, acrobats, magicians, and musicians, and even a comedy impressionist — chosen by Billy Marsh from the agency's stable of acts.

Bernard Delfont need not have worried. Over the two weeks, commencing 25 February, Laurel and Hardy smashed all box-office records for the Embassy Theatre. This did not seem to impress the critic from the *Peterborough Standard*, who had rather fixed ideas of the kind of "business" Laurel and Hardy's act ought to contain. Under the heading, "Not the Laurel & Hardy of Custard Pie Fame," he wrote:

Laurel & Hardy disappointed a section of their admirers. The reason was a matter of style, for they forsook, almost completely, their true 'custard pie roles.' The two presented a new sketch which, although highly amusing, was not typical of the performances which made their reputation. Probably in an effort to modernise the act, the sketch tended to neglect the personalities of Laurel & Hardy and concentrated on witty words and amusing circumstances. That being said it must be stated that many of the audience enjoyed the act. The reputation of the popular comedy team satisfied some, and others, taking the act at face value and ignoring precedent, found in it a welcome relief from the normal round of music hall turns.

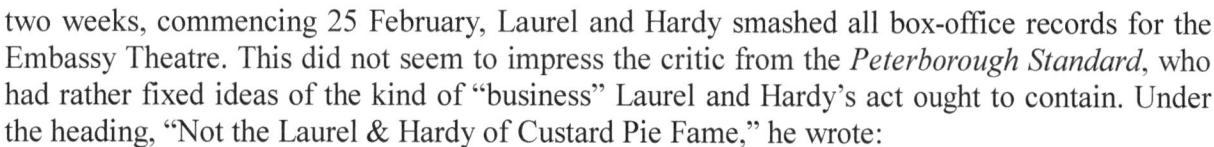

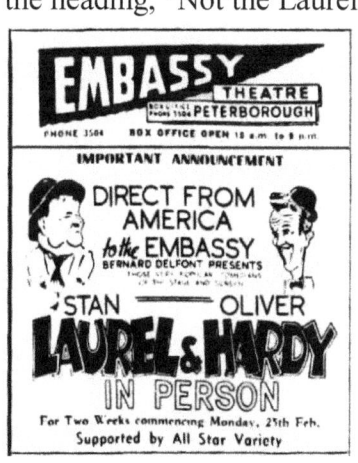

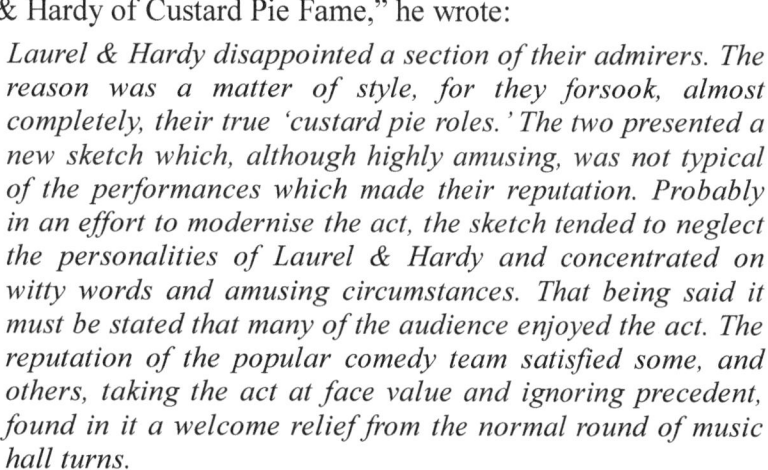

In analysing the above, a Laurel and Hardy buff would immediately take exception to the phrase, "of custard pie fame." In *Battle of the Century*, one of the earliest Laurel & Hardy films, Stan had tried to bury the custard pie image once and for all by having so many pies thrown, that no-one would even contemplate trying to follow it with a film in which only a fraction of the alleged two thousand thrown in "*Battle*" would be used. It is therefore hard to comprehend why the reviewer should choose to select a single scene from a silent-film in the 1920s, and relate it to a stage sketch in the 1950s. One must accept that Laurel and Hardy *did* have a slapstick image; but, with Laurel still not over his illness; and Hardy at his lifetime's heaviest, plus their now being elderly men, anything too physical was ruled out. Slapstick though *was* still a major part of the act, as the following review from *The Stage* will testify:

> The sketch is on the lines of the comedians' old comedies, and contains many of the hilarious situations associated with them. The setting is first a railway station, and then the living-room of a police chief's house. At the beginning we are treated to some typical Laurel & Hardy patter, and the scene where they both try to sleep on a small bench is particularly funny. In the house, where the two comedians are supposed to be burglars, the sketch builds up to one of those slapstick affairs, in which the police chief chases the police officer round the room, while Laurel & Hardy make a quick exit.

The line from the latter: "The sketch is on the lines of the comedians' old comedies, and contains many of the hilarious situations associated with them," totally contradicts the line in the former, which went: "The two presented a new sketch which was not typical of the performances which made their reputation." How could it *not* be typical, when the main plot is a near scene-by-scene recreation of one of the Laurel & Hardy films?

The line from the former: "the sketch tended to neglect the personalities of Laurel & Hardy and concentrated on witty words," is also contradicted by the prevalence of visual business in the sketch; what with the 'bench' scene, 'the break-in,' 'the burglary,' 'and 'the chase' as the finale – one can clearly gauge that dialogue was limited, and slapstick was prevalent.

It really does make one wonder how one critic can see the total opposite to what everyone in the theatre is watching, and is the reason why I shan't be taking up much more space to pick holes in future reviews.

Our subjects stayed at the Great North Station Hotel, adjacent to Peterborough Railway Station, from where Laurel wrote another exposé to his friend Booth Colman (1 March):

```
Happy to tell you the act was a huge success & has been
every show. We are doing capacity Bus. - really wonderful
our popularity over here. Needless to tell you, I am
getting a thrill out of it - a new lease on life, after
sitting home for months watching my garden grow! Glad to
tell you - I am feeling good & no ill effects from the hard
work & anxiety I went through before opening. It was quite
a strain & you know what I mean.
```

On Thursday 28 February, Stan, Ida, Lucille and Babe were driven from their Peterborough hotel to Grantham – thirty-miles northward. After a civic luncheon at the Red Lion Hotel, their hosts, the Lady Mayoress & Mayor of Grantham – Ald. & Lady W. Goodliffe, took them to the Guildhall.

Red Lion Hotel

Accompanying the Mayoress are Mrs. J. Godber (wife of the MP), Mrs. Sandall (wife of the chairman), and Gladys Foster (who later, herself, became the Lady Mayoress)

A Posh Do

As soon as their car arrived, a crowd of several hundred surrounded it, and jostled to see them. Upon emerging, the two comedians used the top of the Guildhall steps as a platform on which to perform to the crowd, and provide a great photo opportunity.

GUILDHALL, Grantham
Ida Laurel – behind her, Stan's sister Olga – behind Stan is Lucille Hardy, behind pillar is Leslie Spurling, who plays the cop in the sketch.
Far right is the Lady Mayoress and her husband – Ald. & Lady W. Goodliffe.

As they don't have their own headwear with them, Colin Tipler provides Stan and Babe with a couple of Bowlers from his dealer's display stand.

Inside the Guildhall, the party ascended to the ballroom on the second floor to view the display stands, laid out by local businesses, as part of the 'Chamber of Trade Exhibition.' Stan's sister Olga and brother-in-law Bill took advantage of the visit, and accompanied them on their rounds.

On the second Monday of their stay in Peterborough, the Boys had a look around the offices of the Peterborough *Citizen & Advertiser*, where Hardy revealed that he had worked in a printing office, when a small boy. [Thought to be the *Union Recorder* newspaper company, in Milledgeville – circa 1906.]

ABOVE: Mr. E. Yandell watches anxiously as Laurel and Hardy operate the first stage of newspaper half-tone block production, using the new vertical process camera.

RIGHT: Hardy trims a flong ready for casting one of the printing plates, much to the amusement of the machine room staff.

Next visit was not by Stan and Ollie, but by a comedy duo who had come to see their show. Morecambe and Wise were pretty much unknown then, but went on to become Britain's most-loved TV double-act. Eric & Ernie said of the show:

> Though they (L&H) were past their best, we loved them just the same, and can vividly remember their clearly-defined roles, with Stan doing most of the comedy, while Oliver stood beside him, using his great stage presence, his huge frame shaking with laughter.

A Posh Do

Ernie Wise added:

> They were close to the end of their career and their sketch was not very good, but it was enough to see them, two master craftsmen at work.

Come the end of the two-week run in Peterborough, it was Laurel's turn to be reminded of his boyhood when, on Sunday 9 March, the Laurels and Hardys took the show up to Glasgow. Arriving late evening, the party was met by several hundred fans at the Queen Street Station. After police had forced a way through for the VIPs, many of the spectators simply followed them to the Central Hotel; but, mercifully, the terrifying scenes of 1932 and 1947 weren't repeated.

Everyone doing their best to smile for the Glasgow newspaper photographer, in one of their suites in the Central Hotel.

In the Scottish accent he had picked up when living in Glasgow (1905-1910) Stan enquired of the staff, *"Oh aye, how are ye?"* To reporters, he hinted that the current seven-month tour might be extended, because of the proposal for them to play the 'robbers' in the London pantomime *Babes in the Wood* (originally planned for 1948). Hardy offered: *"Or we may go back home and do television work. We'd do complete new shows on film for this medium."*

The talk of television was causing a lot of excitement that week, not solely because the Scots might soon be able to see Laurel & Hardy on TV, but simply because Scotland had received its very first television transmission.

Meanwhile it was on with the *live* appearance at the Glasgow Empire, the review for which appeared in the *Evening News* under the headline, "The Screen Magic is not there":

> On what all the best critics call a well-balanced bill, there emerge Laurel & Hardy, two comedians who have made me laugh uproariously on the screen, and made me smile last night. They are a preposterously engaging couple, but they have to struggle with the sort of sketch which is only funny if it's performed in a kirk [church] hall with your cousin in the cast.
>
> It just comes to this – that you can't imitate on stage what you do on the screen.

Gordon Irving, from the *Daily Record*, thought that their appeal lay with the children:

Laurel & Hardy offer simple, homely fun. It's the kind of absurd knockabout comedy which made them famous in so many film comedies, and without which, as they say, 'we'd not be Laurel & Hardy.' Their new sketch is 'cops and burglars' stuff, with no subtlety and demanding nothing of intelligence.

The fans will relish it as a flashback to happy times spent at film matinees. And the 1952 child who has not come to expect anything too sophisticated will still laugh at this funny pair of opposites. The whole variety bill is ideal kiddies' fare.

This is Master J. McCorkindale, meeting his comedy heroes, backstage at the Glasgow Empire.

Below is a publicity shot, which L&H had printed onto postcard-size handouts, which they would sign and give to fans.

Now take a VERY close look at both photos.

Did you spot it? It's the same photo, but the boy has been cut out, and Ollie moved over. [And you thought Photoshop was something new.]

The local papers gave no coverage whatsoever of the two Hollywood Stars' stay in their city, but a letter written by Stan on the Saturday, reveals a visit they had made the previous day:

```
Alhambra, Glasgow
My Dear Harry Condos,
Just a wee note to let you know how much I enjoyed meeting
you yesterday at the Memorial Club. It was indeed a great
pleasure Harry & I certainly appreciated your kindness &
courtesy & I hope it won't be long before we meet again & I
shall have the opportunity to reciprocate.
The club is delightful & enjoyable, a great credit is due
you & all involved for a wonderful thought & gesture which
could only be conceived by a Swell Guy.
```

The visit to the Stage and Screen Memorial Club may not have registered any interest with the newspapers, but it certainly meant a great deal to Laurel, as there he met up with Albert Pickard (*ibid.*). Thankfully, the occasion also meant something to Albert Pickard, as he commissioned some footage to be shot. **[FILM]**

With the lack of fuss and attention being given to Stan, on his return to the city he loved so much, maybe his having to leave would not have been as hard to bear as on previous occasions. Hopefully, as his next stop-over was at the place to which he felt he *belonged*, Tyneside, he would be treated with more respect and affection. Or would he?

o-o-0-o-o

Chapter 4

STAN MEETS JEFFERSON

Arriving at Newcastle on Sunday, Laurel was again reminded of his strong ties with the area, by the great reception given by the huge crowd.

Above: Mr. A. Nesbitt, journalist for the Newcastle *Sun* newspaper, obtaining Hardy's autograph.

Left: A reserved wave from Hardy as the comedy giants arrive at Newcastle North Station.

When Stan joined in with the waving, he confided: "*I get a great kick out of coming back to Tyneside.*" But things got off to a bad start. Having been unable to obtain a reservation at the Royal Station Hotel, in Newcastle, Stan and Babe ended up at the Grand Hotel, Tynemouth, only as a last option. Laurel griped to a friend, some years later:

```
We spent a miserable two weeks. The place was so dilapi-
dated & run down & most uncomfortable - was happy to leave
the place. I wouldn't have stayed there one night if we
could have found other accommodations.
```

First public appearance was on the day they arrived, Sunday 16 March, at the Gaumont Cinema, North Shields. There, on arrival, they were immediately mobbed by the hundreds of fans unable to gain admission. Inside, in the manager's office, the Mayor of South Shields – Councillor Oliver, bade them welcome. On stage, twenty-seven year-old Eric Nicholson was compering a *Charity Gala Concert*. In 1987 he recalled his feelings at the time, in a private letter to me:

> I do not think any experience ever brought the drama, immense enchantment, and sheer exhilaration which I felt that night. During one of my long rambling stories, the laughs were coming along nicely, and getting stronger by the second. I was thrilled. Great guffaws were greeting me, and at the end of the story there was rapturous applause. Just then, I saw two very good reasons for all the laughter and applause. There, walking towards me down the centre aisles were Stan Laurel and Oliver Hardy.

> The audience was going spare. What was I to do? There was I, a nobody, and bearing down on me were the world's two greatest comedians. Silently, I pleaded for help. The great men were now just a few rows away, and the audience were "tearing the place apart." Two spotlights hit them, and I blurted out, 'Just you two wait till I get you up here.'

> They stopped advancing, paused, then Ollie slowly put his hand up to his bowler hat and wiggled it. His hand descended to his tie which he pulled out and wiggled in turn.

Stan's reaction to my 'telling them off' was to burst into tears. At this, I, along with the audience collapsed in total hysteria.

The furore lasted a full five minutes during which they ascended to the stage. The show was now well and truly stopped, and the two stars spent many minutes apologising to me for interrupting my act. I needed no apologies at all. They'd made me that night. I was in ecstasy.

The *Shields Evening* News added:

On stage, Stan and Oliver – accompanied by their wives – were given a civic welcome by the Mayor of Tynemouth, Councillor T.A.M. Hails. Introductions over, Oliver spoke first – 'This is going to be Stan's night. Tonight I'm going to let him be General Buller again' [the part Stan had played in the "Relief of Mafeking" celebrations, when he was just ten]. To more cheers, Hardy added: 'Your boy and my boy, Stan Laurel.' To which Laurel replied:

It will be kinda difficult for me to express my, and our, grateful thanks ... it really is wonderful to be back in my old home town ... it brings back memories.

To remind him of the Mafeking celebrations, his old pal Roland Park, who had played Lord Roberts, came forward (pictured bottom left). Then to the wild cheering and clapping of fourteen hundred people, the local-boy-made-good wound his way to the circle, to watch the rest of the show.

[AJM: There has been some confusion as to which soldier in the Boer War the young Stan Jefferson was portraying at the Relief of Mafeking Celebrations, in Dockwray Square on 19 May 1900. A contemporary newspaper account says only that "Masters Jefferson, Walton and Davidson were attired in the uniform of the Imperial Yeomanry." In in his speech, Hardy seemed to suggest Stan was portraying General Buller, whereas another source thinks Baden Powell (Yes, he of the later Scout movement). In the following letter, though, Stan reveals a hitherto unknown character:]

```
Dear Mr. Newham:-
Regarding my taking part
in the celebration at
North Shields on the
event of "Relief of
Mafeking" in 1900. My
Dad (Arthur Jefferson)
on the same night
produced a show battle
of Boers & Britons in
Dockwray Square -
Fireworks & bonfires etc. with
impersonations of Lord (Bob)
Roberts - Kitchener - Buller -
Kruger etc. & myself as bugler
Dunne - I still have a
photograph of myself taken that day.
```

Taken in Dockway Square, in front of the High Lighthouse, on the embankment of the River Tyne.

LEFT: Roland Park as Lord Roberts.

[AJM: Bernie Hogya, who runs the magnificent website – www.lettersfromstan.com, found the following about Dunne: "The celebrated 14-year-old hero—'Bugler Dunne'—was wounded at the Battle of Colenso (the third and final battle of the Second Boer War) and lost his bugle in the attack."]

Here in 1952, Laurel and Hardy went backstage during the interval to speak to the other acts on the show. Sunderland-born Billy "Uke" Scott's recollection of his feelings, after they'd complimented him on his banjo playing, was:

> I was surprised how much bigger Ollie was than the impression one got from the films. That might seem surprising as we knew he was big; but when a screen image comes to life, you feel dwarfed. There was a slight unreality about it. I began to wonder if they were there in a real life, or if I was part of one of their films.

Even though Stan had so many people to see, and so many wanted to see him, he managed to find time for everyone. Observing how happy and smiling Laurel and Hardy remained under a deluge of autograph hunters, a reporter asked Hardy: "Don't you get sick of this continual signing of autographs?" Without hesitation Babe replied, "I'd get more sick if they didn't ask."

The two of them then went off to perform another service – this time, to present "Stars of Merit" to two of the Gaumont's staff — the lady, here, being Gladys Kent:

The next night, the two comedians were to reappear at the venue where, in 1947, they had made their British debut – the Newcastle Empire. The press made only two superficial comments:

> Laurel & Hardy have shattered theatre records at Peterborough and Glasgow, and it would not be surprising if they did it here.

The second statement was made in the "review" of the first night's performance, and stretched to the following:

> In a programme embracing many top-line variety acts, Laurel & Hardy have to be at their best, and they are.

The manager wrote in his notes at the end of the week:

> Both scenes get loud laughter, but lack a good finishing tag.

During the week, Stan met the son of his sister Olga for the first time. The nephew, professional organist-entertainer Huntley Jefferson Woods, recalled in a letter to the author:

> I approached the meeting with 'Uncle Stan' with mixed feelings. After all, I didn't know what the reaction of such a famous star would be, even to a relation – especially as he had never seen me, and knew me by name only.
>
> As it turned out, he was pleased to see me, and showed interest in my musical career. I also met his wife, who was equally charming.
>
> All in all, a marvellous night, which I shall always cherish.

Of his overall impression of Uncle Stan, Jefferson was to say: "*A great man, with the common touch.*"

Be that as it may, there were still old times to talk about and, after visiting his boyhood pal Roland Park (*ibid.*), Stan sought out William Henry Harmon, who had worked at the Theatre Royal in North Shields during the time Stan's father was lessee and manager (1895-1905).

As the black saloon carrying Stan pulled up outside Mr. Harmon's house, Stan was treated to a big cheer from a huge congregation of neighbours. Inside, he was told he hadn't changed a bit – William could still picture him stood in the wings of the theatre in his conventional Eton collar. "How old are you," enquired Stan. "Seventy-two," came back the reply. "Then I'll race you down the street," said Stan.

OH, THE THINGS THEY DID!
It was Stan Laurel's turn to laugh when the famous comedian visited Mr William H. Harmon, of West Percy Street, North Shields, and heard his boyhood escapades recalled. Mr Harmon at one time worked for Stan's father in a North Shields theatre.

Asked where Ollie was, Stan said: *"The fog has made him lose his voice a bit."* Then he laughed, *"He's not a Geordie, like us."* After meeting William's family, Stan was thoughtful enough to make the offer: *"If any of the neighbours out there have autograph books, just tell them to hand them in."*

Obviously, Stan couldn't visit all his boyhood pals or others he had spent time with during the years he had lived in North Shields (circa 1897 – 1905), but he always had an open door at the theatre, and would arrange meets with them at the hotel, as he discloses in this letter (written a year later):

```
                                          February 26th.'53.
My Dear Bill:-
I never had the pleasure of meeting your Dad, but remember
him a few years ago as "Len Long" when I was a kid in North
Shields during the time my Dad had the old Theatre Royal
there.

I got quite a kick out of your Dad's letter, mentioning
names of the old timers I used to remember seeing. I was
playing in Newcastle & Sunderland last march, Hardy & me
stayed at the old Grand Hotel in Tynemouth for the two
weeks. Am sorry your Dad did'nt contact me, as I met quite
a few of the Sons & Daughters of the old gang & thoroughly
enjoyed the exchange of memoirs, but felt a bit sad to see
the unhappy appearance of Canny aud Shields. I visited
Dockwray Square where I used to live, it certainly was a
sad sight.
```

As stated in the letter, Stan and Babe stayed on for second week at the Grand Hotel, Tynemouth, during their week of appearances at the Sunderland Empire. This was because of the advantageous location of the hotel, as each evening they would go down to the quayside at North Shields, get on the ferry and go over the river Tyne, to South Shields. The rest of the journey from the ferry port to Sunderland would then be completed by car. After the show, they would do the journey in reverse order.

```
                                                24-3-52.
My Dear Booth-
Had a wonderful week in Glasgow, Bus. terrific also
Newcastle. Opening at above today - Big advance sale. We
are certainly very lucky as the Theatre Bus. is awfully bad
here in this Country - not due to TV, but things are tough
financially. It's really amazing the popularity we have
here. The name seems to be quite magic!
```

Stan's wife Ida, who also classed Booth Colman as a friend, added her sentiments:

```
Hello dear, dear Booth: Thank you for your sweet letters
and the flowers—your sweet thought touched me very much.
Finally, I can breathe the ocean air, our hotel just right
on the beach but too cold to swim and no sun. Our room is
in penthouse. Well I am quite busy with all the packings
every week. Lots of Stan's old friends coming—you have to
talk, smile, be sweet with everybody, quite a job.
```

Backstage at the *Sunderland Empire*, a face from the past appeared to remind Stan of the time they had toured together in the Levy & Cardwell Company pantomime *Sleeping Beauty* [September 1907 – April 1908]. The face belonged to seventy-year-old Benny Barron, whose visit came as a pleasant surprise. Whilst waiting for the start of rehearsals, the two old troupers were soon lost in reminiscences of those "good old days of music hall." The *Sunderland Echo* recorded the conversation as follows:

'And they were grand times,' said Stan. 'The money wasn't much but we were happy all the same. I remember playing in Sunderland years ago – was it the Villiers Institute? Times have changed a lot since then though, but there's one thing that remains the same – Northern audiences. They're wonderful.'

The article continued:

On one point Stan and Benny agreed: 'You miss all that grand slapstick humour today. The new generation has never even seen that humour of the past.' This week Stan & Ollie bring back to Wearside just that. As they settled down to rehearsal Benny quietly left by the stage door, still chuckling over the memory when he too was 'one of the gang' and Stan Laurel was a pantomime golliwog.

A little of Stan and Benny's views on humour of the past was echoed in the review of the opening night, given by the aptly named, *Sunderland Echo*:

Perhaps the finest tribute to Stan & Ollie is that they remain the same on the stage as they do on the screen. For that I am deeply thankful. To have emulated the style of Danny Kaye, or even the brisker and less ingenuous slapstick of Abbott and Costello, would have been a betrayal of their reputation.

The material they use seems like a chunk of film-script. If today people find it feeble and unfunny, it is only because the funniest things about Laurel & Hardy films have always been Laurel and Hardy. Nobody cared then what their films were about, and those enthusiasts who learnt to recognise and appreciate their particular brand of humour, won't fail to miss it in their stage appearance now.

After the opening show, Benny Barron proudly took his son backstage. Billy Barron, who played trumpet in the theatre's Empire Orchestra, found both Stan and Babe to be extremely pleasant. Of Stan's past relationship with his father, Billy wrote to me:

Stan Meets Jefferson

> My dad toured with the 'Levy & Cardwell Company,' in a double-act known as 'Graham & Barron.' They were well-established, and Stan saw them perform many times. The facial expressions Stan adopted were exactly the ones my father used in his act, as he was the one who got everything wrong, and used to 'cry' when his partner knocked off his straw-boater.

[AJM: Just how Benny had managed to be in a "juvenile" company at the age of twenty-six is rather puzzling, but that he was is beyond doubt. There is also a strong possibility that Billy Barron's version of the origin of Stan's "cry" is correct. All comedians in their formative years have a tendency to copy those comedians to whom they have regular exposure. Bear in mind also that Stan never felt comfortable doing "the cry," which might imply that it did not come from "within," and was thus borrowed. It is a proven fact, too, that the soft-shoe shuffle – which Laurel performs to Hardy's rendition of *Lazy Moon* in the 1932 Laurel & Hardy feature-film *Pardon Us* – was lifted step-by-step from Graham & Barron's act. Read my book: "*LAUREL — Stage by Stage.*"]

Yet another backstage visitor at the Sunderland Empire was Father John Caden who, in his autobiography, *Game, Set, and Match*, gave the following account of his meeting with the two stars.

> My second lesson in humility, and undoubtedly the most memorable lesson of my life, was my meeting with Laurel and Hardy. At that time, they were huge stars – legends in their own lifetime. Consequently, when a rather nervous young priest knocked at the door of the No.1 dressing room and said, "I'm Father Caden, the priest from the Catholic Stage Guild," the door was opened by Stan Laurel with a welcoming smile, and I was graciously ushered into their holy-of-holies!

> He led me over to the other side of the dressing room where Oliver Hardy was relaxing with a book. He was seated at the performers' black worktop, with its large mirror "haloed" with a dozen bright bulbs. He hauled himself out of his chair and, with a wonderful "Ollie" smile, shook my hand and drawled, "It's a pleasure to meet you Father. Would you care for a drink?"

> I declined with a stammered, "No thank you, all the same."

> "Please do take a seat, Father," Ollie insisted.

> If I had been the Pope, I could not have been made to feel more welcome! They talked to me about England, about my work as a priest and why I chose it, about the influence of the Catholic Church and the Episcopalian Church in America, and many other topics. As I sat there, I had to pinch myself to be sure that these were really the men who had enriched my schoolboy years and early manhood with so much laughter and pathos. They never once alluded to their film fame during our forty-minute conversation.

> When I tried to say how much happiness they had given me and millions more. Ollie, with a deprecating smile, merely said, "Thank you, Father, that's very gracious of you ..." and gently changed the subject!

> As a priest, I had often been intrigued with the personification of "Wisdom" in the *Old Testament Book of Wisdom*. Since 1952, I have never ceased to marvel at "Humility" personified in the very disparate persons of Stan Laurel and Oliver Hardy.

Stan was very pleased with the week in Sunderland, as this letter to Dorathi Bock Pierre (a theatrical publicist and dance writer) and husband Jacques J. Pierre (a theatrical producer) will confirm. At the time, both were living in Los Angeles.

```
                                               March 27th.'52.
My Dear Dorathi:-
Glad to tell you I am still feeling good, the act is going
wonderful & so far playing to record Bus. We are very
lucky, as the show Bus. is having a hard time just now, &
money is tight. Have to go now, we travel by car from here
to Sunderland (20 odd miles) so have to leave early as the
first show starts 6-15.
```

EMPIRE
SUNDERLAND
Managing Director: RICHARD REED
Manager: JESSE J. S. CHALLONS
Booked by MOSS' EMPIRES, Ltd.
Telephone: 3374-5
MONDAY, MARCH 24
ONE WEEK ONLY
6.15 TWICE NIGHTLY 8.30
MATINEE ON SAT. AT 2.15
HOLLYWOOD'S
GREATEST
COMEDY COUPLE!
HERE IN PERSON
STAN
BERNARD DELFONT
presents
OLIVER
LAUREL AND HARDY
LORRAINE
Singing Cartoonist
THREE
ADAIRS
THE CAPTIVATING STARLET
DAISY MAY
assisted by
SAVEEN
JIMMY
ELLIOTT
ANIMAL MIMIC
MACKENZIE
REID &
DOROTHY
VOLTAIRE
OUT OF THIS WORLD
THE AERIAL
KENWAYS

Stan Meets Jefferson

After leaving Tynemouth to travel to Sunderland for the last six days, Laurel and Hardy next left there to travel to Hanley, in Staffordshire. The theatre critic for the *Evening Sentinel* wrote:

> The undiminishing popularity of the famous film and stage comedians was clearly demonstrated at the Theatre Royal. Their appearance was the signal for roars of anticipatory laughter, and their many smart comedy moves, familiarised by their many successful films, kept the audience highly amused.

The happiness Laurel had expressed in the letter sent while in Sunderland, was still being expressed by him in Hanley. He and Hardy told the reporter they were enjoying the tour, and that British audiences were, "the best in the world."

Of his partner, Hardy revealed: "When we are rehearsing, he still seems so funny to me that I often burst out laughing." He went on to describe their partnership as not only one of the longest in show business, but "certainly the happiest." The article said of Stan:

> He has not been well of late, and, although a variety tour is no rest cure, he is enjoying the change. 'The stage is in my blood,' he said, 'and British audiences are so wonderful to play to. We don't go in for the sophisticated type of thing. It is the real, old-fashioned knock-about stuff, and people seem to like it, for it is the kind of thing they used to love in the old variety halls.
>
> Our act is really a pantomime out of season. We both like the provincial theatres. It is here where our act is best appreciated - especially by the children.'

Photo by picture editor of the *Sentinel* – Huston Spratt

The Laurels and the Hardys stayed the week at the North Stafford Hotel, a couple of miles outside Hanley, opposite Stoke railway station. Although the newspapers reported only Laurel as being unwell, others noted Hardy to be constantly breathless, and finding it difficult to rise from his chair once he had sat down.

An insider also revealed that Hardy felt it necessary to bathe three times daily, as he was constantly perspiring. Between shows, however, Hardy managed frequent trips to the pub, the Mechanic's Inn, at the rear of the Theatre Royal.

Several years after Stan and Babe had left Hanley, Fred Peake, owner of the Theatre Royal, was asked why he kept a dirty, worn, and battered settee in his front room, when he could so easily afford a new one. He replied: "Laurel and Hardy sat on that settee, and when that goes out of the house – so do I." Apparently Fred had loaned the settee as a prop for the second scene of the Boys' sketch, where they break into the police chief's home.

```
My Dear Booth,                                          7-4-52.
Had a letter from Ben Shipman, who is trying to make a deal
for us to make more TV & appearances in various Foreign
Countries - Egypt - Turkey - Greece - Italy & Israel -
which sounds bloody silly to me - there was also a guy
named Pascal (I think Paramount) with them who has the idea
for a series of MOLNAR Stories with us - am not familiar
with those stories - so don't know if any good for us or
not.
   Am feeling fine - get a bit tired once in a while - but
manage to keep going.
   Terrific Bus. in Hanley last week. Opening tonight here
with big advance Booking so looking forward to another
Bumper week.
```

[AJM: Again we are indebted to Bernie Hogya for some additional information: "Ferenc Molnár (1878-1952) was a Hungarian-born dramatist and novelist who is now best remembered for the play *Liliom* on which the Rodgers & Hammerstein's musical *Carousel* is based."]

From Hanley, the company made the relatively short journey to Leeds, a place Stan had first worked whilst in his teens – for which no newspaper coverage could be found. In 1952, little had changed, with there being no press write-up of Laurel and Hardy's arrival or departure. The review of the first night's performance was also in danger of being overlooked. It read:

> There is no doubting the popularity of Laurel & Hardy, to judge by the packed first house at Leeds Empire last night. The two went through their film antics in a comedy sketch and the result was uproarious. If you like Laurel & Hardy then you will not be disappointed in their real selves as compared with their celluloid ones.

The *Yorkshire Evening News* wasn't much better:

> Laurel & Hardy's sketch is amusing without being hilarious – for the obvious reason that they are not backed by all the tricks and paraphernalia of film making. A legitimate complaint will be that, having come all the way from Hollywood, their appearance is all too brief.

Nor the *Yorkshire Post*:

> A two-sketch act with Stan Laurel and Oliver Hardy up to all the silly tricks that made them famous is the chief attraction in the Leeds Theatre. Despite the limitations of the stage, this couple are as funny as we have known them in films. Laurel saying little, but always the wrong thing, and Hardy sums up: "This is another fine mess you've gotten me into!" But a most enjoyable mess.

[AJM: Before Laurel and Hardy nit-pickers become enraged, I ought to point out the actual comment Oliver Hardy made on screen was: "Here's another *nice* mess you've gotten me into." The phrase "*fine* mess" became the popularised version because one of Laurel & Hardy's early films was titled: *Another Fine Mess*. 1930.]

After neglectful coverage of their stage characters, no less than three Leeds' journalists sought to find out what Laurel and Hardy were like in private life. Just what caused the sudden fixation remains a mystery; but, for posterity, below are the "facts" as discovered by Edgar Craven and Con Gordon, of the *Yorkshire Evening Post*; and R.C. Scriven, from the *Yorkshire Observer*.

> The star dressing room at Leeds Empire is small anyway. Occupied by the 6ft 1in, 22st. presence of Oliver Hardy, duplicated in wall mirrors, it seemed as though I was interviewing the great man in a telephone kiosk. There was an air of unreality about the proceedings. It seemed so improbable that the idol of one's boyhood could be there in the flesh – all 22st. of him. It seemed even odder that there was no Laurel. Then the door opened a few inches and Stan Laurel managed to enter. At once everything seemed natural. One somehow felt the vague pervading influence of the Mad Hatter, an impression heightened when Hardy boomed, 'Boy', could you find some tea?'

Stan Meets Jefferson

[AJM: The 'Boy' was Bert Tracey, a former film actor, who had worked with Babe Hardy during Hardy's pre-Laurel days with Vim Comedies, Jacksonville, Florida, 1916. Now needing a job, Tracey had been appointed by Hardy as his dresser.]

> He brought a very English tea tray complete with brown teapot and rich plum cake. 'Stan converted me to English afternoon tea,' said Ollie. He cut the plum cake into enormous slabs and handed them round. Laurel reached out eagerly. 'Stanley!' said Hardy at his most magisterial, 'Visitors.' Abashed, Laurel fidgeted with his tie. It was rather like the dormouse and the teapot. In fact in real life Laurel & Hardy are each rather the opposite of their screen personalities. Laurel is a quick, lively, facetious talker, always ready to crack a joke at his friend's expense.

Either Hardy is teaching the manager an uncomfortable way to do his trademark tie-twiddle, or he is trying to strangle him owing to the mixed reviews.

Con Gordon said of Stan: "He's no fool. He has in fact a touch of intellectual acerbity." And of Hardy:

> Hardy is no bulky egotist. He is a big, simple, friendly soul, who every day says his prayers, and reads the Bible. He is proud that their stage act is clean enough to be commended by the clergy and simple enough to be applauded by children.

> On the present day state of British music hall, Stan said:

> What I miss, is the sort of comic we had in my early days on the stage – men who played comic characters – George Formby Snr., Harry Weldon, Mark Sheridan, Tom Foy, and a lot more. They didn't just walk out in a dinner suit and reel off gags. They were funny to see, as well. You seem to have only a few of that sort left.

Later in the week, the *Evening News* chose to submit yet more trivia:

> Quite a few people I know, who rarely go to see a variety show, have been to Leeds Empire this week. They went, I think, not merely because this droll pair epitomise a type of comedy which never palls and, despite modern sophistication, never will. To many they were the first favourites of childhood cinema-going and, in twenty five years of film-making, they must have amused several generations of youngsters.

> Have they had as much fun out of it as they gave? I put the question to them during a chat this week.

'It used to be fun,' replied Stan Laurel, 'but now it's different. It is all too commercialised, too much production, too many people telling you what to do. Nothing is done spontaneously – and spontaneity is the essence of our work.'

Oliver Hardy put in, 'For eighteen years Stan produced and wrote all our pictures. We made things up as we went along. That was the best time.'

The two are housed in separate dressing rooms – Stan in a large one, Ollie fitting his bulk into about one-third of the space, next door. But Stan needed the larger accommodation. He has been receiving the family between shows. Quite a crowd of them were in the other night – mostly cousins who live in Dewsbury, Castleford, and other parts of the West Riding.

The relatives mentioned above were Stan's Aunt and Uncle – Mr. & Mrs. John Shaw, and three cousins. On Sunday, all had been entertained by Stan at the Queen's Hotel.

Stan's wife Ida had rather less luck with her visitor. Whilst allowing herself an uncustomary afternoon away from the theatre, a caller arrived at Stan's dressing room and announced: "I'm your wife's cousin, from Shanghai." After enduring dressing rooms full of Stan's visitors, it was just Ida's luck that, on the one day a visitor came to see her, she wasn't there to meet him.

Fortunately her cousin was resident at the City University, in Leeds, so the two were soon reunited. Stan, meanwhile, was about to enjoy a reunion with other family members when he and Hardy next stopped off for a week in Nottingham.

o-o-0-o-o

Chapter 5

HIGHLANDS and MIDLANDS

It was a glorious hot Easter Sunday and, after signing in at the County Hotel, in Nottingham, the Laurel and Hardy party were driven on a further fifteen miles to go and have lunch at Stan's sister's. Olga and her husband Bill were now at the Bull Inn, Bottesford, having moved from nearby Barkston shortly after Stan's father, Arthur Jefferson, passed away (15 January 1949).

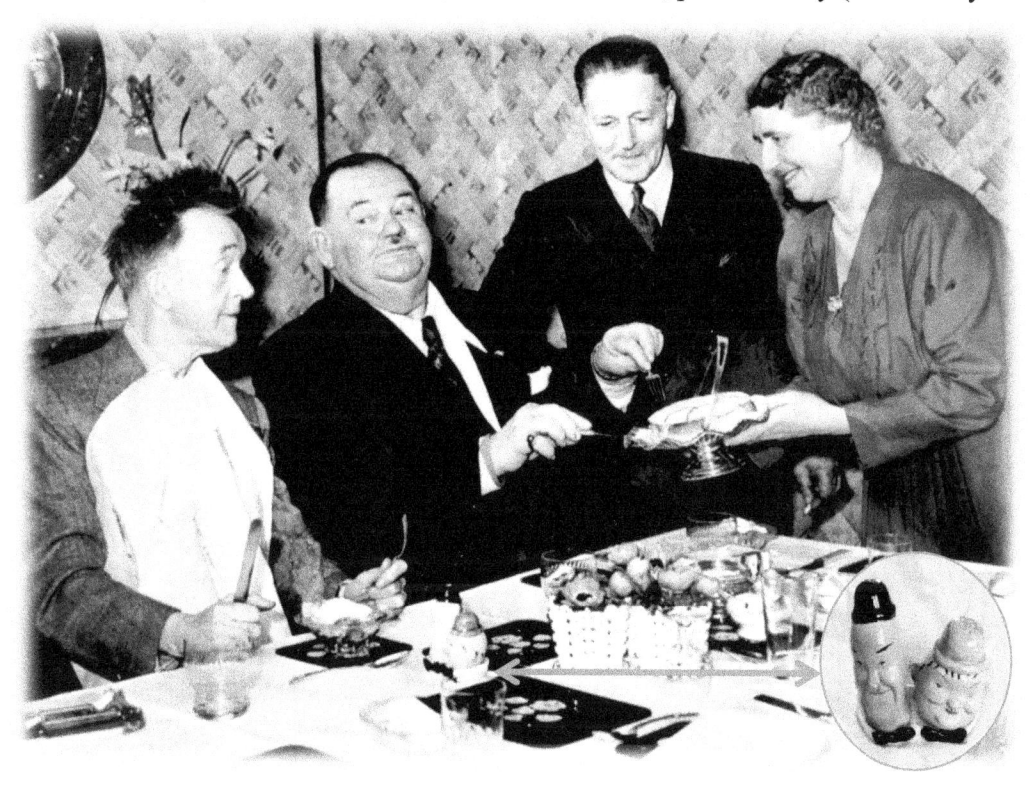

It was gone 2 o'clock when the visitors arrived, by which time the pub had been cleared of patrons — leaving the VIPs alone to enjoy Sunday roast, a few English beers, and five hours of privacy before the pub reopened. That was the plan, but Dick Bradshaw provided us with this account, which goes along with the old adage of: "The best laid plans of mice and men ...":

> My grandfather was Arthur Bradshaw, the local police sergeant. Doing his rounds of the three pubs in the village, to make sure Sunday licensing hours were being upheld, he spotted a party of people inside the Bull. Imagine his utter surprise when, in going to investigate, he found the out-of-hours drinkers were Laurel and Hardy.
>
> When he went into the usual lecture he gave to offenders, it developed into a farce (just like Laurel & Hardy's brushes with the law in their films). When he threatened to lock them up in the local police cells, they actually went along with it. Upon arrival, Ollie, who had expressed interest in the Victorian cells, went inside one to get the feel. Big mistake! Stan gave the wink to Arthur, locked the cell door, and left Ollie hollering to be let out. All was forgiven when granddad next took them home for tea and cakes, where they kept the Bradshaw family amused around the table.
>
> Then it was back to the Bull Inn, for the evening session. Stan, being careful not to break the law again, reacted to one patron's request for "a pint" by serving him a glass of water. The rest of the evening went off like a normal pub night, with drinks and a game of darts for the two Hollywood stars, who were happy to mix with Olga's invited circle of friends.

The evening ended with their hosts, Olga and Bill, promising to go and see the show during the week, whilst bidding the VIPs a fond farewell when the car came to take them back to their hotel. Dematerialising from Bottesford, the twosome re-appeared in Nottingham – if the review in the Journal is to be believed:

> Had anyone asked 'Do you believe in fairies?' at the Nottingham Empire last night, the whole audience would have roared 'YES'. They could not have helped it. For the fairies were there in person – Laurel & Hardy. There they were, materialised in the flesh, exactly as the screen had always told us. It was a lesson to all unbelief. Their panto on stage seems even more exquisite than it is on the screen. **[AUDIO]**

It took Jeff Cragg, who was a small boy at the time, to provide a little more of what it felt like to be in that theatre, observing these two great comics:

> What really made an impression on me was the applause. Their act wasn't very much: there were one or two typical bits from their films. I now realise that the audience had, like us, paid to go in so as to be able to clap for all the films they had seen. When the pair first appeared on stage it just went on and on, past all reason. It must have been several minutes. None of us wanted to stop.
>
> Despite being obviously two elderly non-too-strong men, their performance was professional and seemed, in retrospect (40 years), to have been the best they could do. All they needed to have done was stand on the stage and bow, and take their hats off, but they gave a little demonstration of what they did in the pictures as well.

The two comedians next materialised in Shrewsbury, where the press were at pains to string together two sentences regarding their presence there:

> Laurel & Hardy's names still have the magic to pull in their audiences at the Granada Cinema, Shrewsbury, and if their appearance continues on the same lines as Monday's show, then all box office records will be broken. Their act is very much on the lines of their films – two down-and-outs in trouble with authority – and despite their mellow years the comedy couple still invest it with some energy.

Little too was reported outside the theatre, except for Wednesday, when the Boys and their wives attended a Police Ball, at the Music Hall. There, when pausing to sign one of many autographs, Laurel remarked to the Chief Constable, Douglas Osmond: "It's a change not to be asked for fingerprints."

Highlands and Midlands

It was Lucille's birthday, and she was able to celebrate in the company of scores of policemen. Three days earlier she had had fifty-five pounds stolen from her room at the Raven Hotel. (There's never one around when you need one!) The detectives sent to investigate the theft reported back that Mrs. Hardy was an exceedingly difficult person to deal with, whereas Mr. Hardy treated the whole incident as a great joke. Laurel, too, dismissed it on the lines of: "It's no use crying over split milk." [*sic*]

```
My Dear Booth-                                    30-4-52.
Had big excitement last Saturday night at the Hotel in
Shrewsbury while we were at the Theatre - someone robbed
our room (Hotel) & took £50.00 in notes - Eda had locked
away in her make-up kit - They took it out of room & forced
it open in a Public Toilet in the hallway. It was
discovered by the management & when we got back a dozen
detectives were investigating etc. I think an inside job.
Of course we shall never see it again - so no use worrying
about it - or writing about - could have been worse.
```

The Officials and committee of the Police Ball, pictured at the Music Hall, Shrewsbury.

Two eye-witness reports refer to Laurel's movements outside of the theatre. In one, he visited a chiropodist, and in the other it is claimed he stayed with a Wallace and Martha Riley, in the nearby village of Longden Coleham. It is further speculated in the article (*Shrewsbury Chronicle* 7 March 2002) that the Rileys may have been distant relatives. However, upon further inspection of this article it appears that the two accounts are both concerning *the Rileys*. So the more likely scenario is simply that Laurel went to see Mr. Riley purely to have his feet treated, and the claims of staying there, and of being related, are totally unfounded.

[AJM: Taken in isolation, the probability of Stan and/or Hardy staying at someone's house, when a hotel would seem to be the most popular choice, is hard to believe. However, other such claims are dotted throughout the British tours. Alec Frutin (*ibid.*) stated (in a personal letter to me) that, in 1947, during the Laurels' and the Hardys' two-week stay in Glasgow, all four stayed at his house. And, for the same period, Alexander Gibson (a manager for MGM) claimed (in a newspaper article in the *Glasgow Extra* – 22 November 2001) that both couples stayed at his house in Atholl Drive, Giffnock. And yet a third Glasgow resident making a similar claim was Alex King (*ibid.*) – and yet it is a fact that the Laurel and Hardy party was booked into the Central Hotel (which, of course, doesn't prove they slept there on all fourteen nights). [Refer back to the chapter dealing with the Glasgow 1947 visit!]

Then there was the visit, in 1947, to a guest house in Manchester. More examples of visits to the homes of members of the public can also be found throughout this narrative so, working on the adage: "There's no smoke without fire," it would seem that there is a distinct possibility that at least some of these claims are correct – although I would not consider the Shrewsbury claim to be one of them.]

Continuing this 1952 tour, the Boys where next in Edinburgh. Mass hysteria had erupted on their two previous arrivals at Scotland's second city, so barriers had been erected to keep back the fans. Ironically they weren't needed this time around, as the expected thousands turned out to be just one hundred.

The worry was that fans would break through the barriers at the train station, but here the two stars are having trouble breaking OUT.

Once inside their hotel, the Caledonian, Stan and Babe were told of the precautions which had been taken to protect them from being kidnapped. This was only a light-hearted threat made by the Students Union, whose members were holding their annual 'Rag Week.' Laughing it off, Hardy said of the kidnappers: "They would have a load on their hands."

Despite the smaller turnout at the station, the show itself did good business, as the *Evening News* will confirm:

> Laurel & Hardy had no reason to complain of their reception at Edinburgh Empire, a full house giving them a cordial reception both before and after their sketch. It was typical Laurel & Hardy stuff, and if the stage does not give them the elbow-room of the film, the couple put over the laughter raising antics with genuine artistry.

The reviewer is quite right when he opined that Laurel & Hardy had no reason to complain, as Stan, for one, was well-pleased with the audience's reception, and even got in an unusual (for him) humorous comment in this letter written from his room in the Caledonian Hotel:

```
My Dear Booth-
Just getting over a lousey cold otherwise am fine - opened
Edinburgh here last night (28TH) show went well - Bus.
swell - our Hotel room is facing Edinburgh Castle, a lovely
sight but so bloody old fashioned - so far behind the
times! Now in Hollywood, we —
```

In May – the month in which the headlines were for Queen Elizabeth taking up residence at Buckingham Palace – Laurel and Hardy had to content themselves with being mentioned only in theatrical reviews. In writing of their next show, in Birmingham, Norman Holbrook, of the *Evening Despatch*, questioned his own merits as a member of the audience:

> Twenty years ago Laurel & Hardy were names to conjure with. If the ecstatic behaviour of last night's near-capacity audience is any criterion, they are still. Which, when you come to think of it, is quite an achievement. Their sketch is woefully thin, but what of it? The old, odd antics are still there, although perhaps less exuberant than in the old days. As one of their fans of 1932 I was a shade disappointed when I saw my old comical heroes at close quarters. But then I usually am.

Brian Harvey of the Birmingham *Post & Mail* did not give any quarter. Although his review would send any Laurel and Hardy *fan* running to find a pair of boxing gloves, a *buff* would accept most of the overall sentiments expressed therein:

> As you come away from Birmingham Hippodrome this week, you can assure yourself that you have seen Laurel & Hardy 'in person,' as the posters say. What more? Little, I'm afraid. Last night, at their opening performance, the greeting they received was shrill with delighted anticipation in a way which made the applause at the end of their twenty minute sketch seem tame. The sketch itself is flimsy material; and, to do them credit, they do not waste any exertion in trying to stretch it beyond its somewhat pathetic limits. Frankly, any pantomime producer would be accounted a failure who could not put more pace and more 'gags' into these proceedings. But then, we are seeing Laurel & Hardy – 'in person,' and most people will be satisfied to know that Oliver's size is really as massive as it appears on the screen, and that Stanley does scratch his own head.

The above phrase, questioning the pace and the gags, would seem to be more than a little over-critical, considering the sketch was written by one of the best film gagmen in the business. But then this wasn't film – it was live stage. The rest of the review is simply the compiler's opinion of what he observed; although, to be honest, he was looking through the eyes of a humourless man. To a lesser degree, aspects of his opinion were by no means isolated – as other reviews will show. But no-one was about to tell the old master

Billy Nelson introducing his former Roach co-Stars to his son, who was working at the Birmingham Hippodrome.

anything he did not already know. According to biographer John McCabe, Stan said of the script of *A Spot of Trouble*: "It worked for us at the time, but I wouldn't like to be remembered for it."

For the second week in a row, the Laurel & Hardy show now had to travel half the length of England to fulfil the next booking. Even though the two stars had landed at the port of Southampton on three different occasions, the local press had allowed their comings and goings to pass almost unnoticed – dare I say: "like ships in the night." Now that the two comedy stars were actually about to spend time in Southampton itself, at the Polygon Hotel and the Gaumont Cinema, no attempt was made to redress the balance. The *Southern Daily Echo* said only:

> This is probably the best variety programme the Gaumont has put on since stage facilities were restored in 1950. Stan & Ollie themselves are a riot; they are just as much at home (and just as funny) before the footlights as before the cameras. None of the old magic has gone, and although the sketch does not, perhaps, do them full justice. Stan can still bring the house down just by looking at his audience (those famous eyebrows!). And what a joy to hear that comic little signature tune; from a real live orchestra; in a real live theatre; to introduce a real live Laurel & Hardy.

John Fisher [producer of top TV magic shows, and author of several books on magic] gave me some of his local knowledge:

> There was a cut that reached down from the Polygon Hotel, to the Gaumont Theatre, and Stan and Ollie were known to walk the short distance to the theatre using this route. To this day, it is still known by some locals as "Laurel and Hardy Way."

The following week, in what was literally their second port of call, the Boys arrived in Liverpool. The *Liverpool Echo* was none too complimentary:

> Laurel & Hardy's 'bit of nonsense' – their own description* provides glimpses of this famous comedy team at their best, but suffers from a flimsy plot. The act follows much along the line of their film shorts, and the audience delight in their slapstick, 'double-takes' – but even the best of nonsense requires some sense of reality.

[*Hardy was still using the closing-line, "We hoped you enjoyed our bit of nonsense," from the 1947 tour.]

And that was just about the sum of Laurel & Hardy's impact on the press of Liverpool. In 1947 they had been mobbed in scenes that would only be repeated some seventeen years later, when the Beatles were to hit their peak. But it is the ticket-buying public whose views really count. Here is what the theatre manager of the Liverpool Empire had to say in his end-of-week report:

> Excellently received wonderful performers but rather dated in their generation & with material which is hardly likely to beat what is almost a heat-wave. Their sketch brings continual laughs & they work to a storming finish. The kind of stuff that children would love & yet our audiences are normal – practically all grown-ups.

The box-office (children or no children) did excellent business, with a 75% excess, and the manager stating that he would have the Hollywood comedy couple back.

Stan had 'happy added to happy' when an old friend from his days in panto paid him a visit:

```
My Dear Trixie,
Jackie Harrison came to
Liverpool & spent Saturday
night with me, so you can
imagine the Gab Fest we had -
talking over the old days,
needless to tell you we had a
grand time & a lot of laughs
over The Armstrong Bros.
Randy Cutter etc. I really
enjoyed it. We are having a
nice Time here.
```

To give you a flavour of the panto, and a few of the names which Laurel mentions in various letters, on the right is a review from 1907.

> **CONSETT - NEW THEATRE**
> Lessee: Mr Hugh Robertson;
> Resident Manager Mr. Lloyd Clarence.
> Messrs. Levy and Cardwell's company, with the pantomime *The Sleeping Beauty*, opened to a packed house on Monday. Miss Isa Gibson in the title-role was a complete success; whilst Miss Kitty Trewitt as "Prince Florizel" was very pleasing; Miss Marie Lumberg, as "Sir Alphonso", Miss Trixie Wyatt, and Miss Daisy Thompson Wood as the "Heralds" were well received. Master Jack Harrison as "King Dreadnought" and the Brothers Armstrong as the "Queen" and "Asbestos" were an excellent trio. Wee Georgie Wood as "Bertie Dalrymple" kept the audience in roars of laughter, his comic business being exceptionally funny. Master Jack Adamson as "Julius Caesar" and Master Stanley Jefferson as "Ebeneezer" were very good, and the dancing of Mlle. Adele quite a speciality. The Ballets were well arranged, and the scenery and dresses elaborate.

Highlands and Midlands

Back to 1952, and here is a photograph from an event I can provide the details of, but which, despite dedicated research, have never been able to accurately date.

The best guesstimate I can make is that this visit was made during the week at Liverpool, wherein Laurel and Hardy may have been hoping to encourage the people of Warrington to make their way to Liverpool to watch the show. [**AUDIO**]

Manager of the Ritz Cinema, Bob Parsons, holds the mic' of a tape-recorder, as Stan and Ollie read out a scripted message, which will then be played to the audience at Saturday's 'ABC Minors Club.'

Although the Liverpool engagement came only a third of the way into the tour, Laurel was concerning himself with bookings for when the tour had finished:

```
                                    Empire Theatre,
                                    Liverpool, Eng.
                                    23-5-52.
My Dear Booth-
We may do Panto here at the London Palladium, Xmas - Ben
Shipman is coming over to look into the deal - will let you
know if anything happens.
South Africa deal is off - can't get Dollars out of there.
Too bad - I would have liked to have gone - but of course
not for my health.
```

Although South Africa was out, the Laurel & Hardy Company were still going to have to travel overseas for their next few shows.

o-o-0-o-o

Chapter 6

DUBLIN UP

The aforementioned sea journey began on Sunday 25 May, and ended on Monday 26th. That may make it seem like a long voyage, but it was only across the Irish Sea, from Holyhead to Dublin. The change in date was caused by the voyage being on the overnight ferry service. But the car journey from Liverpool to the ferry port at Holyhead, on the Isle of Anglesey, North Wales, added to the length and fatigue factor of the total journey, which resulted in the touring party being too tired to make it for breakfast. It was 11:30am before a reporter from the *Dublin Evening Mail* witnessed any indication of life at the Gresham Hotel, Dublin:

> Stan Laurel was the first on the scene looking every inch like that silly little man who was guaranteed to get his partner into every conceivable mess. Immediately he spoke, however, a big difference was noticeable. Instead of that squeaky high pitched voice which comes from the screen, one listened to a soft, deeper toned voice from a quiet man who had not a great deal to say but a very charming and rather shy way of saying it. Then came Oliver Hardy, looming even larger in life than he does on the screen, and still sporting his tiny moustache. This is their first visit to this country.

That night, the party had a chance to catch up on some well-earned rest, as the show was cancelled because it had not been possible to get the props and scenery over in time.

Come Tuesday, Laurel and Hardy's first show on Irish soil got under way. The *Evening Mail* saw it as follows:

> A howl of laughter greeted Laurel & Hardy as they walked on stage at the Olympia Theatre, looking exactly as they do in all their films. The laughter came from the adult members of the audience who had been fans for the past twenty-five years and were obviously delighted to see all their old mannerisms and facial expressions brought so wonderfully to life before their eyes. Their act is ideal for children of all ages, containing the maximum of slapstick [not according to the *Peterborough Standard*, it isn't], but it has a very special appeal for those who have been faithful followers and will, therefore, recognise many of the scenes. There is not enough of them, but the time they are with us is filled with laughter.

The *Evening Herald* was also much taken with the Boys:

> On to the stage strode a little man wearing a broad benign grin, a pair of big baggy trousers, a battered bowler, and carrying what once upon a time might have been a respectable-looking violin case. The crowd roared with delight, only to break into a howl of mirth a moment later when he was followed by a somewhat large gentleman, with a worried countenance, and a gleam in his eye that spelled trouble for the little man with the benign grin. Yes, it was Dublin's welcome for those famous comedians, Laurel & Hardy. Personally I found them much more entertaining in person than in celluloid. In two short scenes they manage to convey their genius for the trade that has kept them in the forefront for so long.

The *Dublin Times* wasn't going to spoil the party:

> Laurel & Hardy merely have to appear on stage, and the house rocks, shrieks and hoots with laughter. The verbal jokes are good old music-hall jokes, but the real felicity of the comedy lies in situation, slapstick and facial expression. It's all childishly simple; it's all clean; and it's all uproariously funny. Much of the laughter came from children, but their parents were spellbound, too.

Good to note the presence of children in the audience, this time around. But it certainly wasn't just children who loved our comedy characters. Pretty well anyone who grew up on a diet of their films still loved them. One such man was Earl Connolly, who was able to use his 'licence' as the entertainments writer for the *Limerick Leader*, to get himself, his wife Callie and some friends, backstage to meet his idols. Callie told a friend:

> They were very down to earth. Just before the photo was taken of them together Stan said, "I just have to do my hair," and he did the famous 'hand through the hair' - as we have seen him do many times in film.

DUBLIN EMPIRE – 27 May 1952
Callie Connolly, Earl Connolly, Jim Marshall, Jim O' Carroll, Mrs. Murphy and Ida Laurel.
(With a special 'thank you' to Derek Ward for the story and photo.)

With two shows per night for *thirteen* nights, plus matinees; a guest appearance at The Crystal Rooms; and nightly cinema showings of the 1951 Laurel & Hardy film, *Robinson Crusoeland* (*ibid.*); it would appear that every Dubliner had been satisfied, so the theatre company moved on to Belfast, a hundred miles due north, to play the Grand Opera House. This magnificent theatre, with its splendid mixture of Baroque, Flemish, and Oriental architecture holds one thousand people but, even so, it was necessary for Laurel and Hardy to play two weeks there to cater for demand. This is what the *Belfast Telegraph* thought of the show:

> The sketch shows much of the hilarious technique so familiar on the screen. Its best moments are when the two comics tie themselves in knots trying to find comfort on a railway waiting room seat. In the second part, a burglary scene, there is less of the knockabout fun that one might have expected, but the drole [*sic*] appearance of the two loveable characters should satisfy most patrons. A tribute in itself to their skill is that their patter is spotlessly clean.

Laurel was thrilled with their reception — both off-stage and on:

```
My Dear Booth-                                              24-6-52
Sorry so long in answer yours of the 9th. inst. Haven't had
much chance to get down to personal correspondence due to
the exciting visit to Ireland. Being our first time here,
they went ALL OUT to give us a true Irish Welcome & didn't
miss a thing. Bus. as you can imagine was enormous - broke
house record here (57 years)
```

Being seen in the theatre by two thousand people per night, didn't seem to staunch the flow of people who also wanted to see them by day. Come Saturday, one article in the *Belfast Telegraph* ran the headline: "Laurel & Hardy are 'prisoners' in Belfast."

In a second-floor apartment of the Midland Hotel this afternoon, the two loneliest men in the city sat silently listening to the radio. To the hotel staff they have become known as 'the prisoners of Room 113.' The only contact with the life of the hotel comes when a waiter takes them food. The 'prisoners' would very much like to go out, but that is impossible.

Since they arrived their only glimpse of Royal Avenue has been from a speeding car. When they are due to go to the theatre the car draws up at the Midland, and a few seconds later they make a dash through the hotel lobby and drive away.

The pair are so well known, they attract crowds whenever they appear in public. Oliver Hardy told me: 'we've had a wonderful reception in Belfast – and we'd hate it too if we weren't recognised – but as things are we just have to stay locked up in here.' Then Oliver put the phone down and went back to his easy chair and the radio.

If the above can be taken seriously – one young man must consider himself very fortunate to have met the Boys in the way he did:

> One afternoon, I was passing the Midland Hotel when out of the front door came Laurel and Hardy. I couldn't believe my eyes, and immediately smiled at both of them. Then I said: 'Good afternoon Mr. Hardy, good afternoon Mr. Laurel.' – It was like looking at a movie. I said: 'Thank you for the many hours of happiness you have given me.'
>
> They both reached out their hands and Ollie pushed Stan's hand away as he had done a thousand times in the movies. I was convulsed. They got into a taxi, obviously to go to the theatre. The longest day I live I can still see them, as they waved me goodbye.

In the 1970s and '80s there was hardly a week went by when this man's face was not on the telly. It was Irish comedian, Frank Carson (1926–2012); a man who didn't just kiss the Blarney Stone – he swallowed it.

On the first night of the second week in Belfast, an incident happened almost identical to the one during Laurel and Hardy's second week in Glasgow in 1947 — when accordionist McKenzie Reid had walked on stage at the end of *The Driver's Licence* sketch. Here in 1952, Reid reprised his walk-on part, playing the accordion, followed by the rest of the cast who lined up and sang (Yes! you've guessed it) "Happy Birthday to Stan."

Laurel always enjoyed celebrating his birthday, but I don't think Hardy gave a hoot about his own — although he was never one to refuse cake. Hardy was, however, so in love with Lucille, that he celebrated their Wedding Anniversary – EVERY WEEK. [Yes! I know anniversaries are yearly – but try telling that to the Hardys.]

Laurel gives us more background information in this extract from a letter to Booth Colman:

```
Had a birthday
last week. Eda
arranged a
surprise party
for me at the
Theatre - after
our act -
orchestra struck
up "Happy
Birthday" Dept. &
the whole Co.
came on stage &
audience joined
in - Three cakes
in dressing room
(couldn't get all
the candles on one). Plenty to drink - a regular "Come Ye
Come All" stage hands, musicians, theatre staff etc. even
the Lord Mayor of Belfast - so a good time was had by all.
```

And yet more revelations from Stan:

```
Ben Shipman was there busy with his
camera as usual. He flew back home
last Sunday. Give him a call & see
the pictures - & news etc. Know he
will be delighted. I was presented
with 3 Shilleaglies (good luck
Bus.) & will be able to cut a few
notches in them when I make a round
of the Hollywood Producers!
```

[With thanks to Tyler St. Mark]

The following night, Stan and Ollie got themselves roped in to judging a Talent Show — not at the Belfast Grand Opera House, but at the Tonic Cinema, Bangor. And they did it without leaving their dressing rooms. So how was this managed in pre-computer, pre Skype times. For the answer, see the "lost" photo which follows!

Dublin Up

By tuning in to the BBC broadcast from the Bangor cinema on the radio (seen behind them), the Boys were able to listen to the acts, and then make comments and award their marks.

After seventeen weeks of working at a high energy level, the Boys were finally forced to take a week off. Babe was in need of a rest and, along with Lucille, took a holiday in Dublin.

Poor old Stan though was in a bad way. He had been suppressing his diabetic condition for a while, but it had now got all too much for him; and so, wisely, he had himself admitted to the Musgrave & Clark Clinic, in Belfast.

He told a reporter: *"I'm only going in for a check-up. It's nothing serious."* But he was wrong. A fully-trained nurse, Nancy Jane Reid, was assigned to look after him. She remembered Laurel looking like "a little, lost soul," and added:

> He was painfully thin, and the dressing-gown he wore didn't do anything for him – but when he got up and put on his suit, he looked very nice.
>
> I remember a desk was brought up to his room, for he seemed to be always writing. I thought perhaps he was writing a book, or a script for his show. He was a very nice writer.
>
> His room was at the end of the building. It had a big window which looked out onto a nice lawn, and a tall chestnut tree. He used to sit and look out quite a bit, watching the birds. He was quite sneaky, as the following incident will show:
>
> Dr. Smith, who specialised in diabetes, was looking after Mr. Laurel. He was very worried that he couldn't get him 'stabilised.' Then one afternoon Mrs. Laurel phoned Dr. Smith's office to inquire about Stan's progress. When told he was having trouble getting him stabilised, his wife said:
>
> 'Don't say I told you, but Stan has a very sweet tooth, and you might be enlightened if you took a look under his pillow.'
>
> So next morning the doctor came in and Mr. Laurel was sitting up in bed – the picture of innocence, and Dr. Smith said:
>
> 'How are you this morning, my good man?'
>
> Mr. Laurel said: 'Fine'.
>
> By this time, the doctor had edged up towards the top of the bed and slipped his hand under the pillow, and sure enough, there was a box of chocolate and papers from other candies. Poor Mr. Laurel! What a mess he had got himself into. He wasn't even able to scratch his head. He wouldn't say where he got the chocolate. I think he brought a good supply with him, for when we searched, he had some in his case.
>
> After that, his blood checks soon became normal, and he was able to be discharged. Before he left he signed autographs for all the domestic staff, from a pile of photographs he brought with him. He was a real gentleman!

Stan wasn't, of course, writing a book (as suggested by Nancy), but taking the opportunity to reply to the mountain of letters he had accumulated, including yet another to Booth Colman.

```
We are laying off this week so decided to go into Hospital
here for rest & check up, so am able to get a chance to
clean up my desk with the mail dept. away from the
maddening crowd.
```

> Eda sends love & everything. She is staying at hotel &
> visits me every day. She has a bit of a cold but otherwise
> OK. I am feeling fine - the rest doing me a lot of good.

[AJM: I wonder if Stan knew that the Thomas Hardy book title is actually "Far From the *Madding* Crowd" and had changed it for comic effect, or if he had misquoted it, like many others have.]

The convalescence seemed to do the trick, and Stan was able to complete the rest of the fourteen-week schedule without any stoppages. Upon hearing that Laurel was fit again, Bernard Delfont informed the Boys there was a distinct possibility that he could get them the parts of 'Captain' and 'Mate' in the pantomime *Dick Whittington*, at the London Palladium, for the forthcoming Christmas season. (*Babes in the Wood* had obviously fallen through). Laurel further explained the situation to Booth Colman:

> Panto at the Palladium not definite yet due to the tax
> situation if we come back for Xmas. We have to leave here
> in Oct. otherwise we are liable for Tax on this present
> whole trip plus the States. We have So. Africa & Australia
> offered. but can't get Dollars out, so of course no good
> for us, so all we have open is Italy - Belgium - Holland &
> Scandinavia but will have to do a Pantomime act instead of
> this one.

It was back in 1947 that Laurel and Hardy's tour had opened the doors for other American acts to play Britain, and now their appearances were frequent. Laurel himself was keeping his eye on how well they were doing, of which here are some examples:

> Jack Benny & Dennis Day opened Big at the Palladium - we
> follow them in at the Palace Manchester July 14th & Sophie
> Tucker follows us. Sophie, I understand, hasn't done well
> this trip - she should worry!

Meanwhile, the tour continued. Laurel makes no mention in his letters of how the L&H Company travelled. It is only when newspapers write articles about their arrival that we get to know what transport they used for those particular journeys. In this instance, there would be a mix of modes. First would have come a train journey from Belfast to Dublin; then the ferry crossing from Dublin back to Holyhead, North Wales. How they did the next leg, to Sheffield, whether by car or train is not known. Either way, it was a long journey.

On the way over to Ireland, they had been totally exhausted after the journey from Liverpool to Dublin. But this latest one had the addition of the Belfast leg, plus Sheffield was some distance further on than Liverpool. As it was though, the show hadn't played the week before the Sheffield appearance, so there was not the pressure of having to vacate the theatre on the Saturday night, travel on Sunday, and be ready and set up for Monday morning rehearsals.

In 1932, the Boys had seen little more of Sheffield than the railway station and the inside of the Grand Hotel; but now were able to go wherever they wished. The *Sheffield Telegraph*, however, credited them only with attending the prize-presentation of a competition run by their newspaper; but did get a reporter to interview them:

> It must come as a relief to Sheffielders who have seen their film comedies, that Laurel
> & Hardy are just the same off screen as on. In baggy trousers, tattered white shirt with
> string in place of cuff-links, Stan was sipping pop in his dressing room, at the
> Sheffield Empire. With him was his wife, who was born in Siberia, brought up in

China, became a naturalised American, and is now British on Stan's passport. Complete with his doleful expression, Stan butted in, 'But she loves Yorkshire pud'.'

Hardy was next door, with his very charming wife who comes from Texas. In terrible French, Hardy shouted 'Entrez-vous' as I knocked on his door, and we immediately got down to the question of bowler hats. With a delicately poised finger and an authoritative air, he took a relic down from the shelf, used his sleeve with mock care to 'dust' it and said: 'This one is over twenty years old. We used to buy them by the dozen until we got hold of some which were practicably indestructible.'

As soon as the signature tune trickled out to a darkened stage, the applause was spontaneous with neither of the team yet in view. Briefly, they break into the house of the chief of police with enough commotion to wake the dead.

The critic from the *Sheffield Star*, too, wasn't very informative about the content of the sketch:

Bereft of many of the mechanical aids to humour with which Hollywood has garnished their films, the pair will have to rely mainly on verbal comedy for their success. Will they make it? Certainly! Both Stan and Ollie are natural comics, and if their scope is limited, their wit will be as crazily fanciful as ever.

After seeing the two in action, the same reviewer followed up with:

The genius of Laurel & Hardy is that their comic situations are based firmly on reality. The things that happen to them could happen to anybody – or almost anybody – but their treatment of events is highly individual. In fact, they turn life inside out. On the whole they translate well the atmosphere of live theatre. The two scenes of the sketch are often very funny, especially in the comedians' attempts at burglary, but the slapstick ending would profit from extension.

[AJM: Although the sketch had many good moments of business, the ending *was* very weak. During a chase around the house by the two policemen, Hardy would sit down, exhausted, and utter the immortal words: "Well! here's another nice mess you've gotten me into," and the curtain would come down.]

As a rule, a Wedding Day is the greatest day of a bride's life. This one was made even greater, when two surprise guests walked into the reception, at the Sheffield Grand Hotel. When Stan removed his hat, at the request of wedding-photographer Eric Bellwood, Hardy impishly slipped *his* hat back on. This prompted an improvised "hat fight" from the comedy couple; much to the amusement of the transfixed guest, before Eric finally captured this delightful shot.

Grand Hotel
SHEFFIELD
Eric Bellwood photograph

Travelling from Sheffield to Brighton is not a journey one would relish undertaking with any regularity and, during their stay in this South Coast resort, Stan and Babe were going to need all the recuperative powers it could offer. Not that this one journey was to blame, but the accumulated toll of travelling, twinned with the incredible number of shows performed, was beginning to tell. So much so that, even after the recent week off in Belfast, Laurel had again to see a doctor. He mused: *"I'm like a car battery – I need a spot of recharging now and again."* It then emerged that Laurel had been under medical supervision for quite a while; but, defying doctors' advice, had refused to cancel any tour dates.

One would presume that, because of the distance involved, they did this journey by train. Laurel revealed of the trip, in a letter written from the Royal Crescent Hotel, Brighton, that they had paid a surprise visit to his sister Olga at the *Bull Inn*, Bottesford, on the way down.

Lucille, Babe, Olga, and Ida posing for Stan outside the Bull Inn, Bottesford.

As similar visits had been made when changing trains at Grantham, this would strengthen my theory for the Sheffield-Brighton run being done by train. (The car parked by the pub was most likely used to take them from and to the railway station.)

Most of the Brighton papers printed ready-written trash about the show and its stars (gleaned from the poor press releases in circulation), but the *Brighton Evening Argus* came up with a personal and affectionate account:

> Laurel & Hardy showed us at the Hippodrome Theatre, why they are still the most popular film and comic-strip team. After their act had been duly acclaimed by the audience, a smiling Hardy walked up to the microphone to tell us that watching the show in a box was none other than George Robey. Slowly a surprised Mr. Robey got to his feet – and lifted those famous eyebrows. Then all three stood in humble acknowledgement of the crowd's expression of gratitude for many an hour of entertainment.
>
> It was a simple, sincere gesture from two grand troupers to the greatest figure in English Music Hall. And that simplicity and sincerity are the secret of the Laurel & Hardy success story. They try no tricks, no subtlety, no sophistication. They know the audience want only to see them as they are on the screen and in the comics [comic strips]. It is the good old slapstick action stuff that first put Hollywood in the money. And the audience love it.

To meet the great music-hall comedian George Robey backstage after the show was a great thrill for Stan, as he had been a fan from before the days he himself became a comedian. Stan loved Robey's 'dame' and also took from him the use of a monologue, compiled from extremely long and over-complicated words – an example of which is heard in the attic scene of the Laurel & Hardy film *Sons of the Desert*. (It starts: "For the meticulous care with which you have executed your finely formulated machinations ...").

Joan Turner, top female impressionist of her time, was on the bill that week and, in an interview with the author, gave her personal opinion of Laurel and Hardy as follows:

GEORGE ROBEY

After the first show, Stan came to my dressing room to congratulate me on my act, and apologised that they [Laurel & Hardy] 'didn't have better to offer.' Their timing was dreadful. You see, they weren't really a theatre act. They were used only to working on film sets, where – because there is no audience – timing is totally different. Later in the week, when I accepted an invitation to go to Babe's dressing room for coffee, he too apologised for the poor standard of their act, whilst congratulating me on mine with, 'Sure did like your Gracie Fields, Miss Turner.'

Considering the reception Laurel and Hardy had received, and that it was their name, and theirs alone, which filled the theatre, it is hard to understand why they found a need to apologise at all. It was, however, this almost constant awareness of the strength of their act, and the desire to continually improve it, which kept the comedy duo at the top of their profession for so many years, and one of the reasons why no other act will ever replace them.

Laurel had never stopped believing that he and Ollie would again make films and, while in Brighton, events happened which raised his expectations: The following letter, written by Stan a year later, will explain:

```
                                                June 26th. '53.
Dear Ed [Patterson]:-
Funny you should mention about us doing a picture in Eng. for
Balcon, he sent a fellow to see us when we played in
Brighton, his name was W. P. Lipscomb, he came back to see us
after he had seen the show & seemed very interested, but
nothing has developed to date.
```

The project was a little more than a casual statement made to Laurel, as an American newspaper picked up the story (dated 12 August):

English producer Michael Balcon has writers working on a new Stan Laurel and Oliver Hardy comedy feature, to be made in England.

One of Stan's backstage visitors that week was local author John Montgomery, whom he had first met at Hannen Swaffer's flat in 1947. Offering his services as a guide, John asked if there was any part of Brighton Stan would particularly like to see. The Royal Pavilion having been selected, the two duly met up the following morning. Babe, meanwhile, was at the West Brighton Golf Course. John recalled:

Although Stan was now an elderly man, he was immediately recognisable, and people stopped all along the street and in the Pavilion Gardens to shake his hand, ask for his autograph, and grin at him. During the walk, Stan revealed he had played Brighton as a boy, but couldn't remember in which theatre or what production.

Royal Pavilion, Brighton

John didn't press him to remember, as the idea was for Stan to enjoy a relaxing stroll, and not to be badgered for an interview so, disappointingly, this little piece of information is still unknown — despite extensive efforts by the author to locate at least one solo appearance.

So, after a week of reaching parts of Brighton he had never reached before, Stan contentedly left this seaside resort, and headed back up North, to the city he had visited most in pursuing the stage part of his career — Manchester.

o-o-0-o-o

Chapter 7

SOUTHEND, SOUTHPORT

The press coverage for Laurel and Hardy's 1947 Manchester visit had been exceedingly poor and, in 1952, showed no sign of improvement. Of their show at the Palace Theatre the *Evening Chronicle* revealed:

> Said the small man to the fat man: 'Are you really all one person?' Said the fat man to the small man: 'Shut up and go to bed.'* Laurel & Hardy have been doing this kind of thing for years and years and it is still whole-hearted fun – and clean as a whistle. They have the sense not to stay on the stage too long; nor to attempt anything they can't do. But everything we wanted was there – Oliver wagging his forefinger, Stan bursting into tears and telling the cop: 'I'll sue you for inflammation of character' and remembering, after looking through the wrong end of his field glasses, that he can't read anyway.

A second review, in the *Manchester Guardian*, ran:

> There is no denying those unequalled film clowns Laurel & Hardy are somewhat diminished in a stage appearance. It may be that we have been used for so long to their screen predicaments in close-up form. The enormous time-bomb of Hardy's patience and Laurel's sad but hopeful attempts to do the right thing, like a small boy tinkering with the fuse, seem to need those long excruciating silences that they get on the screen, but did not get last night. Yet their dramatic sketch had some wonderfully funny moments. Particularly when they were trying to sleep on a bench.

[AJM: *The quote in the first review – "Said the small man to the fat man: 'Are you really all one person?' Said the fat man to the small man: 'Shut up and go to bed'." – is part of the dialogue between Stan and Ollie, as they prepare to bed down for the night on the railway bench.]

Sometime during the Manchester stay, comedy actor Michael Bentine got into Stan and Babe's company. In 1994, John Stoker interviewed Bentine, from which he compiled the following:

> Bentine had only recently left 'The Goons' [a team of anarchic comedians comprising of Spike Milligan, Peter Sellers, and Hardy Secombe.] He was surprised to notice that Ollie twiddled his tie while he was talking, and that Stan still had a North Country accent. What amazed him most was that the great comic duo appeared to be more interested in the people who they met. They watched Michael do his famous "Chair-back" routine, and thought that it was hilarious.
>
> Stan was fascinated by the mechanics of comedy and particularly fond of variety theatre, which was still very much alive at the time. He and Michael had much in common, for they had both come up the hard way by learning their craft in provincial theatres.

On the Wednesday night, Laurel and Hardy met an even more famous person – celebrated actor, author, singer, songwriter, playwright, wit, and raconteur Noel Coward. This was at the Midland Hotel, where he was staying during a visit to attend the opening of his play *Quadrille*, at the Opera House — a fact which was duly noted by Stan in a letter dated 17 December 1958:

```
Dear Earl,
I met Noel Coward once in Manchester England in '52. He was
dining with Lunt & Fontaine at the hotel - they were playing
in one of his shows which had just opened - I was introduced
to him, so did'nt have a chance to talk with him at the time.
I saw his "Cavalcade" show at Drury Lane in '32. it was a
magnificent production - I agree with you, he is a genius -
amazing talent.
```

LAUREL and HARDY – The British Tours
MANCHESTER – Midland Hotel

LOST PHOTOS
Noel Coward chatting with Lynn Fontanne and Alfred Lunt, the stars of Coward's new play "Quadrille" – which opens at the Manchester Opera House tomorrow night.

Stan tries one of his film tricks – producing a flame from his thumb – to light Ollie's cigarette.

Lucille showing Ida some dolls in Irish and Scottish national costume, which she bought to send to a niece in America.

And that would have been the sum total of coverage of Laurel and Hardy's week in Manchester until, that is, 2013 when I was sent the following account from a Gordon Bailey:

In July 1952 the Manchester Evening Chronicle announced a new competition. Young readers were asked to draw a cartoon of Laurel and Hardy, who would be appearing at Manchester's Palace Theatre later that month. Laurel and Hardy were my comedy heroes. I had been interested in making people laugh since seeing clowns at the Bell Vue Circus every Christmas time. So, a keen cartoonist, I entered and awaited the results. I was the runner-up in the older age group; 14–16. I was then in a state of counting the days until Laurel and Hardy came to Manchester.

My father and I, with my younger brother, sat in the front row of the stalls and enjoyed the first half of the show. As the curtains closed at the interval, the theatre manager walked to the stage centre and announced the special event: the awarding of prizes to the winners of the newspapers competition, then inviting the winners onto the stage. Laurel and Hardy awarded the prizes, making a joke about my height: I was six foot two inches and towered over the other winners. We were then photographed, before being invited to spend the next twenty minutes behind the curtains with Laurel and Hardy. I was in heaven, sitting and chatting to them, enjoying squash and cakes with them, wanting that interval to go on and on and on.

HERE is an opportunity for youngsters between the ages of 8 and 16 to show what they can do as budding artists. And the 8-year-olds stand an equal chance with the 16-year-olds of winning a prize.
You all know the features of those world-famous comedians, Stan Laurel and Oliver Hardy, who appear at the Manchester Palace Theatre next week?
What you have to do is fill in the eyes, nose, mouth and characteristic expression of each in the two blank faces given above. You may use either paints, crayons, pencil or ink.
There will be THREE CLASSES. 1, For children 8-10 years; 2, 11-13 years; 3, 14-16 years.
The winner of each class will have the choice of a tennis racket, cricket bat, football, swim costume, or hockey stick.
In addition 6 prizes of suitable books will be awarded in each class as consolation prizes.
There will thus be a grand total of 21 winners who will be able to meet Laurel and Hardy in person.
Each winner will receive two tickets (bring Mum along) for the matinee performance at the Manchester Palace Theatre on Saturday, July 19 —and there Laurel and Hardy will present them with their prizes.
Now, kiddies, out with the paints, pen and ink and crayons. Let's see what you can do with this grand little competition.
Address your entry to "Laurel and Hardy," "Evening Chronicle," Kemsley House, Manchester 4, and enclose your full name, address, and age. It should reach us not later than Wednesday, July 16. Look out for the prizewinners on Thursday, July 17.

Gordon is easy to pick out. Although only sixteen, he was 6ft 2ins. tall, which is actually one inch taller than Hardy (whom he is standing behind).

Being told we had to leave and return to our seats caused some disappointment, a feeling that was blown away by the shows second half. And, I could go to school the next morning and tell my schoolmates that I had appeared on stage with Laurel and Hardy. Wow! This experience still excites me whenever I recall it and I still love to tell people, "I appeared on stage with Laurel and Hardy."

The newspaper colouring competition was a regular ploy to attract kids and parents to the Saturday matinee, of which more, later. Meanwhile, it's on with the tour:

Playing inland theatres during the summer months can be the kiss of death, for people are disinclined to sit in a hot stuffy theatre when all outside is bright and sunny. People at seaside resorts, however, go by tradition to theatres. To them, a holiday would not be a holiday without the sun by day and the shows by night. Thus, after having met indifference from some of the places they had played, Laurel and Hardy were both heartened by, and genuinely thankful for, the reception they received in Rhyl – a North Wales seaside resort, in peak season. On the first night outside the Queen's Theatre, queues extended along the promenade in both directions, and the police had to be called to control the crowds who had besieged the stage door. The "House Full" signs stayed in use throughout the week, and potential customers were turned away nightly. The *Rhyl Leader* reported:

> It is saying a lot to say that Stan & Ollie are just as funny on the stage as they are on the screen. In a screamingly funny two-act sketch [were they doing the same one?] they prove that they are born comedians, whose popularity will never wane. Their actions in the waiting room at the station are the quintessence of good comedy, and when they 'break in' to the Chief of Police's home, nobody but Laurel & Hardy could possibly concentrate so many laughs into such a brief space of time.

Having had no problems filling the Queen's Theatre all week, on Friday morning Stan and Babe were asked if they would go along and do the same for a little theatre in Deiniolen. This tiny village, near Bangor, housed one of Britain's first, if not *the* first, "16mm cinema" – The Hanroy. After a warm welcome by the delighted village residents, the comedy couple were treated to a showing of one of their greatest, if not *the* greatest, of their films, *Way Out West*.

At the Saturday afternoon show, back in Rhyl, Stan and Ollie met the winners of the now-customary local newspaper painting/drawing competition. On these occasions there was never any attempt by the Boys to fob the children off with a quickly given prize and a brief handshake. They always went to great lengths to ensure that it was a truly memorable occasion. The children would firstly be taken backstage and shown around; allowed to watch the show; then invited on stage to receive their prizes. Prize-giving ceremonies in the hands of bad presenters can be dull affairs but, in the hands of these two masters of mirth, the event would become a scenario of helpless laughter for both participants and on-lookers, alike.

The Laurels and the Hardys stayed at the Westminster Hotel, in Rhyl, where some of the acts from other shows in town would nightly congregate in the bar. One of these was 'Prince' – proprietor of 'Prince's International Circus' – who was in summer season at the Pavilion Theatre. From the letter he wrote to them, on the Monday following their week in Rhyl, one has an illuminating insight into just how the two comedians' wives, and Hardy himself, socialised off-stage. The following is a transcript of the text:

> Firstly, may I say how extremely delighted we were to have had the real pleasure of meeting you great folks. It was a most pleasurable week for us I can honestly assure you. I sadly miss you for it is like a 'morgue' in the hotel without your grand presence. I have no boozing pals and all the people staying here are 'Tea-Cup' merchants. I think they have all been weaned on blasted 'tea'. Oh for a few nights like we had together. I am sure I shall sign the teetotal pledge and go 'crackers' before the week is over, so do not be surprised if I rush over to Bradford to break it.
>
> May I heartily congratulate you on a very fine performance, but perhaps only what one expects from two such grand troupers. I suppose we all get a little hard-boiled at times, but I honestly laughed more at your brilliant comedy than anything I have seen for ages, especially after watching our 'lousy' clowns doing their best to send the customers to the undertakers to get measured up.
>
> Do trust that you have settled in at Bradford nicely and that The Ladies are happy, also your goodselves. Hope Mrs. Laurel is feeling better and that the old throat is much easier and that the "Gargle" department is having the desired effect, also hope that Stan is feeling better and that you will soon be able to join us in a little 'Jack the Dandy'.
>
> Well old Pals, good luck, good health and God Bless is the sincere wish of the trio with an extra whack from your humble
> "Prince"

In the Yorkshire town of Bradford – a first-time visit for Laurel and Hardy (although Stan had worked there in 1910 with the Karno Company, in *Jimmy the Fearless*) – the reviewer from the *Yorkshire Observer* would have been better classed a *non-observer* when he wrote:

> Last night at the Bradford Alhambra, Laurel & Hardy opened to a capacity house. They brought back to Bradford slapstick comedy which had the entire audience rocking in their seats and one particular sequence when Stan's foot became entangled with Hardy's braces almost stopped the show.
>
> [That's all folks, although there is a short piece of footage taken of Stan by a relative, backstage.]   See [**FILM**] page 161

The Manager's Report adds little:

> Very well received indeed. Maintain their cinema reputation & and are proving a very big attraction.

Local boy Joseph Ellis recalled:

When Stan & Ollie made their entrance, they stood centre stage for a full five minutes or more, and the audience simply laughed and laughed continuously. Everyone was mesmerised – we just couldn't believe we were actually seeing the lovable pair in the flesh. What followed was just like watching one of their films. They were just as funny on stage – in fact, they could have been filming, their timing was so perfect. But it is the memory of that initial entrance, a magical moment, which will always stay with me.

The family foursome stayed at the Midland Hotel, in Bradford, where the hotel receptionist, Bea Winterburn, thought she was doing the Hardys a favour by booking them into a room with twin beds. The Laurels, she thought, could far more easily fit into one double-bed. "Imagine my surprise," she said, "when they came downstairs and told me they'd swapped rooms." Bea found them to be charming people, and popular with the hotel staff.

An alleged visit only came to light in 2011, through a website detailing "Forgotten Pubs." On the day of their arrival in Bradford. Laurel and Hardy took a ten-mile car journey north west of Bradford, to Keighley, where they popped into the Queen St. Arms public house, in Queen Street. There, Stan said "Hello" to the landlady, Edith Riley, who, so the story goes, "was a childhood friend when their parents were involved in travelling theatricals." [Sorry I can't add to that.] The story goes on to inform us that during Edith Riley's remarkable sixty-three-year residence [sic], all the famous theatrical visitors used the pub, but adds: "*Most of their names are now sadly completely forgotten.*" Well, we are pleased to inform Bradfordians that the names "Laurel & Hardy" have not been forgotten, and are not likely to be so for *hundreds of centuries of generations* to come.

Except for going on a trip through the Yorkshire Dales, little else is known of the Laurels' and the Hardys' movements during their week in Bradford. Even one of Stan's regular letters to his friend Booth failed to cover the subject:

```
Don't think we will bother with offers on the Continent -
don't think it's worth the time & trouble due to money
exchange etc. so much Red Tape - plus no trust in them.
Contracts & agreements mean nothing. The only way is to
have them put up the cash in the States - otherwise you are
at their mercy & they have very little of that.
They are still trying to arrange for us to stay for
Palladium Panto but don't think it's possible, so will
```

```
probably return home end of Oct. I can do with a rest
anyway. Will let you know what happens. Having another
smash week here in Bradford - Terrific Bus. its really
amazing!
```

On Sunday 3 August the party arrived in Southend-on-Sea for their one and only appearance in the county of Essex. On Tuesday, the *Southend Times and Recorder* dutifully recorded their show as follows:

> Laurel & Hardy began a week on the stage of the Southend Odeon, on Monday. They were given a great reception by a large August Bank Holiday crowd as the band struck up their familiar signature tune, and all the familiar grimaces with their own brand of droll humour, make the twenty minutes as well worth-while as any ever spent in the Odeon.

As it turned out, spending time inside the Odeon was a pretty good idea, seeing as the whole weekend was rained out and billed as "the worst Bank Holiday in years."

While presenting a 'Star of Merit' to Odeon usherette Eileen Winfield,
Ollie ensures he is the only one who gets to kiss her.

Southend, Southport

Laurel and Hardy stayed at The Palace – an enormous hotel built on the seafront, overlooking the Thames estuary. The hotel is directly facing Southend Pier – which, at 1.34 miles long since 1929, has been billed as "The Longest Pleasure Pier in the World." From there, Laurel wrote a letter describing both the weather and working conditions:

```
Dear Stan [Anniston],                          Aug.5th.'52.
Had three shows here (Monday 4th) Band call 10 am so in
theatre all day & night - glad that's over. Weather here
cold - wind & rain, so not too pleasant - but of course
good for bus. (Big theatre here - seats 3,000.)
```

With the rain killing off the prospects of a walk down the pier and a stroll along the prom, it was left to a Friday luncheon in the Pier Hotel to provide the first bit of news coverage. Laurel and Hardy were guests of a group of cinema managers from the Odeon circuit in Essex, and reciprocated by presenting many of them with long service brooches, which they personally pinned onto the lapels of the recipients.

Stan and Ollie are amused by the demeanour of the recipient of the Star of Merit – Mr. E. Pike – who looks totally awestruck at meeting his comedy heroes close up.
But then, who wouldn't be?

On the Saturday afternoon, Stan and Babe popped over to the Regal Theatre, in Southend, to plug their show to the audience there. Backstage, they had a photograph taken with the members of one of the acts on the show — Burton Lester's Midgets.

[Had troupe member Kenny Baker not contacted the author some fifty years later, details of the visit, and the existence of this photograph, would have remained unknown.]

Kenny Baker later went on to find fame in the cabaret act 'The MiniTones,' and then as a film actor. He is best-known for being the animator of R2D2 in the early *Star Wars* films.

LEFT: Henry Behrens gets an even greater thrill than his fellow cast members, when Babe and Stan get close up and personal.

And here is another story sent to me long after the first-edition of this book went to print. I have to thank Laurel & Hardy fans Ian Piley, and Andrew and Colin Sheehan, for giving me permission to use it here:

> Harry Day and William Barton were regular musicians at the Palace Hotel in Southend, and were playing there whilst Laurel and Hardy were performing at the Odeon. After the performance one night, Stan Laurel was relaxing in the Palace Hotel bar listening to the band. Inevitably they got chatting and, during the course of the conversation, Harry Day happens to mention that he and his wife have just had a baby. Stan is genuinely thrilled and, incredibly, says that he'd like to meet Harry's wife Rose to congratulate her, and toast the baby's health! Harry says OK, but wonders when they could possibly do it? "How about now" says the enthusiastic Mr. Laurel! So without further ado the pair set off for Harry's home in Westcliff.
>
> It's getting late by this time, and the sound of the key in the door, followed by voices, initially brings a lukewarm response from Rose ... "Harry, you brought someone home with you?" she warns.... "Erm, yes" comes the rather sheepish reply ... "It's Stan Laurel." Rose changed her tune pretty sharpish after that, and offered them both a cup of tea, to which Harry replied "We're not here to drink tea." A full bottle of whisky was found, and the three of them sat up until the early hours of the morning chatting and drinking. Around 4 or 5 in the morning, Stan said that he should be going and Harry drove Stan back to the Palace hotel. (I don't suppose drink driving had been invented back then!).

This story would be easy to fob off as just tosh. What doesn't ring true is the part about Laurel helping to drink a half a bottle of whisky. As has been previously confirmed, by the letter written by 'Prince' from Rhyl, Laurel had been off the drink since his worsening diabetic symptoms had led to his being admitted to the Musgrave Clinic in Belfast. However, the bit about Stan being overly keen to see the baby does kind of ring true, as it bears a striking similarity to the events at a party Laurel went to in America, in 1941. On that occasion, the hostess – Virginia Karns (who played 'Mother Goose' in the Laurel & Hardy film *Babes in Toyland*) – had recently given birth to twins. Laurel was fascinated, and kept popping upstairs during the house party, to view them. Not only that, but he kept taking other guests with him to have a look at them. So! The 1952 Southend story may well have some credence.

And here is a third story which didn't make the First Edition. Thankfully, this one has provenance to back it up. One of Laurel's backstage visitors was Teddy Desmond, whom Stan had first reunited with on the 1932 Glasgow visit. Then, Teddy was the leader of a jazz band – the *Savannas Orchestra* – a position he had held for some twenty-five years: but now he was the manager of a Southend amusement arcade.

This extract from the press-notes on the back of the photo tells us:

> The act was financed with £6 borrowed from Mr. Desmond's sister, and they pushed their props on a wheelbarrow, from Camberwell to the Old Vic where they performed on Saturday night. Lilian Bayliss saw the act and said "You'll go far with that."

> "We did", said Laurel, "we went to the continent and nearly starved".

> Laurel was ambitious and decided to go to the USA. Desmond, however, was married and more cautious.

[AJM: In the spring of 1912, Stan and Ted were performing in a double-act known as 'The Barto Brothers,' playing the sketch: *The Rum 'Uns From Rome*. They then joined 'The Eight Comiques' along with Jimmy Reed, and played Rotterdam and Liége with another sketch, plus their own. (Ref: Page 33 in book 1. Full story, plus contemporary photographs, in my book: "LAUREL – Stage by Stage")]

Another line in the press-notes reads:

> They reminisced on the old days, but there was no celebrating. Laurel is on a strict diet which forbids alcohol.

So, yet more testimony that Laurel was off the drink, which would seem to cast doubt on the story of the drinking session at the home of the Southend musician.

Between visits from old friends, Laurel continued writing letters to others — this one to Betty Healy (dated 7 August):

> I was in hospital for a week in Belfast. Nothing serious, just went in for a check up & rest, was a bit run down after Five months straight work. It did me a lot of good & am feeling fine again.
>
> Ben Shipman was over, but it is not possible for us to stay here after October, due to the Tax situation - we can't pay tax in both Countries, so the Palladium Pantomime deal is off it as we can't return here for Six Months. I am very disappointed, but nothing can be done about it, so guess we shall leave for home sometime in Oct. 'We could go to Australia & South Africa, but can't take Dollars out, so that no use. Ben Shipman phoned me from Santiago Chile last week, they have offered us a lot of time in South America, but they are Big Night Clubs, we are not suitable for those places, so I guess a good rest back home won't do me any harm.

Delfont had kept Laurel and Hardy out of London purely so as not to over-expose the two stars before booking them into a major London venue for the pantomime season. So now, not only was the pantomime booking lost but those for other London theatres they could have played during this current tour.

[AJM: For those who need to know, the roles of 'Captain' and 'Mate' in the 1952 pantomime *Dick Whittington* at the London Palladium were filled by David Dale and Richard Hearne (Mr. Pastry), with Frankie Howard as 'Idle Jack'. (I suppose you now want to know who played 'Dick.' Well this will surprise you. It was a girl — Vanessa Lee. That's panto for you).]

Coventry, where Laurel and Hardy had received such an enthusiastic welcome in 1947, was the next stopover on the tour. Here, the *Evening Telegraph* commented on their performance at Coventry Hippodrome:

> The fun is as fresh as ever. The pair have lost none of those characteristics so typically 'Laurel & Hardy' – they are all there. The pace of the sketch never flags, the comedy is wholesome, and all together it is no trouble for onlookers to get a good laugh out of Stan and Ollie's latest dilemma.

The *Coventry Standard* too, waxed lyrical:

> Laurel & Hardy do rather more than prove the indestructibility of slapstick as a medium for laughter; they provide an object lesson for all would-be comedians by giving us nearly a half-an-hour of high-pressure, unadulterated nonsense in which there is not a single word out of place, which can be remotely called indelicate.
>
> If ever proof were needed that it is possible to be clever and clean, this is it and for that reason, in these days of innuendo, double-meanings, and blue-edged gags, I salute these masters for reducing their audience to the point of near-hysteria simply by exploiting absurdities; and for leaving us limp with laughter, but refreshed.

Even though the two comedy stars had no background in the area, the people of Coventry had built up a special affinity for them. In an article in the *Evening Telegraph*, Hardy reciprocated the feeling to some extent. Under the heading, "Ollie may become a Warwickshire man," it ran:

> Off-stage, Mr. Laurel and Mr. Hardy are very modest people. Says Mr. Laurel: 'We know what we can do, and we stick to that. Why should we change? Neither of us is a great talking comedian, so we just say enough and carry on as we always have.'
>
> Asked if they were enjoying their second tour of Britain, Hardy gave the very definite answer, 'Yes, my wife and I think the English countryside is beautiful. I like the English provinces – after all, big cities are the same all over the world – and I like the people. I've never seen such hospitality. I like the way people live over here, too.' Then he let me into a little secret: 'Mrs. Hardy and I have often thought that when I retire we would like to settle somewhere in Warwickshire, because we both think this is the most beautiful part of England.'

Southend, Southport

The following week, the comedy duo were back among the holidaymakers, this time in Southport – a coastal resort located half-way between Blackpool, in Lancashire, and Liverpool, on Merseyside. The standing joke about Southport is that the tide recedes so far out that it becomes virtually an inland town. The day before Stan and Babe arrived, though, the joking had stopped when a thirty-foot high tide damaged the Marina at the north end of town. Mercifully the storms and flooding did not recur, and another fine mess was averted.

Of their live appearance, the *Southport Visiter* [*sic*] wrote:

> Crowds gathered at the stage door of the Garrick Theatre to catch a glimpse of Laurel & Hardy, and inside the theatre was full to capacity. 'Here in person' announced the placard outside. When I was a small boy, if anyone had offered me £100 or the chance of seeing these screen buffoons in person, I would have refused the money. Accordingly the small boy in me rose in delight to greet Stan & Ollie when they appeared on the stage. They had the audience rocking with laughter, which grew even more uproarious as they blundered about as housebreakers. The old tricks and the familiar mannerisms were present, and it was truly Laurel & Hardy IN PERSON.

The tour had now been running for six months, and both comedians were feeling particularly tired and weak. Stan was receiving constant attention from a doctor, and being given daily injections of drugs specially flown in from America.

On their arrival on Sunday both celebrities were jostled by a crowd so, throughout the week, Hardy requested a police escort. He was later reported as saying: "We don't want to go anywhere except the back of the stage and our hotel."

And it was in the Prince of Wales Hotel that Laurel wrote the following letter, in which he reiterated the cancellation of an extended tour, but then introduced the subject of television:

```
                                                  Aug.19th.'52.
Dear Stan [Anniston]:- Opened here last night to Big Bus.
looks like we shall have another good week. We sail back to
the States again Oct 8th "Queen Elizabeth" so only have six
more weeks to play. Really hate to leave, but have to on
account of Tax situation - Understand if we don't return
here till Oct 1953 - we can stay a whole year. So all being
```

```
well, we intend to do that - except if we don't get tied up
in TV. Anyway a good rest won't do me any harm & will give
me plenty of time to prepare another act.
```

The *Southport Guardian* gave more insider information:

> Once their two hundred yard car ride to the Prince of Wales Hotel is over, Stan Laurel goes to his room on the first floor, and Oliver Hardy to his on the second. Behind the safety of his bedroom door, Laurel can relax, for doctors have told him he must do nothing else but. His twenty-five minute turn on the stage is his only exertion.
>
> Said a friend of Stan's: "We often wonder how he carries on. He is a very sick man. A special diet has been arranged for him, but he takes his trouble cheerfully."
>
> At the hotel, special instructions were put into force. Neither comic was to be disturbed, and phone calls could not be put through until a certain hour – and even then only friends and managers could be connected. The hotel restaurant and public lounges remained unused by the Laurels and the Hardys, and all services were done in their private suites. During the week, the Boys turned down an invitation to judge a heat of the "English Rose" [a beauty competition for young ladies] — fearing the strain of facing the crowds would be too much for Laurel.

Touring wasn't fun anymore.

o-o-0-o-o

Chapter 8

THE LAST LEGS

Having spent three out of the last five weeks at holiday resorts, Laurel and Hardy were next precipitated into the residential atmosphere of the London suburb of Sutton. This is as near as Laurel and Hardy came to playing in London during the 1952 tour, but was far enough out so as not to compete with the catchment area from which audience members would have been drawn if the pantomime had gone ahead.

Upon their arrival at Monday morning rehearsals at the Granada Cinema, Sutton, the two former screen stars were besieged by youngsters demanding autographs. A press photographer naively invited them go to Manor Park to meet some more youngsters.

> 'No thank you – no parks' responded Stan. 'We have tried that before, and had the police on us for causing an obstruction. Hundreds of kids just float in from nowhere.
>
> 'It's sort of funny too, when some old man with a long beard comes up and says that he saw you on the screen when he was a little boy.'

At the Burford Bridge Hotel, Box-hill, where Stan and Babe were staying, their meals were being supervised by floor-waiter, Claude Johnston, whom they had brought over from the Palace Hotel, Southend. Johnston said of Hardy's eating habits: "He has a big breakfast with plenty of bacon and eggs, but no lunch. Then he has a very big meal at night with plenty of ham and chicken." Stan, it was revealed, was eating very little since his illness the previous year. Hardy had again brought over lots of tinned food from America, but the food situation had improved so much since 1947 that he found little need of it. It was added that neither of them drank anything stronger that orange juice. [I would think that last claim applies to Hardy, only at meal times.]

A *Surrey Herald* reporter interviewed the Boys backstage at Monday morning rehearsals, and wrote:

'It's been tough going,' smiled Ollie, 'two shows a night, three on Saturday, but we have enjoyed every minute of it.'

The two return to Hollywood next month, but hope to be back before long to make a picture in this country. At present they are mostly tied up with making short films for American television.

[AJM: At present they are mostly tied up with touring Britain – doing two shows a night and three on Saturday].

Looking very fit after his recent operation in Paris, Stan had plenty of praise for one exclusive English topic – the Weather. 'It's been really grand; almost like dear old sunny California,' he laughed.

While the reporter was talking to them, Bert Tracey (*ibid.*) brought in a pile of autograph books, and enquired, "There are a lot more people waiting; can I bring their books in?" "Sure," said Ollie, "bring 'em all. If people are kind enough to stand and wait for our signatures, who are we to refuse?"

Of their stage work, the *Advertiser* wrote:

LAUREL and HARDY – The British Tours

Laurel & Hardy at the Granada, Sutton, are proving to the audiences that they are still in the first flight of comedy teams. Their comedy is the inimitable fare that they have presented for so long, but their technique and artistry make it evergreen. Their patter and clowning is rich in humour and throughout their act their team work is brilliant. Their timing in everything they do is faultless.

> Knowing they would get mobbed if they went to meet the gang of kids outside the stage door, Stan and Ollie wisely wave to them from an upper floor.
> [Lost photo – Croydon]

One member of the audience, Kevin Henriques, was less kind, but honest, when he wrote of his memories of the show:

> I was seventeen at the time and recall how excited I was to have the chance to actually see on stage two of the funniest men I had ever seen on the screen. Alas, my certain and clear recollection of my visit to the first house, Monday night, is total disappointment. Maybe it was because it was opening night, but the audience was surprisingly small and the two funny film men were decidedly unfunny on stage.

Henriques' opinion of Laurel and Hardy's reception is rather hard to take, especially when one compares it with the glowing review in the *Sutton Advertiser*. However, that for once the enthusiasm of the press outshone that of the public is confirmed by a letter written by Stan on 25 April 1953. Those eight months later he still felt embittered enough to write:

```
Delfont wants us to do panto at the London Casino this year
[Christmas 1953], but am afraid that's out & if we come
over in Oct. I don't know where the hell we could play
during the Panto Season as all the Variety [venues] change
policy for that Period & I certainly don't want to play
places like Sutton!
```

Maybe Laurel and Hardy had come away from Sutton feeling unhappy, but they left behind two young boys who certainly weren't so – as this excellent human interest story from the *Sutton Times* will confirm:

> TWELVE-YEAR-OLD Peter Kavanagh and his school friend, Patrick Walsh, aged 10, dangled their legs over the edge of a comfortable settee in a backstage dressing room at Sutton Granada on Monday night and cheerfully munched cookies with the stars of the show – Laurel and Hardy.
>
> It was the perfect ending to the happiest day of their young lives. Early that morning the two boys had set off from their home in Constance-road, Sutton to try and collect the stars autographs. Instead it was just like a Cinderella story. They met, talked, laughed, and had their pictures taken with the screen's funniest funnymen.

The Last Legs

And how did it all happen? Peter explained it this way: "When we heard that Stan and Ollie were coming to Sutton Granada this morning to start a week's variety, we made up our minds to get their autographs. We waited a long time outside the cinema, and then, what do you think, a gentleman came out and asked us if we would like to have our pictures taken with the stars."

Here Peters young friend, Patrick, chipped in: "When we got inside we had to clamber over coils of wire and bits of scenery because everybody was rushing round getting ready for the opening performance.

"Then we saw them, Laurel and Hardy, I mean. They were surrounded by lots of reporters asking questions, and photographers were taking their pictures. It was smashing."

Peter took over again. "The next thing we knew we were standing right beside them having our picture taken. They asked us our names and where we lived and if we liked school. They were very funny and made us laugh, specially Ollie. He kept waving his tie at us.

"Afterwards one of the reporters took as along to see Mr. Ken Brierley, the cinema manager, and he asked us if we would like to see the opening show. At first we thought he was joking. Then he told us to come back just before the show opened and he would take us in as his personal guests," said Peter.

That afternoon seemed the longest the two boys had ever spent. But soon it was time for the show, so, dressed in their Sunday best, the excited youngsters presented themselves outside Mr. Brierley's office and then settled down to enjoy themselves in two of the best seats in the house.

After the show the boys went backstage to meet the stars and say "Thank you" for such a wonderful time. They also met Mrs. Laurel and Mrs. Hardy. Mrs. Hardy gave them lots of cookies and chatted away about Hollywood and the sort of things all boys and girls like to hear about. It was, the boys agreed, the happiest day of their lives.

It is amazing to think that, even though they weren't enamoured with the populace of Sutton; weren't in the best of health; and were counting the days till the tour ended; the two Hollywood legends still took time out to give the thrill of a lifetime to two young boys.

Following the blasé reception at Sutton, the picture brightened for the two stars in Bristol, when the reviewer from the *Bristol Evening World* was prompted to write:

> Laurel & Hardy were cheered and whistled for a whole minute when they walked on stage at the Bristol Hippodrome. It seemed as though half the children of Bristol had persuaded their parents to take them along to see this popular screen couple. Or did the parents need persuasion? No, I don't think they did. For Stan & Ollie, who have been amusing us on the screen for more years than we like to remember, have a brand of nonsensical fun that endures because it is so human and so very clean.
>
> Laurel getting pushed off the seat when Hardy wants to curl up and go to sleep, and Ollie trying to saw his way through the window while Stan, having found the door unlocked, watches him with interest from the inside, are lovely moments of silent burlesque in their act, and although it is nonsense, meant only for broad laughs, it is as refreshing as a cool breeze in a stage world in which the titter too often takes the place of the guffaw. Laurel & Hardy give us plain, hearty guffaws, and it's grand to hear them again.

It was Friday before the comedy couple gained any further press coverage; when, after the Friday night show, they and their wives were whisked over to the Grand Spa Hotel, Clifton (not to be confused with the Grand Hotel, Bristol, where the Laurels and the Hardys were staying). They were there as special guests at a Ball in aid of the "Lynmouth Relief Fund" – for victims of the terrible floods which had occurred in Lynmouth three weeks earlier. Amongst those present were the Lady Mayoress and the Lord Mayor of Bristol; plus the Duchess of Beaufort. After supper the guests were treated to a cabaret show from the Western Bros, Fayne & Evans, Len Marten, Fred Ferrari, Ken Morris, and Laurel & Hardy. Talk about singing for your supper.

At Portsmouth the following week, the *Evening News* came up with a short exclusive:

> Double Tax Sends Stan & Ollie Home – Five years have made a big difference to this country say Laurel & Hardy. 'When we were last here there were so many shortages,' said Stan. 'You couldn't get lemons, grapefruit, or bananas. Vegetables were hard to get, the bread was coarse and dark, and people's clothes looked shabby. Now everything is better.'
>
> He and Ollie have been delighted with the receptions from British audiences. Stan & Ollie were asked to stay to do a pantomime, but if they had done so they would have had to pay tax here as well as in America. As Stan put it, 'We would have owed ourselves money.' But they are coming back next year for a longer visit and hope to do a pantomime then.

But the possibility of a pantomime was trumped by the offer of being in a Hollywood film, as Stan revealed to confidante, Booth, in this letter written from the Theatre Royal, Portsmouth:

```
Had a cable last week re a deal with
Paramount for a color Feature cartoon "Tom
Thumb" (Geo. Pal) They have been considering
us in this thing for over two years - so it
may develop to start in January. You didn't
mention re my letter telling you that we
leave here Oct. 8th. "Elizabeth" & will be
home around 18th.

Still doing Big Bus - hate to leave, but of course have to
on account of Tax Dept. however - can't grumble, have had
an exceptional good trip & expect to return in '53.
```

Of their theatre work, local writer Tony Wheatley gave the following personal view:

> I went to see Laurel & Hardy through utter devotion to their screen personalities, and for the laughter they caused in me through their films. The opportunity to see them personally, so close to home, was too good to miss.
>
> Sitting in the Theatre Royal awaiting their entrance, I had a sense of disbelief that they were actually going to set foot on that stage within a few minutes. All around was a quiet air of expectancy, and a general hum of excitement. As they walked on stage they were given a huge, warm, welcoming reception. For their stand-up, cross-over routine. The Theatre Royal stage mic' would appear out of the stage floor, front centre, and I can remember Stan feigning fright by flinching backwards as it shot up.
>
> They were very, very funny. Their age did not appear to have diminished their skills. Everything anticipated was met and surpassed, their timing superb, their rapport with the audience, perfect.

Les Pudney saw the Boys in an entirely different light:

> They were really on their last legs – completely worn out. When they tottered on to the stage, we were all pleased to see them, and the theatre was crowded – standing room only. Everyone stood and cheered them for about five minutes, but it was a sad occasion, as they were so obviously tired out. Hardy had to sit down, and said softly: 'Another nice mess' etc. However, they were a delight to see in the flesh, and afterwards went into the lounge, where everyone present shook hands with them.

Les is quite right in saying the Boys were absolutely worn out. After all, here they were, both gone sixty, having done thirteen shows a week for the last twenty-seven weeks. They had criss-crossed the length and breadth of England, Scotland, and Ireland; made numerous public appearances; been to late-night functions; and stayed behind after shows to mingle with their fans. Both, too, had their illnesses, so it's a wonder they were able to even *totter* on stage. The manager of the Portsmouth Theatre Royal, however, allowed them no excuses and, after reporting them on his Weekly Report Sheet as being "very disappointing," stated that he would not have them back.

Hopefully, the two former screen stars would fare better in Dudley, a Midlands' town they had last visited in 1947

Dudley Station

Bob Kennedy, who was still director at the Dudley Hippodrome, told the following story of one happening that week:

> One night I suggested to them that, as there was a big crowd outside the stage door, we could get them out of the theatre another way. But Laurel insisted on going out that way, remarking: 'When they are not there, we shall know we are not wanted.'

Doris Payne, who had been working at Dudley Hippodrome since its opening night in 1938, gave a very unusual insight into the business mind of Babe Hardy:

> At the Hippodrome we had a clientele of around two thousand, who came every week, regardless of who was appearing. I would put tickets by for these people, and just wait for them to turn up on the evening. Hardy, though, didn't retain my faith. If all the seats weren't taken by fifteen minutes before "curtain up," he would come round to the box-office, and say things like, 'You'll have to let the tickets go, Mrs. Payne, [i.e. Sell them to people waiting, without tickets]. We can't let there be any empty seats.' As it was, the seats were filled all week, but Hardy would not rest until he'd seen it for himself.

From Dudley in the West Midlands, the cast headed south west to Swansea, a Welsh port on the inlet to the Bristol Channel. There, the *South Wales Evening Post* printed little more than a synopsis of the sketch:

> Adult fans who recall Laurel & Hardy's popular two-reelers, and children who know them from comic-strips and their full-length films will not be disappointed by Laurel & Hardy at Swansea Empire. The well-loved gestures and fondly remembered expressions of their screen shadows are re-created in substance on the stage. Stan & Ollie make the audience roar without recourse to the frenzied knockabout of modern slapstick comics. They know the value of stillness in their gentle nonsense, and were given a warm ovation, which left Hardy shaking with merriment.

Of their "welcome in the hillsides" the two comedians later reported:

> 'Welsh audiences,' said Stan, 'are good. You know as well as I do that audiences differ, and in Swansea the people were wonderful. You can feel the warmth, you know.' Ollie nodded. 'Wonderful reception,' he said.

So pleased were Stan and Babe with the warmth of their reception that, during the day, they were often to be seen on the balcony outside their rooms at the Mackworth Hotel, waving to the passers-by below.

In the theatre, at the Saturday afternoon prize-giving-presentation for the "Laurel & Hardy painting competition," one young lady, Carole Anne Williams, distinctly remembers that when Hardy gave her a peck on the cheek, his breath smelled of vinegar. In later years she came to learn that this smell came from a clear brown drinking liquid, quite different to vinegar.

Mackworth Hotel

The Last Legs

Carole Anne Williams

Upon leaving Swansea, the company had only a short trip to Cardiff, for what was the last engagement of the tour. Only the *South Wales Echo and Express* bothered to do a story on the two comedians, after sending round a reporter to interview them at rehearsals at the Cardiff New Theatre. Talking on his favourite subject of comedy, Stan said:

People are fed up with looking at stuffed shirts on stage. They like action and human characters. Too many would-be comedians today want to take the easy way. They don't want funny clothes or dirty faces. They want to throw away their tramp's outfit and walk on stage in evening dress ... and talk. Words ... words ... no action, no characters.

Hardy added:

There's a careful design behind slapstick stuff. As we talk, we act. You've got an awkward situation and two funny characters who make it laughable. Take out the funny characters and put in straight players and you've got drama. See what I mean?

A sour note also hangs over the week, in the form of a story which originated from the hotel where Stan and Babe stayed.

> When that great comedy duo Laurel & Hardy stayed at the Park Hotel it posed problems for the staff, as they weren't on speaking terms. They also insisted on taking their breakfast at the nearby New Theatre, so that they weren't disturbed by the attentions of their fans. This curious arrangement meant the hotel staff had to carry their breakfast over the road to the theatre, where Stan Laurel and Oliver Hardy sat grimly uncommunicative in their separate dressing rooms.

Subsequent cross-examination of the Head Hall Porter, Frank Bois – who was there at the time – revealed that it was not the Boys who had argued, but *their wives*. The compiler of the brochure from whence this story came, must have switched the roles for added effect, and thus blotted the proud record which Stan and Babe held for never having fallen out in all their years together. Shame on you, sir!

The New Theatre manager, Reg Phillips, welcoming the Hollywood legends, outside the Stage Door. See previous picture!

Laurel and Hardy paying a visit to the Capitol Cinema, to poach the audience, but disguising it as a presentation of long-service awards to some of the staff from the Odeon and Capitol cinemas. At left, watching Laurel enjoying some "good old fish & chips," are W.C. Hall, manager of the Capitol Theatre, and Ian Craig, manager of the Odeon Cinema.

In other local papers, headlines like: "Tea Rationing Ends Today," and: "Chaplin Invited to Appear on 'Royal Variety Performance'," took preference over Laurel and Hardy's appearance, and the tour ended in an anti-climax

The Last Legs

It was also a time for tearful farewells, as the acts on the show said "Goodbye" after most had toured together for these thirty-two weeks.

Above is a signed farewell photo to the Lonsdale Sisters, a dance act, who also doubled as Cingalee's assistants. They were Pauline Banks, the daughter of Claude Banks, and her friend, Florence Samuels — so not sisters at all.

Sharing company, from the company, is Leslie Spurling 'the Cop', and Claude Banks – aka: 'The Great Cingalee.' [Signed to Claude – at the end of the 1952 tour)
(Both photos by kind courtesy of Charlie Cairoli Jnr. and Claudi.)

The day after, Sunday 5 October, the Grand Order of Water Rats held a dinner at the Park Lane Hotel, in London. Amongst those present was Charlie Chaplin; and the highlights of the evening were shown on television. Stan and Babe, for whom the occasion would have been an ideal farewell, did not attend. With the Boys conspicuous by their absence, it is strange to learn that the following night they *were* in London – at the Prince of Wales Theatre.

It was a few minutes before the star of the show spotted them sitting in the audience; but, when he did, he ad-libbed his way into coming off the stage, climbed over the seats, and accosted them. Needless to say, the house was in uproar.

In Norman's book of memoirs, titled: "*NORMAN WISDOM – My Turn*" he recounts the surprise visit as follows:

> *Paris to Piccadilly* won some marvellous notices. It also became the show that celebrities wanted to see. One night there was a flurry of excitement, and a stage hand said to me: 'You'll never guess who's out front, Norman – Laurel & Hardy!' And there they were, four rows back in the stalls.
>
> I did something extremely rare that night: I asked permission to go out front during the interval and chat with them – and the whole audience cheered us to the echo! Stan and Ollie stood up and took a bow, and then Stan said to me: 'Bit different from Brussels, eh?'
>
> 'Not arf!' I agreed. 'How did you get on there?'
>
> 'We survived,' said Ollie. 'By the seat of our pants.'

[AJM: To uncover the significance of the reference to Brussels, read my book: "The European Tours."]

After the show Stan and Babe went backstage to congratulate the comic genius on his fantastic success. In 1947 he had been taking his first faltering steps into comedy. Now, only five years later, he was headlining a show which was to run for over eighteen months. What was lovely to see was that, after their own phenomenal career, Laurel and Hardy's last gesture before they left Britain was to go and pass on their best wishes to him. Norman Wisdom had come a long way.

On 8 October the Laurel and Hardy Family boarded the *Queen Elizabeth* at Southampton Docks for their return trip. It had been a totally exhausting tour, and neither Stan nor Babe was getting any younger. All doors leading to work prospects now seemed to have closed and, as they sailed home, the two greatest comics of the silver screen must have had it in mind that spending the rest of their days behind closed doors was a real possibility.

Hopefully, Stan's mailbag, awaiting him back home, would contain a viable offer. Hopefully!!

o-o-0-o-o

Chapter 9

ONE IN A HUNDRED

After a smooth Atlantic crossing on the *Queen Elizabeth*; an overnight stay in New York; and the coast-to-coast train journey to Los Angeles, the two fatigued former film stars were delighted to be back where they could enjoy all the comforts of home.

> Leaving London on the boat train, bound for Southampton, at the end of the 1952 tour.

At his home, at Franklin Ave., Santa Monica, Stan began to wade through a mountain of mail, and then reply to fans and agents alike. Back in March 1952 he had aired an offer of a theatre engagement, to Dorathi Pierre (*ibid*):

```
We just had an offer to play the
Palace New York, for a run,
starting in June or is open to us
any time we return to the States.
I'm afraid they are going to have a tough time getting
attractions there to follow Judy Garland, she was such a
smash hit.
```

Obviously, this had not come to fruition, as Laurel and Hardy would have taken the opportunity to sign the deal, during their stay-over in New York on 17 October.

And in September 1952, while the Boys were still playing theatres in Britain, word had come through that, as soon as they returned home, they would resume talks with the Hal Roach Studios about a TV show. But, in the first four months, only three offers came in. None were from Roach.

The first was an update of the film offer made the previous month, as revealed in a newspaper column (dated 23 October 1952):

> George Pal tells us that he still has the film version of "Tom Thumb" on his schedule. He's already tested a boy for the title role and made him pint-size by trick photography. Stan Laurel and Oliver Hardy, just back from a long tour of Europe, will likely play the two thieves who kidnap Tom and endeavour to enlist him in their life of crime. The story will stick closely to the original fairy tale.

This is one of the rare instances when a film offered to Laurel and Hardy was actually made. Sorry to say, when it was finally made in 1958, it came too late for our comedy heroes; but two other comedy heroes did justice to the parts they would have played – namely Terry-Thomas and Peter Sellers (with Russ Tamblyn in the eponymous role).

But then came an offer to play a venue much nearer to home — one which was more than a little surprising:

```
Dear Betty -                                          Nov. 17th. '52
We have been contacted again to play the SAHARA in Las
Vegas, but don't think we could manage with our scenery
etc. Stage isn't big enough - but may take a trip there &
```

look it over. Anyway I don't intend to do anything till after New Year.

If you found the Vegas offer surprising, read the follow-up to Betty – dated 29 November.

Ted and Betty Healy

I went to Las Vegas a week ago last Tuesday [18 November] & came back next day. a quick trip to see the place & find out re size of Stage etc. Too small & no facilities to hang scenery - so impossible for us to play there with this act. They want us to put on a new act - more suitable for night Clubs where we wouldn't require a lot of scenery & props. Am not too enthusiastic about it - especially that type of audiences. Anyway, I can't be bothered right now.

Just had an offer to go to the Malay States - Singapore - Hong Kong etc. & Japan & Bangkok (Siam) which sounds interesting - but will have to do a pantomime act to avoid language difficulties. We have a terrific following in these places & they are anxious for us to open next March - we are checking now re getting Dollars out. Will let you know if anything develops.

So the offer of driving two hundred and seventy miles to work in Las Vegas, in front of Americans, had now been turned down in favour of flying over seven thousand miles to work in the Far East, in front of Asians.

If that weren't a poor enough alternative, then consider that the next one was again to fly over seven thousand miles, this time to Australia; drive for thousands of miles when they got there, and then fly over ten thousand miles to Ireland, in time for a Christmas panto — as described in this letter from Stan – 4 February 1953:

We have offers to play in Tokio for eight weeks also a tour of Australia & Panto at the Opera House in Belfast this next Xmas for a 10 week run "Babes In The Wood" & of course a tour in Variety to follow in England again, but nothing definite to date.

That's an awful lot of flying for two men who have an aversion to flying. Unless, of course, they intended sailing everywhere; which would mean spending more time at sea than on land, over the remaining weeks in 1952.

Even some ten weeks later when Laurel wrote to Claude Cingalee, over in England, the "Land of Aus" was still being considered:

April 25 1953

Funny you should happen to mention Belfast, remember Geo. Lodge the managing director? well, he has been visiting here for a couple of weeks & is leaving for home on Monday next. He wanted us to play Panto this Xmas in Belfast, but Babe is not too hot about it - too much work, so that's out. However we have promised to play Variety for him when we come over again.

All here as usual, just taking it easy, but have the feeling to get going again. Delfont wants us to do Panto at

```
the London Casino this year, but am afraid that's out & if
we come over in Oct. I don't know where the hell we could
play during the Panto Season as all the variety change
policy for that Period & I certainly don't want to play
places like Sutton!
```

Claude Cingalee, alias — "The Great Cingalee – Oriental Magician"
[Sounds a lot more impressive than 'Claude Banks,' doesn't it – which was his real name.]

The letter continued:

```
We have a deal pending for Australia & New Zealand & if
that goes through, we may come to Eng. to play variety till
Dec. & then go down there, so don't know as yet what will
happen. The picture bus. is very quiet at present, most of
the studios closed down owing to this 3rd dimension
situation. A lot of the producers not sure how good it will
be after the novelty wears off as it takes a terrific
investment.
```

It is amazing to count just how many times Laurel and Hardy *had* been offered to play Australia. The first time was, would you believe, some thirteen years earlier, as this Australian newspaper clip will confirm:

THE [ADELAIDE] NEWS, JULY 5, 1940

Gracie Fields and the film comedians, Laurel and Hardy, and the Ritz brothers may be seen in Adelaide as a result of negotiations now in progress between the artists and the Australian chain of Tivoli Theatres.

Mr. Clyde Waterman. who returned to Adelaide today after having completed the Adelaide link with Tivoli Theatres Ltd. to present star variety programmes at the Majestic Theatre, said that Tivoli Theatres were already in communication with these famous artists, and that if these were successful they would appear at the Majestic Theatre as part of their Australian tours.

Ten months later, terms were still being negotiated:

LAUREL and HARDY – The British Tours

SYDNEY MORNING HERALD, WEDNESDAY, MAY 21, 1941

Mr. Wallace Parnell, general manager of the Tivoli Theatre, will leave by Clipper next month for the U.S.A. to book new acts. He is trying to negotiate a contract with Gracie Fields and Laurel and Hardy to tour Australia.

This next clipping reveals another city on the proposed tour:

THE MERCURY [HOBART, TAS] SATURDAY, JUNE 14, 1941

Efforts are being made to bring Gracie Fields and the comedy team of Laurel and Hardy to Australia. Gracie Fields is Englands No.1 screen comedienne and vocalist. Laurel and Hardy are a popular comedy team. The partnership was temporarily broken some months ago, but has since been re-established.

In June 1945 Gracie Fields *did* go to Australia, but the Boys stayed home. A little under two years on, and the trip was on, again, for Stan and Babe:

THE CAIRNS POST 21 APRIL 1947

BRISBANE, Apr. 19. – Two Australian theatrical firms are battling to handle the Australian tour of comedians Stan Laurel and Oliver Hardy, probably next year. They are Harry Wren Theatres Ltd. and J. C. Williamson Ltd.

A cable message on Thursday reported Oliver Hardy as saying that J. C. Williamson would probably handle their arrangements – taking in all Australian capitals. The cable said that they would reach Australia in March next year for a four months tour.

When a statement, reported to have been made by Mr. Wren, that the comedians had accepted a lucrative offer from Harry Wren Theatres Ltd., was referred to Mr. Wren in Sydney by telephone last night, he said:

"I understand that they have accepted my offer, but I cannot be sure without reference to the file, which is in Brisbane. We have been negotiating for some time with Forsters Agency, In London, which is handling Laurel and Hardys tour overseas ."

The general manager of J. C. Williamson Ltd. (Mr. Harald Bowden) said that negotiations were proceeding in London for Laurel and Hardy to come to Australia under contract with his firm. He believed that these negotiations were well under way.

Roll forward another twenty two months, and we find yet another proposed tour of Australia:

PORT LINCOLN TIMES

Thursday, February 24, 1949

Laurel And Hardy May Visit Port Lincoln

Shirley Testrow, of Port Lincoln – who is the representative for Rand Brooks Fan Club, of California – has received a personal letter from the well-known Hollywood comedy team, Laurel and Hardy, stating that they may visit Port Lincoln during their proposed trip to Australia later this year. The actual wording of the letter reads — *"Mr. Hardy and myself expect to be in Australia sometime this year to make personal appearances. We are anxious to visit your beautiful country and if we happen to be near Port Lincoln, we hope to have the pleasure of meeting you all. (Signed) Stan Laurel."* The letter is dated February 5.

[AJM: Rand Brooks was a screen actor, who went on to play in TV westerns. Between 1948 and 1976 he was married to Stan Laurel's daughter.]

Talking of TV, Laurel wrote this to a fan:

```
                                               March 14th.'53.
My Dear Charles:-
I very much appreciate your loyalty as a L&H Fan, but
frankly I think you are crazy to spend all the time &
effort to see an old picture when you can see them so often
at home on TV. They have been running here once a week for
over three years & still continue under different
sponsorship.
```

One in a Hundred

Back to the proposed tour of Asia:

>   March 31st.'53.
> Dear Teddy Desmond:-
> The Singapore deal is off, conditions don't look so good
> down there & we don't want to get in the middle of
> anything. It looks now we will return to England again in
> October.

However, Australia was still under consideration:

>   April 25th.'53.
> My Dear Betty-
> I am feeling lots better, & getting the urge to get moving
> again. We are either going to England or Australia this
> year or maybe both, arrangements not completed as yet, but
> will be, pretty soon now, so am busy preparing a new act.

So here we are in 1953, with seemingly nothing learned from all the pitfalls of planning previous visits to down under. But then ...

>   June 4th. '53.
> My Dear Betty:-
> The Australian trip has been postponed, we will have to
> wait till the Tax situation is cleared up or no use of us
> going. So now its back to England for a year & maybe by
> that time things will get straightened out for Australia.
> We open in London for eight weeks in Oct. then tour the
> provinces again.

Meanwhile, Stan was enjoying the rest; putting on weight (he was now back to 155lbs.); and watching TV. Stan watched a lot of TV — comedy shows, chat shows, boxing, and plays. Oh! and this one-off programme:

>   July 1st.'53.
> Dear Nellie [Bushby]-
> Eda & I saw the Coronation film at home here on our
> Television, just eight hours after the ceremony! was'nt
> that amazing? what an age we are living in. We thought it
> was wonderful, needless to tell you I felt very proud &
> thrilled. A credit to Dear Old England, it was magnificent.

[Princess Elizabeth, the older daughter of King George VI, was crowned Queen Elizabeth II on June 2, 1953, at the age of twenty-seven.]

As for Laurel and Hardy, finally, after eleven months of deliberation over which far-flung corner of the globe to pitch their tent, they settled for the UK. Why all the other offers had been considered is puzzling, as the one they eventually chose was one they had pretty well accepted some *thirteen months earlier*. On 19 August 1952, during Laurel's confinement to his room at the Prince of Wales Hotel, in Southport, he had written to English comic Stan Anniston:

> We sail back to the States again Oct 8th "Queen Elizabeth"
> so only have six more weeks to play. Really hate to leave,
> but have to on account of Tax situation - Understand if we
> don't return here till Oct 1953 - we can stay a whole year.
> So all being well, we intend to do that - except if we
> don't get tied up in TV. Anyway a good rest won't do me any
> harm & will give me plenty of time to prepare another act.

With the 1953 British tour finally agreed to, Stan began to release details of their preparations:

```
We are leaving here in September for England, but will
first go to Dublin for about a month, to rehearse & prepare
a new act to open in Eng. in October sometime. Our reason
for going to Eire is, to avoid using up some of our working
time allowed - if we rehearsed in London, that month would
be deducted from our time limit, even tho' we were not
working.
```

A second letter, to cartoonist Lorraine, added a few more details:

```
                                           August 10th.'53.
My Dear Lawrie & Jeanette:-
Our reason for going direct to Dublin is, we are not
allowed to enter Eng. until Oct.5th. & as we open the 19th.
we have'nt time to get ready, being a new act, scenery to
make, rehearsals etc. Its a nuisance, but the only way we
can manage it. We leave here this Aug.30th. sail from New
York Sept.3rd. SS "America", due in Cobh, Eire. the 9th.
then train to Dublin. All for now, busy as hell packing,
seems like we'll never get through with so many other
things to do.
```

So, using the loophole in the labour restrictions placed on US citizen Oliver Hardy, the plan went ahead; and on 9 September 1953 the *SS America* duly deposited the Laurels and the Hardys at Cork Harbour, a deep-water port, just outside Cobh, on the south coast of Ireland.

o-o-o-0-o-o-o

Chapter 10

THE BELLS ARE RINGING

(For Me and My Pal)

"Well, we've found the girls' luggage. Now to find our two cases.

The Laurel and Hardy party where up at 5:30 am, to get ready in time ready to disembark when the *SS America* dropped anchor at 7am. I say "dropped anchor" as the ship couldn't be moored at the dockside, and all the passengers had to be brought to shore via a tender.

It had been requested beforehand that there be no advance publicity, and no reception party at the docks — to which the liner company faithfully acceded. This would leave Stan and Babe free to walk quietly to their chauffeured cars, and be driven away, unnoticed. What everyone concerned had failed to take into account was the fascination of little children for these two funny men. As at Christmas time, when children know instinctively that Father Christmas is coming, so it was here that they knew of the coming of not one, but two equally adored characters. Thus, almost every child in Cobh had played truant, and neither parents, teachers, nor police were going to send them away before they had set eyes on their screen idols.

Adults and children alike poured down to the quayside in a constant stream, blocking traffic to and from the docks. The air was filled with the noise of sirens, hooters, and whistles being sounded by every vessel in dock. Those who had taken to the water in pleasure-craft followed the tender from the liner to the dockside – waving and cheering at the party on deck. As soon as Laurel and Hardy touched dry land, they were mobbed. Children – greeting them like their favourite uncles – climbed on them, hugged them, kissed them, and ruffled their hair. They patted them, squeezed them, and begged for autographs. Policemen stood aside in amusement, as there was nothing to do but just allow the tide of love to wash over the two subjects. Being genuinely touched by the display of affection, Stan and Babe made every effort to satisfy the desires of the whole assembly, and to sign as many autographs as physically possible.

LAUREL and HARDY – The British Tours

Yet another game of "Where's Ollie?"

Before being led away, Hardy managed to say to a reporter:

> We were absolutely overwhelmed. There scarcely ever was a film scene like it. They are grand children, and Stan and I are grateful to them.

Still reeling from the unexpected sentimentality of the reception, the comedians' show of emotion finally burst forth when the air was filled with the sound of St. Colman's Cathedral forty-seven Carillon bells ringing out *The Dance of the Cuckoos*. Both Stan and Babe wept openly, and later described the moment as one of the greatest thrills of their lives.

That was somewhat like the account given by the newspapers at the time. Here is how Stan Laurel perceived it:

```
                                               Sept.18th.'53.

My Dear Booth [Colman]-
A wonderful reception on our arrival in Cobh, seemed like
everybody turned out to meet us as we came in on a tender,
people came out in row boats, boat whistles blowing, the
Cathedral chimes playing the Cuckoo, the schools had
specially closed so the kids could be there with the
cheering crowds. I never saw such a sight, this was all on
the level, no publicity stunt.
I have since had a letter from a guy at the Bank of Ireland
there, telling me that all the staff, due to the
excitement, left the bank wide open to come and see us,
then realising, they all rushed back! can you imagine. It
was murder getting through the crowds to our cars, the
police force being small & unable to handle them
(5000.Population).
```

And now a personalised and insightful account of the proceedings, sent to me by a local – Adrian Patrick Gebruers KSG, who wrote:

> The story begins in the picture palaces of Antwerp back in the early 1920s, when my father, Staf Gebruers (1902-1970), then an impecunious young music student, earned much needed pocket money as a temporary cinema pianist.

The Bells Are Ringing

On the morning in question [in Cobh, in 1953], a little drama was unfolding at St. Joseph's Boys' Primary School. As a ten year-old pupil, I was not only a first-hand observer, but very much a participant in these events. The thought that our favourite film comedians might be a stone's throw away, down town, while we scholars sat in our classrooms, was more than any human being could be asked to endure. We therefore took advantage of the morning yard break to petition the school principal to allow us out to see the film stars. The ageing Br. Eugenius was probably not in the best of health, so the collective pressing of hundreds of over-excited boys was probably more than he could take. In what the poor brother might well have considered to be one of his last breaths, he managed to gasp out the words we were longing to hear: "Alright, you can go down to see them."

Housewives going about their daily shopping on "The Beach," Cobh's main thoroughfare, at first thought they were detecting the sound of distant thunder but, with the addition of youngsters' exuberant voices, it soon became obvious that the town's schoolchildren were rushing down West View hill en route to the railway station – where passengers from the liners disembarked.

As my best friend was Seán O'Mahony, and his parents managed the Royal Cork Yacht Club, I was able to get on to the balcony of this building, which commands a fine close-up view of the harbour. When the tender taking the passengers ashore from the liner passed, we waved and shouted and repeatedly rang a ship's bell in welcome, just as everyone else of the thousands lining the waterfront were similarly engaged. The two film stars were completely taken aback by the sheer ecstasy of their reception and, in the years left to them, never tired of reminiscing about that Wednesday – 9 September 1953. Stan Laurel was to say:

"The docks were swarming with many hundreds of people. 'It's strange, a strange thing,' Stan says in recalling that day, '[how] our popularity has lasted so long. Our last good pictures were made in the thirties, and you'd think people would forget, but they don't. The love and affection we found that day at Cobh was simply unbelievable. There were hundreds of boats blowing whistles, and mobs and mobs of people screaming on the docks. We just couldn't understand what it was all about. And then something happened that I can never forget. All the church bells in Cobh started to ring out our theme song, and Babe looked at me, and we cried. Maybe people loved us and our pictures because we put so much love in them. I don't know. I'll never forget that day. Never."

When the two celebrities stepped ashore in Cobh they were immediately surrounded by good humoured milling crowds, all wishing to catch a glimpse of them or even shake their hands or get an autograph. The few local Gardaí fought a losing battle to speed them through immigration and customs formalities and out to a waiting car, and there was some considerable delay before they eventually emerged from the railway station to more cheering masses of fans.

Ollie did not look a well man that morning but, in spite of how he might have been feeling, he and Stan insisted on personally thanking "the bell-ringers." Like most people, they knew next-to-nothing about carillons, and even less of how they're played.*[1] When Seán O'Brien, manager of the U. S. Lines, and a personal friend of my father's, explained that this was an instrument played from a keyboard, by one man, they were even more anxious to make his acquaintance.

A few minutes later, Seán's car sped around Cathedral Corner, followed Pied-Piper-like by hundreds of screaming children. My father was at the main entrance, where I had joined him – standing shyly a few steps behind. My first reaction was one of disappointment as these two elderly gentlemen dressed in modern lounge suits alighted, only vaguely resembling their far more familiar screen personae. But even worse confusion was to follow. When Ollie went to take my father's hand to thank him, the accumulated emotion of that whole morning seemed to suddenly spill over the poor man and words failed him. Tears began to roll down his cheeks as he engulfed Dad in his not inconsiderable embrace.

Alarmed that my father, who in these politically-correct days would be termed vertically-challenged, might not come out intact from that massive bear hug, I was even more unnerved by Stan's contrasting total composure as, dry-eyed, he repeated polite words of appreciation. Shouldn't he be the distraught one, wringing his hands and crying as Ollie yet again admonishes: "That's another fine mess you've gotten us into," when in fact the reverse seemed to be the case?

But there was no denying the sincerity of the film stars' gratitude. Having their theme played on the Carillon, and the great warmth of the welcome they'd witnessed in Cobh, was a genuine public acknowledgment of the innocent fun they had given to millions which seemed to deeply touch them and was to become a landmark experience in their twilight years.

Adrian Patrick Gebruers

[*¹ AJM: Picture the foot-peddles that you see organists dancing their feet across. Now picture those peddles at chest-height, with wires leading to the clappers inside each bell. Now, when you depress the peddles with your hands, the clapper strikes the bell. That is basically how carillon bells are operated.]

When I wrote the First Edition of this book, the only account of the arrival I had to hand was a newspaper article, the content of which had always bothered me, as the description given in the text did not match the scenes in the photographs — and so I was leaning towards believing it was a work of exaggeration. But now, with more witness accounts, including Laurel's, I am happy to accept the scene was as described. Mind you, the photographs still don't match up, but this recently released letter, written by Stan, gives an explanation as to why the pictures don't paint a thousand words:

```
My Dear Booth [Colman]-
Pictures were made of our arrival in Cobh, but, as I told
you it was an impromptu affair & a complete surprise to us
all - as we first saw the crowds all yelling etc. - we
hadn't the slightest idea what it was all about till
someone on board of the Tender told us to listen to the
Cathedral Bells - Then came dawn! There may have been
pictures taken by individuals - There was a news
photographer on the Dock when we got off - but of course
all he did was in the close ups - half of them never think
to photograph the crowd - only the attraction. Had we
known, we could have arranged to have it properly covered -
it's a shame - but just one of those things.
```

Stan than adds some personal comments about the event.

```
We had dozens of letters & notes handed to us - invitations
to homes etc. One pastry shop made a Big cake for us with
our faces designed on it & welcome etc. but of course
didn't go anywhere - Just impossible to move - was glad to
get into the car & away - reminded us of our Glasgow
reception in 32! & Rome in '50. at times. It's terrifying -
just a mass of humanity. It's wonderful, but a terrible
ordeal.
```

Adding, in another letter:

```
A sure hectic way to be pushed around all day!
```

It was reported that fans were most disappointed at Hardy's whole demeanour. He seemed to be disinterested and discourteous to anyone who approached him. Well, there was very good reason for that. Hardy had a medical condition, which needed immediate attention, and needed somewhere private to address the problem. Unable to escape the crowd, he had to suffer in silence, while trying to keep people at a distance.

Continuing Laurel and Hardy's short but memorable arrival at Cobh, the party was next driven six miles north west to Blarney Castle – in whose walls is embedded the legendary "Blarney Stone." This stone, so legend has it, has the powers to impart the gift of flattering speech to those willing to kiss it. To reach it, one has firstly to climb the steps to the top of the ramparts, lie on one's back, and then let one's head drop downwards and backwards (with one's weight supported by an assistant), before administering that life-changing kiss. Uck!! This physical exercise was easily achieved by Stan, but Ida and Lucille declined – as did Babe, who rightly pointed out: "Nobody would hold me. I'm too big."

With this dubious opportunity being lost – which one can rest assured did not seriously affect Mr. Hardy's gift for flattery – the party left Blarney Castle and retired to Cobh City Hall for luncheon, as guests of the Lord Mayor of Cork – Ald. P. McGrath, and other civic dignitaries.

Lord Mayor of Cork – Alderman P. McGrath

All too soon the impromptu sightseeing tour came to an end, and the party left the city of Cobh, a little later than scheduled, with the sights of the children's faces forever etched in their minds, and the sound of its bells echoing in their ears. Having originally planned to arrive unnoticed, Stan Laurel and Oliver Hardy would not have exchanged this reception for the world.

Upon boarding the train that would take them from Cork to Dublin, the Boys may have expected a little respite, but their hopes were soon shattered as they were besieged by autograph-hunters during the entire three-hour journey. Next came a much shorter train journey, about seven miles south-east, to the coastal town of Dun Laoghaire. There, the Hollywood superstars' arrival at the Royal Marine hotel went off with a minimum of fuss — which came as quite a relief.

Thankfully, the Royal Marine Hotel was to prove to be a real sanctuary, with the fan hysteria far behind them. The hotel also provided some very welcome comforts, and good food — two attributes they had not always found in the hotels back in 1947. Stan was particular delighted at having a nice large room, and bath – facing the harbour.

Outside the Royal Marine Hotel. Lucille Hardy looks on from the doorway

Later, a reporter from the *Irish Times* found the Laurels having dinner in the hotels' dining room:

"Ollie is resting," explained Stan. "We had a terrific heat-wave in New York before we left [102 deg.F] and, well, it was just too much for him. He did not quite get over it until a few days out on the boat, and then the journey ..."

The Bells Are Ringing

The following day it was the turn of the *Evening Mail* to pose the questions, and Lucille to act as spokeswoman:

> "We are all very tired after the journey," she told the reporter. "We intend to rest a few days before starting work on our new show. We will probably go into town tonight."

This extract from a Laurel letter re-iterates his wife's comments:

```
We start to work Monday - so glad to have a few days rest.
Bob Hope is playing in Dublin for a couple of nights - too
tired to go & see the show. All for now.
```

[AJM: It is one of those enigmas in life, wherein passengers on liners (and now cruise ships) have nothing to do but eat, sleep, and relax — and yet come off the ship more tired than went they went on it.]

The *Evening Mail* article further revealed:

> Their show will go on a 12-month tour of British theatres. "We will be appearing in Belfast, but I do not know about Dublin yet," Stan added.
>
> The cast which will take part in the show will arrive in Dublin in a fortnight's time, and will rehearse in the Olympia Theatre, where the two comedians appeared last year during their visit to Ireland. The scenery for the show is being made in Belfast and will be brought to Dublin for the rehearsals.

Laurel had started working on the script at his home in California at least some four months earlier, as the extract from this letter of 4 June will show:

```
I am busy trying to work
out a new act, have a
rough idea. Babe is in
the Hospital,
Psychopathic Case by
mistake. I come to visit
him & of course become
involved, finishing up,
the Psychiatrist Dr.
turns out to be the one
that is NUTS. (His name
is Dr. Beserk) It sounds
like it may have some
possibilities for a
funny sketch, however,
if it doesn't pan out,
I'll have to shake my
head again.
```

But the sketch was still very much work in progress.

```
Hotel very nice here. Am
busy getting the script
in shape to start
rehearsals on the 28th
when the cast arrives.
```

If that is writing paper, Laurel must be anticipating throwing a lot of it in the waste-basket, when he starts writing the sketch

During the next three weeks Stan wrote at least four different drafts of the new sketch before he was happy with it. Just why the Laurel and Hardy Family came to Dublin at all, while Stan wrote the script, is beyond my comprehension. Why didn't he just write it at home – thus eliminating the first three weeks of the expensive five-week stay in Dublin, before rehearsals began? Laurel was a real penny-pincher, so this arrangement just doesn't figure.

One member of the cast making preparations to come over from London was Gordon Craig, to whom Laurel wrote the following:

```
We would like you to join us here for rehearsals on Monday
next (28th) kindly contact the Delfont office re transport-
ation matters. Suggest that you arrange to live in Dublin,
as we shall be rehearsing at the Olympia Theatre about
Wednesday of next week. In the meantime we shall have a few
run throughs at the Hotel here with the cast, to get
familiar with the sketch. It is about six miles from here
to Dublin & there is bus or train service.

Re the costumes & wig, regulation Nurses outfit, blue with
white collar & cuffs & white cap. The wig I will leave up
to you, whatever you are accustomed to working in. Get two
outfits & have charged to L&H, Delfont office. Will
appreciate if you will bring them with you.
```

Stan Laurel and Oliver Hardy weren't the kind of Hollywood stars to stay in their hotel rooms, and allow the public to see them only when they were on stage. These too lovable gentlemen not only regularly attend public events, but also spent time with their fans. They were also very charitable – not only lending their names to raise money for charities, but often donating the fees they were paid for public events. So, when they were introduced to polio sufferer Willie O'Reilly, who was used as the flag-waver for the local 'Little Willie Polio Fund,' they were able to present him with a cheque in no time.

Stan and Babe had purloined the cheque off Premier Tailors, who had three shop premises in Dublin. The original plan had been for them to have free suits made, in return for Premier Tailors to use the Laurel & Hardy images in a newspaper advert; but, for the first time in their lives, the Boys were able to broker a better business deal – hence the cheque.

Both Stan and babe loved children, and were always thrilled by the happiness and laughter that always ensued whenever children were introduced to them. And so we give you this happy picture of Little Willie with his little female friend – all made possible by a "cheque suit."

Little Willie, with Big Ollie.

The Bells Are Ringing

Below is proof, if proof were needed, that Laurel was working on the script of *Birds of a Feather* during the weeks at their hotel. The bottom picture shows how much of it made it to Draft 4.

TELEPHONES 81911/3   **WIRE "COMFORT" DUN LAOGHAIRE**

ROYAL MARINE HOTEL
DUN LAOGHAIRE
CO. DUBLIN

B. AT A DISTILLERY — WHAT DOING?

S. WHISKEY TASTING

B. ? whiskey tasting? what's that?

S. ~~well the fellow says you~~ ~~KEEP TASTING WHISKEY~~ TILL WE FIND THE PROOF

B. PROOF OF WHAT.

S. WE'VE GOT TO KNOW IF IT'S A SINGLE OR A DOUBLE THAT'S WHAT THE FELLAR TOLD ME

B. DO YOU KNOW THIS FELLAR?

S. NO, I just met him.

B. what does he look like?

S. kind of Tall. & every time he said something — he kept opening his vest Pocket & did this with his cigarette. (Pantomimes knocking ashes off into vest Pocket.) ~~a habit I guess~~

B. a habit I guess.

S. sure saves carrying an ash Tray.

B. never mind that — Did he tell you what qualifications etc.

OLLY:	What kind of a job? STAN: *At a distillery.*
~~OLLY:~~ *What Doing?*	
STAN:	Whiskey tasters.
OLLY:	Whiskey tasters? Did you get all the details.
STAN:	Sure.
OLLY:	What do we have to do?
STAN:	We have to keep tasting whiskey until we get the proof.
OLLY:	~~What~~ proof *of what*?
STAN:	Whether it's a single or a double.

93

Before starting on the tour proper it was decided, with Laurel and Hardy's typically generous nature, to stage a charity showcase at the Olympia Theatre, where rehearsals had been taking place for the last two weeks.

```
Dear Claude [Cingalee]:-
Appreciate very much, getting the pigeons for us & will let
you know re the shipping of them as soon as we get to
England. On Oct.11th. we are going to break the act in at
the Olympia here, a benefit matinee for the Red Cross, & we
are getting a couple of pigeons here for the one show, so
no use sending yours over, besides there may be difficulty
bringing them in, remember you had some trouble last time
you were here?.
```

To advertise the show, other than the newspaper advert, below, Stan and Ollie did a radio interview with a Mr. Boden. The whole piece was scripted, by Laurel, so that the two of them could best stay in character. Plus of course, it eliminated any embarrassing attempts at ad-libbing, at which they had failed so badly in the past — although, to be fair, it was often the interviewer who lacked the skills to make any conversation work.

[See '**RADIO**' page 163 for an extract of the script.]

So, on Sunday 11 October 1953, *Birds of a Feather* was seen for the first time ever by a paying audience. The *Evening Herald* reported:

> The affection in which Laurel & Hardy are held by young and old was very much in evidence, in the premier of their new playlet. This latest effort, which they will present during their forthcoming tour of Britain, sticks closely to the formula that has served them so well over the years. It provides straight-forward knock-about fun and the two comedians worked with their usual earnestness and to the great delight of the audience.

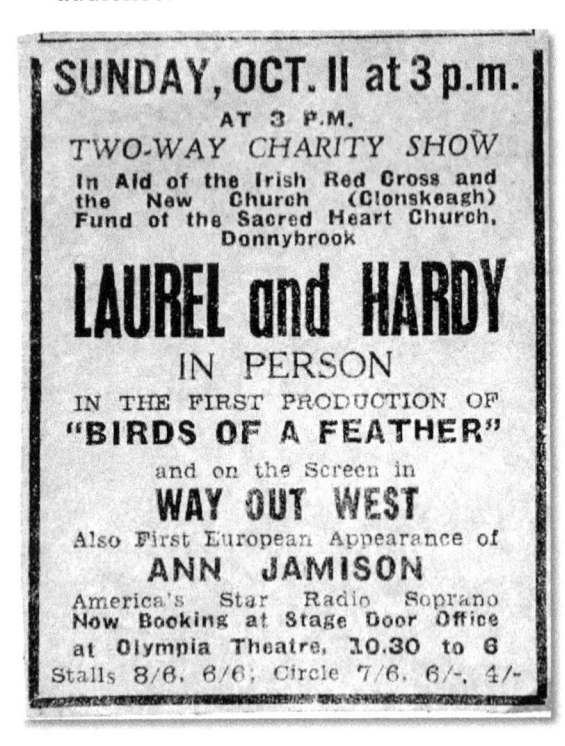

So, had Stan and Babe done enough? Would the sketch still work when played on a regular theatre show? Was it only affection for the two ageing comedians that would see them through the tour, or did they still have enough in their magic-box to justify their booking on a seven-month tour? Let's follow them, and see!

o-o-0-o-o

Chapter 11

PIGEON ENGLISH

On Tuesday 13 October the Laurel and Hardy family sailed across the sea to England – and thus missed seeing the sun go down on Galway Bay. After making their way to London, they checked-in at the Washington Hotel; where, after the obligatory press conference, they pretty much had four days of uninterrupted privacy.

> I brought up a second shot of Hardy (inset), but he doesn't have any eyes in that, either. Maybe he's preventing anyone using them as the windows to his soul.

Saturday found Stan and Babe in the BBC TV studios – being interviewed on the Henry Hall TV show, *Face the Music*. [Pictured below.]

They were against performing their act, or part thereof, on television because, as Hardy explained:

"In the States, the innumerable TV stations use up material so fast that there aren't enough gags and acts to go round. A comedian has to put as much into a one hour television show, as into a theatre show which might run for years."

They therefore performed a very short sketch which Laurel had written specially for this one-off TV appearance.

Page 1 of the FACE THE MUSIC sketch:

Mr. Hardy

FACE THE MUSIC.	**LAUREL AND HARDY INTERVIEW.**
C.U. HENRY HALL.	HENRY: (Intro build-up, finishing...) Well, let's see if these two chaps have arrived, shall we? Has anybody seen Laurel and Hardy?
CALLS OFF	
CUT TO:	
M.L.S. LAUREL & HARDY. LAUREL SMILES AND JOINS IN WITH THE APPLAUSE	LAUREL: (To Hardy) This should be good.
HARDY WATCHES HIM THEN SUDDENLY SMACKS HIS HANDS DOWN.	
	HARDY: Stop that! ~~Pull yourself together.~~ And fix your tie. Don't you know we're going to meet Mr Henry Hall?
STAN FIXES TIE.	LAUREL: Oh, are we? That's swell.
	HARDY: Yes. You've got to look your best. He's going to introduce us.
	LAUREL: Introduce us? ~~But~~ we know each other...we've been together going on thirty years.
	HARDY: Look - he's not going to introduce you to me or me to you.. he's going to introduce us to the audience!
	LAUREL: What audience?
	HARDY: What audience! Don't you realise we have an audience of about six millions tonight?
	LAUREL: ~~Really?~~
	HARDY: Yes...and he's going to introduce us to them.
	LAUREL: That's going to take a long time, isn't it?

Towards the end of the interview, Hardy made a slight mistake:

> "We open," he began, "for Mr. Bernard Delfont at Southampton." After a surprised look from Stan and a gesture from Henry Hall, Babe corrected himself, "I'm sorry! that's **North-**hampton."

The two comedy stars duly travelled to *North*ampton on Sunday, and booked in at the Plough Hotel. At Monday morning rehearsals at the New Theatre, their schedule was interrupted when P.C. Spiller, of the Northamptonshire Constabulary, enticed them outside into Abington Street to pose for photographs. In one, we see Stan with a group of schoolchildren standing by a zebra-crossing, and a rather portly warden, Ollie, holding a huge rectangular sign (a prototype "lollipop") ready to escort the children across. The picture was used in a local newspaper as part of promoting awareness of a nationwide "Road Safety Campaign," aimed at teaching children how to cross the road.

Parked next to the zebra-crossing was a 1902 Wolsey car, in-and-around which Stan and Babe next performed some comedy antics, whilst bringing the serious messages about Road Safety to the attention of the on-lookers.

[It was thought until quite recently that this action was filmed, which is not correct. Good to note, however, that Pathé Newreels did film a comedy sequence of L&H arriving at the theatre in a taxi, and also in the dressing room, just before going on stage.] **[FILM]**

The evening saw Laurel and Hardy performing their new stage sketch for the first time in England. The basic plot for *Birds of a Feather* runs as follows:

> The two friends arrange to meet outside a public house. They arrive individually and go through an extended version of the routine used on the 1952 tour, whereby they keep "missing" one another. This is better effected by the use of two entrances to the public house and, like a novelty weather clock, as one partner goes in one door his counterpart comes out of the other, and vice versa.

by kind courtesy of:
CLIFF TEMPLE
[taken at Norwich Hippodrome]

When finally they accidentally bump into each other, Stan informs Ollie of a vacancy which might suit them. The job entails tasting whisky, with the incentive appearing to be: "The more you drink, the more you earn." They take the job, but strive a little too keenly to fulfil demands, with the result that Ollie ends up in hospital after launching himself through an open window, in an effort to fly.

With the introduction of a doctor, a nurse (Gordon Craig in "drag"), and an undertaker, mix-ups occur over just who is the patient, and who is the visitor. Confusion is increased by the presence of some eggs in Ollie's bedside cabinet which Stanley brought for Ollie, but the nursing staff think were *laid* by Ollie.

The sketch ends with Laurel and Hardy walking around clucking like chickens, after being fed bird seed, and the pandemonium is added to when the doctor opens the cabinet doors and two pigeons fly out.

The two comedians then come front of tabs and sing *Trail of the Lonesome Pine* (from their film *Way Out West*), before saying their customary "Goodnight."

[*Birds of a Feather* is often quoted as being based on the film *County Hospital*. In both, Stan goes to visit Ollie in hospital, but there any similarity ends.]

They finished the act with: *Trail of the Lonesome Pine* (aka: *The Blue Ridge Mountain of Virginia*) – a song they had had the music written for back in June 1947, whilst in Blackpool, but hadn't used on that tour. Recomember? There was no dance to accompany this, which was a very good reason to employ it this time around — especially considering Hardy was now at least four stone heavier, and that his knees were shot.]

Oooo! mi apple.
Stan recovering from an escape attempt, wherein he tied one end of the blanket around his neck, to hold Ollie while lowering him out of the window.

Pigeon English

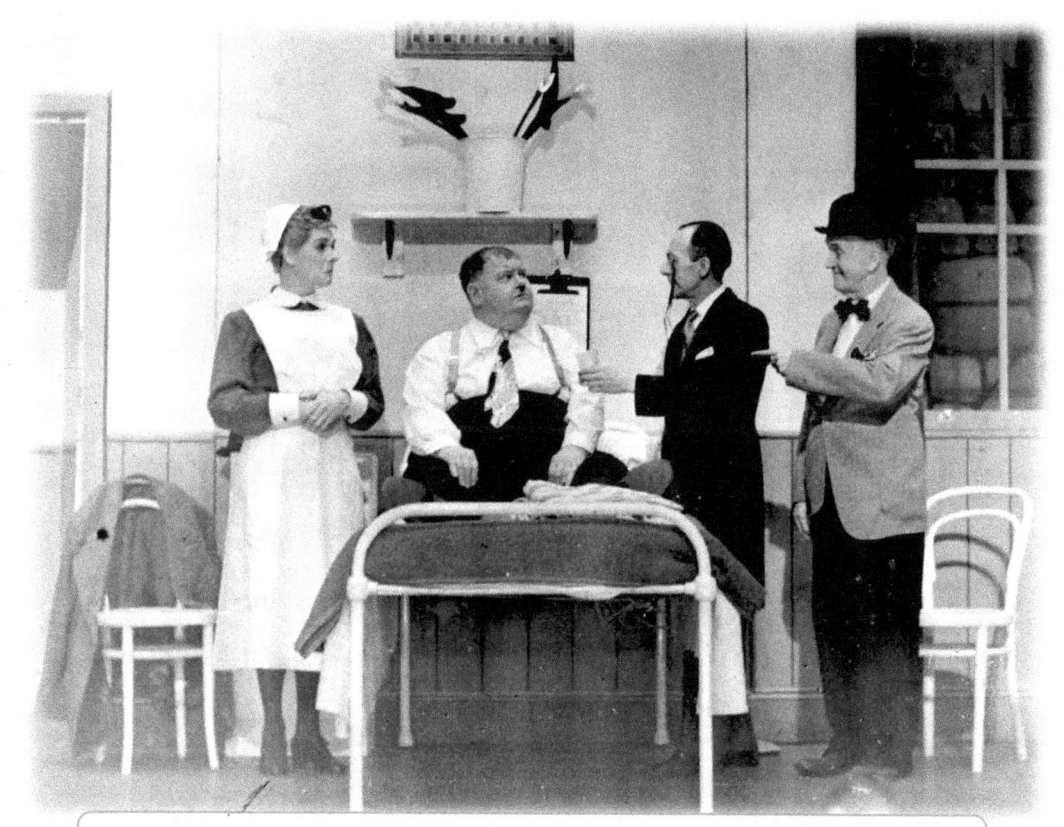

Nurse Rosey Parker looks on as Dr. Beserk tries to get Hardy to take some bird seed, in a glass of water, as a part of "Dr. Wombat's bird seed test."

The Northampton *Chronicle & Echo* reviewed the first performance as follows:

> Laurel & Hardy had a warm reception from an audience that was strangely mixed. There were adults who had rocked at Stan and Ollie when the films were literally the 'flicks'. Secondly, there were the children – before the curtain it was almost like a panto matinee – whose acquaintance probably dated from the time the family TV set was installed.
>
> Nostalgia, and a love for a comedy couple re-born – ironically by a medium the experts say will one day kill the stage – these were two main ingredients in the Laurel & Hardy success. But that was certainly not all. There was for the discerning the pleasure of watching two masters of their craft at work.

Things invariably go wrong on first-nights, and the Boys did not beat the jinx. At the end of the sketch at the first house, when the doctor opened the doors of the bedside cabinet, the two pigeons, instead of flying out, merely dropped to the floor and strutted about the stage. Later, backstage, Laurel suggested to Jack Whitmore, their tour manager, that the pigeons had been fed too much. "Why, they couldn't even take off," he grinned. At the first house on Tuesday night, however, one bird took advantage of its newly-found freedom, and finished up watching the end of the show from a theatre box.

Well I'm sure Claude Cingalee had done his best to "train" these pigeons, but maybe they should have stuck with the ones they used in Ireland. At least they understood pigeon English.

As for the support acts, this was again a mixed bag of spesh-acts, singers and dancers:

> Jill, Jill & Jill – *Steps in Rhythm*; Freddie Harris & Christine – *Magical Entertainers*; Ursula & Gus – *Novelty Jugglers*; Fred Lovelle – *Ventriloquial Humour*; Krista & Kristel – T*win Trapezists*; Keefe Bros. and Annette – *Wonder Balancers*; Roy & Ray – *Singing Accordionists*.

(Laurel & Hardy assisted by: Gordon Craig; Gerald Lennan; Bernard Newson).

And the New Theatre Orchestra

-----o-----

Page 1 of the BIRDS OF A FEATHER sketch:

OLLY DISCOVERED LYING ON THE BED PARTLY DRESSED. HE HAS AN ICE BAG ON HIS HEAD. IT IS A SMALL SINGLE BED TO MAKE OLLY LOOK UNCOMFORTABLE. ON THE LEFT OF THE SET IS A HEAVY DOOR, HALF OF WHICH HAS BARS A LA JAIL. CENTER IS THE BED. AT THE LEFT IS A WINDOW ALSO WITH BARS. LEFT OF CENTER IS A THREE-WAY SCREEN. (A KNOCK IS HEARD ON THE DOOR.)

OLLY: Come in. (THE DOOR OPENS INTO ROOM WHICH REVEALS A SIGN WHICH IS HANGING ON THE OUTSIDE AND READS, "PSYCHOPATHIC CASE. NO VISITORS". STAN ENTERS WITH SOME LILIES AND PAPER BAG.)

STAN: Hello, Ollie. How do you feel?

OLLY: Where have you been? I've been expecting you all day.

STAN: I had a hard time getting in.

OLLY: Why?

STAN: They said no visitors allowed to see you.

OLLY: How did you manage?

STAN: Well, they said it was okay for relatives, so I told them I was your son.

(OLLY DOES BIG TAKEM WHICH SCARES STAN.)

OLLY: You had a lot of nerve telling them I was your father. As if I wasn't in enough trouble already.

STAN: I couldn't say you were my mother.

OLLY: Never mind that. What I want to know is what happened and what am I doing here?

STAN: Didn't you hear? You jumped out of a top floor window.

OLLY: (STARTLED) I jumped out of a top floor window! When?

STAN: Last night.

OLLY: For what?

Page 2 of the BIRDS OF A FEATHER sketch:

STAN:	Remember, yesterday morning, we went to a fellow's office to get a job as whiskey testers?
OLLY:	I remember that.
STAN:	Well, late last night, the fellow said we were the best whiskey tasters he ever had. In fact, he said you were much better than me.
OLLY:	Naturally. Go on.
STAN:	Well, just before the fellow passed out, he told us we could start to work right away.
OLLY:	You mean we got the job?
STAN:	That's what he said.
OLLY:	Wonderful! What luck!
STAN:	Well, it wasn't luck. We worked hard for that job. We didn't even take time off for lunch.
OLLY:	Never mind. Go on.
STAN:	Well, you were so pleased, you took a couple of drinks to celebrate.
OLLY:	Certainly, who wouldn't on an occasion like that?
STAN:	Then you walked over and opened a window.
OLLY:	Opened the window? It must have been hot!
STAN:	No, you said you felt as happy as a lark and you were going to fly around the streets for a while. Then you started to wave your arms, like wings, and jumped out.
OLLY:	(SITS UP IN BED STARTLED.) You mean I jumped out waving my arms?
STAN:	Just like a bird. I can see you now.
OLLY:	Why didn't you stop me?
STAN:	I thought you could do it.

One night, a keen amateur recording enthusiast made a tape of Laurel and Hardy's stage act which turned out so well that Stan considered having it produced commercially. [The tape is now in a secret location.] **[AUDIO]**

On Thursday evening, radio presenter Philip Garston-Jones did an interview with the two stars which was broadcast the following night on Midlands' radio, in *What Goes On*. Earlier that day, Pathé had filmed newsreel footage showing Stan and Babe clowning around in a taxi by the stage door, and then in their dressing room getting ready for the show. The huge disappointment, though, is that, even after the combined presence of such filming and recording equipment and crew, no joint audio AND visual recording of ANY of Laurel and Hardy's stage sketches was ever made. **[RADIO]**

I doubt if the people of Northampton realised that, that week, they had been hosts to a bit of an historic happening, for Laurel and Hardy had been 'live' on TV; were on at the cinema – in *Fraternally Yours* (the British release version of *Sons of the Desert*); were appearing 'live' at the theatre; had made a radio broadcast *and* a newsreel film; had had their sketch taped; and were featured most evenings in local newspaper write-ups. One would be hard pressed to find another time and place where all these media had been employed over such a short period. Liverpool, the next stopover, certainly wasn't going to try to compete.

o-o-0-o-o

Chapter 12

DUMB AND DUMMY

The press in Liverpool were negligent in letting anyone know that Laurel and Hardy were even in the city, and it was only the obligatory review of the opening night at the Liverpool Empire which made it to print. *The Daily Post* was, however, profound in its assessment:

> When Laurel & Hardy take the stage this week, we have to remember they are not there to be judged – merely to be acknowledged in person, as two of the greatest film comedians the world has ever known. Not they, but thirty years of changing tastes and techniques are on trial, to be guilty of failing to raise more than a few laughs despite Stan & Ollie's tremendous sense of comedy, experienced stagecraft, and slapstick script. Their reputation is established and the tricks on which this was built are there for everyone to see. The crushed bowler hat, the falling flower-pot, the battered brolly – everything but the bag of flour and the custard pie.

> The same faultless baby-cries appear on Stan's face – the Lancashire-born comedian has lost none of his skill. Oliver's apoplexy still threatens. But is something missing? Is it that the stage prevents them falling off roofs, or being dragged behind moving cars – or is it that their public has just grown up?

The *Liverpool Echo* too, thought there was something lacking:

> Laurel & Hardy will always be remembered for those two-reel comedies. It is perhaps as well that this should be so. It may well be that the theatre does not offer the scope in action and change of scene which they require, but whatever the reason, their stage appearance provides but a glimpse of the great comedians we knew and loved.

Off-stage Laurel and Hardy were still in demand as the huge celebrities they obviously were, and went along as guests of the Mayor to a dance. Before you start making up your own jokes about "The Mayor's Ball" I should inform you that the person in office at that time was a "lady."

Don't worry! I'll just pin this badge over the hole I burned in your jacket.

Shoot! I've done it again.

The Lady Mayoress and her entourage force themselves to put down their cigarettes, for just the few seconds it took to pose for this photograph.

The manager of the *Liverpool Empire* had his own sympathetic views as to what was wrong with Laurel and Hardy's act. In his weekly report he wrote:

> Very well received. Wonderful performers and they have a good sketch, but it seems that they are "dated" – that they get nothing from the audience like they deserve. Liverpool is not a "children's" town and adult audiences are not falling for this type of comedy. I feel it is a great pity – almost bordering on tragedy – as these artistes are great in their way and deserve a much better welcome.

The above assessment seems a little contradictory, and is also unfair to the paying customer, in that the manager tagged it by saying he would not have them back.

During Stan and Babe's next week-long stopover, in Manchester, the rain swept down with a vengeance, causing widespread flooding. Inside the theatre, things didn't brighten – if the account in the *Evening Chronicle* is anything to go by:

> A not-so-bright Manchester Hippodrome [The "New" Hippodrome – formerly the Ardwick Green Empire] variety bill placed too much responsibility on the shoulders of Laurel & Hardy. Nice to see them back again. Sorry to report that, after twenty-six glorious years of making folk laugh their heads off, that old magic doesn't shine quite so brightly. Still, this act from Lancashire-born Stan and a fatter-than-ever Ollie was streets ahead of anything else offered.

The *Manchester Guardian* reviewer, however, was quite happy to accept the sketch in the capacity in which it had been conceived, i.e. as a vehicle to transpose the comedians' film antics to the stage:

> ... this is genuine clowning which sticks to its mindless principles and has no use for smartness, surrealism, or sex. All we ask is that they should be themselves, and to see them in three-dimensions on the stage meets the demand; their two-scene psychological melodrama uses precisely the same technique as that of their pictures. It is the tactics of elephant and mouse. The elephant feels diminished by the tiny creature that spends its time getting on his nerves and under his feet, and has to inflate his dignity to enormous proportions as a defensive compensation.

Radio and TV comedy impressionist Peter Goodwright, who gave such a good in-depth report on Laurel and Hardy's 1947 Manchester appearance, was on hand to give an equally perceptive view of their latest one.

Their welcome on this occasion was fairly enthusiastic, but contained none of the euphoria of the previous appearance. This time the house was not full and Stan & Ollie had to work very hard for their laughs. It was on this occasion, as Laurel & Hardy took their applause that I realised, for the very first time, that I had been watching two men who were no longer young.

As they stood on the stage, Stan looked gaunt with thinning hair, and Ollie was obviously having difficulty in walking. It came as a shock to me, I recall, and I was filled with a sadness that not even the laughter they had created could erase. I remember thinking 'I shall not see them again,' and of course, I never did. No-one has emerged to take their place, but then – who could?

"A colouring competition" might be the answer to that, as no less than three large features of this nature, in the *News & Recorder*, dominated the interest stakes in Laurel and Hardy, whereas coverage of the comedians in their own merit commanded only half-a-dozen lines. Sadly, this trait by newspapers was becoming all too common – the ultimate irony of which is that the competitions were totally independent of Laurel and Hardy's live appearances.

The following week at the Finsbury Park Empire, London, even worse was to occur when the only mention in the local paper was for the NON-appearance of Laurel and Hardy. Stan had a serious chill, which incapacitated him for a whole week. From his sickbed in the Washington Hotel, he wrote:

```
We did'nt open at Finsbury Park, I caught a hell of a cold
in M'Chester & by the time I got here I was stone cold
deaf. Got an E.N.T. Specialist who decided I must'nt go on,
so have been all week under treatment, Air pressure, short
wave heatbusiness, & glad to say I am starting to get back
my hearing & should be OK again by Monday to open at
Brixton. Too bad this had to happen, as we had a very big
Advance booking & would have done a terrific week's
business. However, we shall play it later on.
```

On what should have been Laurel and Hardy's opening night, Hardy went on stage to announce that Stan was indisposed, and tried to encourage the audience to give every appreciation to the replacements; but, much as the audience were in sympathy, they could not hide their disappointment at missing the opportunity to see two living legends. Consequently, the stand-ins, comedy double-act Jimmy Jewel & Ben Warriss, had to endure a cold reception, followed by four other nights not much better. (On the last night, comedian George Doonan and rag-time pianist Winifred Atwell stood in.)

The only bit of comfort for Jimmy and Ben came from Hardy, who, being quite at liberty to absent himself from the theatre, chose to go in every night – firstly to appease the audience, and secondly to provide moral support for the acts. He actually stayed in Jimmy and Ben's company during the whole time they were in the theatre. If ever a man's heart were in direct proportion to the size of his body – that man was Babe Hardy.

Around this time, Stan and Babe had a reunion with vivacious Hollywood songstress, Vivian Blaine, who was in the middle of a year-long run in the musical *Guys & Dolls*, at the London Coliseum. Miss Blaine had been a shining light in Laurel and Hardy's 1943 film *Jitterbugs*, but was now eager to describe her thrill at having been on the recent *Royal Variety Performance*. In turn, she was delighted to hear of Stan and Babe's tearful welcome at Cobh, which she was later to reveal to millions of American TV viewers on Ralph Edwards' *This Is Your Life* (broadcast 1 December 1954).

Following the enforced week's stay in their North London hotel, while Laurel recovered from the flu, the Boys popped over the River Thames to Brixton, in South London. *The Stage* printed a unique review for the show, which described wholly the on-stage action:

> In *Birds of a Feather*, at the Brixton Empress, Hardy is a patient in a mental hospital. Laurel visits him with a bunch of lilies, and a jam and onion sandwich.
>
> Hardy is indignant at being kept in such a place merely because he tried to fly out of a window after sampling some whisky. (Laurel didn't restrain him because, having had some of the whisky himself, he thought Hardy *could* fly out of the window!) Hardy sends Laurel for a barrister; Laurel returns with a section of banister, a doctor thinks Laurel must be the patient ... and so on. Hardy sighs, looks to the audience for sympathy, and generally finds Laurel's friendship very, very trying. On Monday there was a big audience, and plenty of laughter in all parts of the house.

There may have been laughter in the auditorium, but there was little backstage. Actor, BBC broadcaster, and biographer John M. East (*ibid.*) interviewed the two former screen stars backstage, and came away with a comment Laurel made, forever lodged in his memory – which was: "We should never have come back."

After Stan's illness the previous week it was now Babe's turn, when he was given a very bad heart scare and, by rights, should have had himself admitted to hospital. But, following the old adage "the show must go on," he unwisely continued without resting.

On 23 November the Boys were back at the theatre which had started it all for them in British Variety, the *Newcastle Empire*.

The "review" of the show in the Evening Chronicle was short, but sweet:

> 'Birds of a Feather' provides just the right medium for comedy film stars Laurel & Hardy to indulge their droll slapstick fun, and they well deserved the welcome they received on their return to the city.

That week, one of the other acts was just starting off in his new career. This twenty-three year-old was yet to make his mark as the most technically brilliant ventriloquist of all time; but, then, was happy enough to be fulfilling one of his ambitions – that of meeting his comedy heroes, Laurel and Hardy. In 1988 Ray Alan wrote, in a personal letter to me:

> Meeting them for the first time was something of an experience. I had never met such big stars before. As I entered the theatre the first thing to greet me was Stan's voice saying, 'Hello there! You must be Ray. I'm Stan, and this is Babe. We don't want any of that 'Mister' business, do we? After all we are all pro's doing a job, aren't we?'
>
> When I got to know them a little better, I mentioned to Babe that I had read somewhere about them not talking to each other. Babe Hardy gave me a hearty chuckle, called Stan into the room, and repeated what I'd just said. Stan grinned and replied, 'Oh yeah! We read that too. I'm glad we did 'cos until then we didn't know we weren't talking to each other, did we Babe?' Then the pair of them just laughed.

Of his own spot on the show, Ray Alan revealed:

> Stan would watch my act each night and then ask me to his room where he would suggest a line or a movement. I remember him once telling me that I was losing a laugh by not pausing before the punchline. I tried it his way at the next performance, and as always he was right. To Stan, timing was more important than the spoken word. He had a magical way of doing nothing, hesitating, then either saying something or deciding not to. Whatever way he chose was right and I still use the same pause, the look and the 'slow-burn' when I work now with "Lord Charles," as I did then with the 'cheeky-boy' doll.

And in a newspaper interview:

> Stan said to me, once: "Always remember the audience will never be offended at what you say, as long as they know you are in fun. It's when they think you mean it that it upsets them." I never forgot those wise words.

[AJM: At this early stage in his career, Ray Alan (now sadly deceased) wasn't working with the 'Lord Charles' doll, but a 'cheeky boy' doll named 'Steve.' Ray's bill matter was: "Two Minds With a Single Thought" – which is uncannily similar to the phrase Al Kilgore employed several years later as a motto in his design of the escutcheon for the "Laurel & Hardy Appreciation Society," which reads: "Two Minds With*out* a Single Thought."]

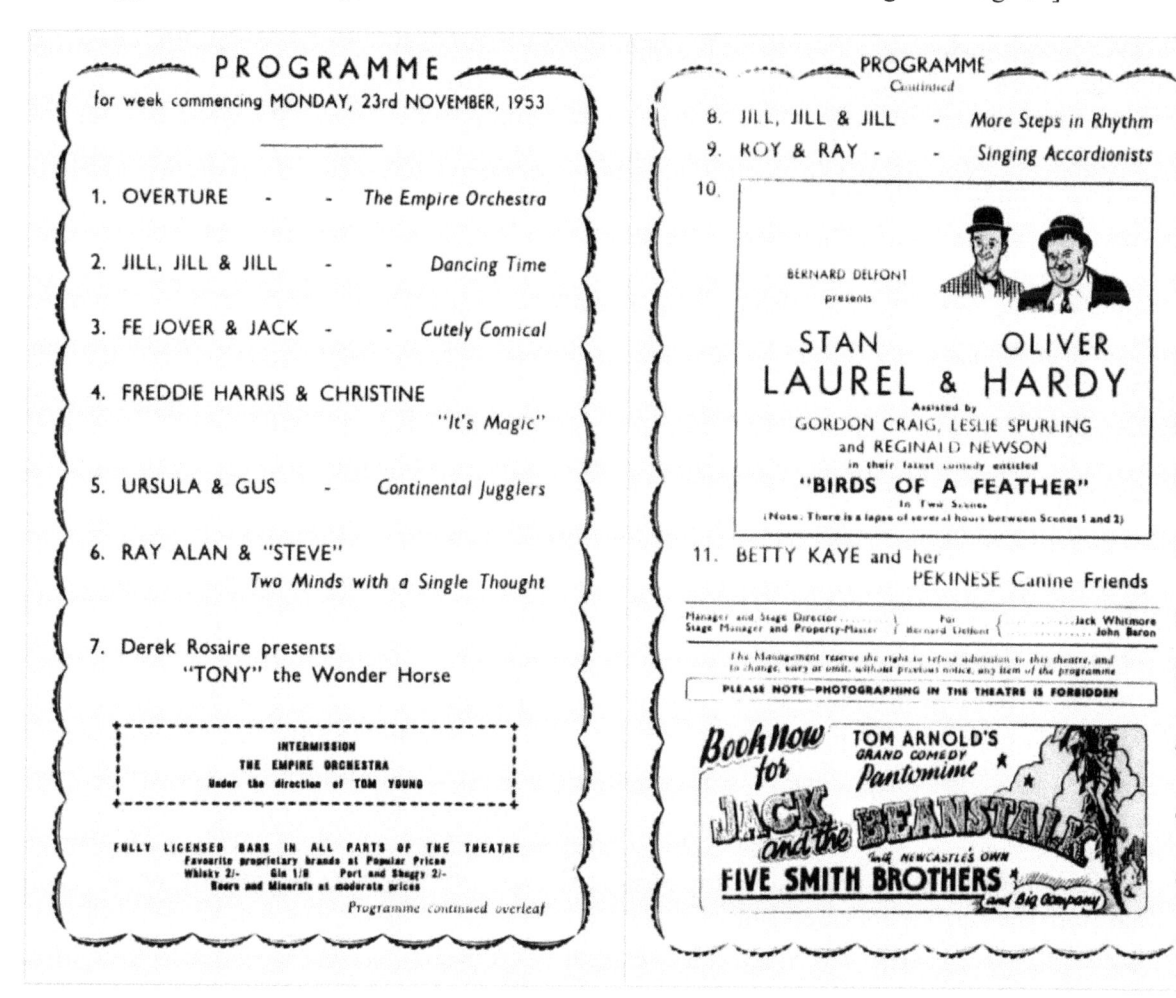

```
PROGRAMME
for week commencing MONDAY, 23rd NOVEMBER, 1953

1. OVERTURE          -   The Empire Orchestra
2. JILL, JILL & JILL -   Dancing Time
3. FE JOVER & JACK   -   Cutely Comical
4. FREDDIE HARRIS & CHRISTINE
                         "It's Magic"
5. URSULA & GUS      -   Continental Jugglers
6. RAY ALAN & "STEVE"
                         Two Minds with a Single Thought
7. Derek Rosaire presents
                         "TONY" the Wonder Horse

            INTERMISSION
         THE EMPIRE ORCHESTRA
      Under the direction of TOM YOUNG

FULLY LICENSED BARS IN ALL PARTS OF THE THEATRE
Favourite proprietary brands at Popular Prices
Whisky 2/-    Gin 1/8    Port and Sherry 2/-
      Beers and Minerals at moderate prices
              Programme continued overleaf
```

```
PROGRAMME
 Continued

8.  JILL, JILL & JILL  -  More Steps in Rhythm
9.  ROY & RAY          -  Singing Accordionists
10.
            BERNARD DELFONT
               presents
          STAN        OLIVER
        LAUREL & HARDY
                Assisted by
       GORDON CRAIG, LESLIE SPURLING
            and REGINALD NEWSON
         in their latest comedy entitled
          "BIRDS OF A FEATHER"
                In Two Scenes
    (Note: There is a lapse of several hours between Scenes 1 and 2)

11. BETTY KAYE and her
                         PEKINESE Canine Friends

PLEASE NOTE—PHOTOGRAPHING IN THE THEATRE IS FORBIDDEN

Book Now for TOM ARNOLD'S GRAND COMEDY Pantomime
JACK and the BEANSTALK
with NEWCASTLE'S OWN
FIVE SMITH BROTHERS
```

Just what kind of welcome, if any, Laurel and Hardy received away from the theatre is not in evidence. On the Monday morning, 'Showman' (theatre reviewer for the *Shields Evening News*) phoned Stan at the Royal Station Hotel, in Newcastle, and recorded the following conversation:

> 'How're y' keepin?' It was a Geordie voice which greeted me when I telephoned Stan Laurel in Newcastle this morning.

'Fine,' I replied. 'And you?'

'Oh, I've had a good rest, put on a little weight and feel much better.'

'And how is Oliver?'

'Fatter than ever. He weighs over 20 stone.'

'Will you be visiting Tynemouth during the week?'

'I'll probably be down one of these days ..... if so, I'll give you a call.'

The article continued:

> Yes, Laurel is back on Tyneside ... Geordie dialect and all. It is his second visit to the area in twenty months. In March last year, he visited Tynemouth where he spent part of his schooldays.
>
> 'We will be in England six months or so and then we may go to Australia,' Laurel told me.
>
> 'How is everyone in Tynemouth? Give them all my love. Tell them I have not forgotten them. God bless.'

Whether Stan bothered to follow up his rather unenthusiastic-sounding intentions to pop over to Tynemouth is unrecorded. After the blasé, treatment the Boys had received on their last visit to Tyneside, perhaps Stan's urge to go back to the place he felt he "belonged" had severely diminished.

What *was* witnessed that week was Stan and Babe's professional dedication in polishing their act. When a show finishes of an evening, many artistes are out of the theatre before the applause has finished. Not so with Laurel and Hardy. If ever Stan felt ill-at-ease with a line, or saw an opening for an extra gag, the two of them would stay behind to rehearse. To get the true feel of the sketch, they would even request the scene-shifters not to "strike" the set, and many were the times it was left up till the following day.

Stan was now in the habit of recording the act, and playing back the audio tape for critical analysis. Sometimes he might feel that a certain line would get a bigger laugh if Babe delivered it, and so would turn the dialogue around to suit. Whatever the case, the following evening they would be in the theatre well before curtain up for another run through, so that, when the new piece was put in the act that night, it would always fit in perfectly.

Billy Marsh and Olga Varona had witnessed this perfectionism back in 1947, when Laurel and Hardy were first adapting to a stage career; whereas Ray Alan was witnessing the same amazing amount of tenacity from the Boys after over two hundred shows (although, admittedly, this sketch was pretty new). The rehearsing obviously paid off as the manager reported:

Excellent reception. These two well-known stage and screen stars return this time with an entirely new sketch. Their comedy of cross patter and actions receives loud laughter, and a big laughable finish.

The Boys may have been going down well with the audiences who were at the theatre each night, but the problem was the people who *weren't* there – as usherette Emily Hopper explains:

> Seeing Laurel & Hardy on stage was something I thought could never happen, after watching them for years at the local cinema. I thoroughly enjoyed the act, but the theatre was only half full, and they didn't go too well. Each night, because there were so few people in, we would move the ones at the back to the seats near the front, so that from the stage it appeared full.

The Boys' disappointment was later confirmed in a backstage conversation between Mrs. Hopper and Babe's wife, Lucille. Trying to determine the reason for the decline in the public's interest for Laurel and Hardy, after the euphoria of the 1947 and 1952 visits, would be very difficult; but, sad to say, they were soon to experience that cold unwelcoming feeling again.

[AJM. When I interviewed Mrs. Hopper, in 1987, she was convinced that she was working as an usherette at the Newcastle Empire at the time of Laurel and Hardy's 1952 visit. However, the low box-office figures suggest it was for this 1953 appearance. Either way, it's an illuminating insight.]

Dumb and Dummy

Ray Alan took away with him that week not only memories that would last him a lifetime, but some very good advice from both these giants of comedy. His final word on his utter respect for the Boys was:

> I don't think Stan and Babe ever refused to say hello to anyone, and I have always believed that, thanks to them, the world became a much happier place. Laurel & Hardy were able to remind adults what fun it was to be children.

Birmingham, like Newcastle, was receiving a fourth visit from Laurel and Hardy. History or reputation, though, didn't enter into the review in the *Birmingham Mail*:

> Laurel & Hardy at the Birmingham Hippodrome were finding the years jading. They showed all the old quirks in a moderate brief farce, but that was all.

The situation wasn't brightened any by Brian Harvey's review in the *Birmingham Gazette*:

> For old time's sake I wish I could say that I enjoyed Laurel & Hardy as much as when they entertained me as a child, with their film antics. At their return visit, however, they are not particularly funny nor has their act any originality. Relying too much on a few time-worn mannerisms, these two comedians must have the most unimaginative gag-writers in show business.

> [AJM: Get the boxing gloves out!]

The Boys must have been reeling on the ropes after being hit a third time – this time by the *Birmingham Post*:

> Laurel & Hardy have been with us for a long time now, and both the formula and reputation of the partnership are well established. That the pair should still be relying on their old formula is nothing remarkable: successful artistes, having recognised their métier, do well to adhere to it. What is significant is that the two clowns, to judge by their performance, are now living on that reputation.

> But it is not really good enough. The sketch is mediocre material as the sort used as make-weight in any of a dozen undistinguished touring revues. It has the slightly sentimental appeal of familiarity, and so has the almost mechanical performance of Laurel & Hardy. The original fire is missing from the drollery, and the pair's enthusiastic reception owed as much, one suspected, to gratitude for past favours, as thankfulness for present laughter.

If ever an ally were needed to champion Laurel and Hardy, then the timing of one young man was impeccable. John McCabe, an American student, was en route to Birmingham Library when he came across Laurel and Hardy's billing outside the Hippodrome and, unable to believe his boyhood heroes were there "in person," ventured inside. After watching their performance, a strong urge led John to meet them backstage. In Stan's dressing room he conversed so intelligently on Stan's favourite subject, the structuring of comedy, that he was invited back a few nights running. By the end of the week, McCabe had enough notes to make a good start on writing the book *Mr. Laurel & Mr. Hardy* which, upon publication eight years later, was to introduce thousands of new fans to "The World of Laurel & Hardy." When in 1987 he saw the review from the *Birmingham Post* (in a draft version of this book, which I sent to him*)*, McCabe was angered enough by the phrase "now living on their reputation" to retort:

> Utter nonsense! Fatuous nonsense! That reviewer was stupid, or inattentive, or both. I saw 'Birds' twelve times, (four in Birmingham), and I heard the uproarious laughter during each performance. I heard the loud cheering that frequently interrupted the performance itself – plain, unadulteratedly [*sic*] funny. Living on their reputation indeed! This is ludicrous.

McCabe's opinion is backed up by the theatre manager, who gave Laurel and Hardy the following report:

> Very excellent reception. These comedians are presenting a very excellent show, which is a "mental" idea, and the comedy they get out of this causes roars of laughter. When this is worked up it will be the best scene they have ever done. Nevertheless in the state it is now it goes excellently.

MOSS'
Hippodrome
BIRMINGHAM
Proprietors: MOSS' EMPIRES, Ltd.
Chairman: PRINCE LITTLER
Managing Director: VAL PARNELL
TELEPHONE - MIDLAND 2576-7
Manager & Licensee: BERTIE ADAMS
6.15 * MONDAY, NOV. 30th * 8.30
HOLLYWOOD'S GREATEST COMEDY COUPLE!
HERE IN PERSON
BERNARD DELFONT presents
STAN LAUREL AND OLIVER HARDY
IN A NEW COMEDY MIRTHQUAKE "BIRDS OF A FEATHER"
PAUL & PETA PAGE
WITH THEIR PUPPETS
FREDDIE HARRIS AND PARTNER
It's Magic
FEJOVER & JACK
Cutely Comical
DEREK ROSAIRE presents his WONDER HORSE TONY
ROY & RAY
ACCORDIONISTS
URSULA AND GUS
CONTINENTAL JUGGLERS
JILL, JILL AND JILL
Dance Team
BETTY KAYE'S PEKINESE PETS
TRIBE BROS., Ltd., London & St. Albans.

Dumb and Dummy

BIRMINGHAM HIPPODROME
Laurel in reflective mood.

This time it's John McCabe caught in reflection, during one of his backstage interviews with both men.

With further material obtained from a continuing friendship with Laurel, and Lucille Hardy, back in America, McCabe was able to compile three more books. Another important spin-off from this friendship was the founding of the "Laurel & Hardy Appreciation Society" – *The Sons of the Desert* – for which McCabe's pioneering efforts cannot be too greatly lauded.

There was no sign of anyone in Hull about to champion Laurel and Hardy's appearance there. In Hull in 1947, Laurel and Hardy had been totally ignored by the press. These six years later, December 1953, Hull still had the least informative newspapers in the nation. The *Hull Daily Mail* gave only the briefest credit:

> Laurel & Hardy were accorded a great reception at the Palace Theatre. Stan & Ollie do not need to speak to raise a laugh. Facial expressions are sufficient. The partnership is perfect in its contrasting humour and though their sketch is comparatively short, they extract every laugh from it.

On Wednesday, a private luncheon given by local cinema managers at the White House Hotel went unrecorded,

Lucille and Babe Hardy look on with polite reserve as Everard Carr Jordan, manager of both the Tower and Regent Cinema, and organiser of the event, seems unable to summon up the words to express his emotions upon having two Hollywood legends as his guests.

And the opening of a jeweller's shop by the two world-famous comedians, in nearby Toll Gavel, Beverley, was given only the merest of mentions. An unknown person breaking into the shop would have gained front page headlines.

Let us hope that this is not a sign that Laurel and Hardy were now regarded as has-beens, the reaction to whose presence was: "So what?"

o-o-0-o-o

Chapter 13

STAN and OLLIE – SANTA and HOLLY

Nottingham, unlike Hull, had done its homework, and gave the fullest of respect to these two living legends – with their appearance having been advertised two months before they had even arrived in England. The Boys now had a free week before the start of their show at the Nottingham Empire, but this was taken up with press and publicity calls, and rehearsing. They did however find time to call in at the Bull Inn, Bottesford, for dinner with the Healeys – Stan's sister Olga and brother-in-law Bill, whom they had also recently visited on their way through to Hull, from Birmingham. This time around, they had just a taster of Christmas-to-come, with mince pies and cake. But then a "white Christmas" almost prevented them getting back to Nottingham, of which Stan wrote: *"Foggy as hell here - (cant see your hand behind your back)."* Thankfully they were able to get back to the County Hotel by car, but at a more leisurely pace.

Could Stan and Babe be getting the chef from the County Hotel to make
a Christmas pudding, for them to take to Stan's sister on Christmas Day?

Even though pantomime is traditional for the Christmas season, the Laurel & Hardy sketch *Birds of a Feather* was retained for the show. When I asked Bernard Delfont why he stuck with the same format of show, he replied: *"There seemed no need to change it."* The support-bill had a heavy leaning towards circus-type acts with: trained pigeons, a 'wonder horse,' performing Pekinese dogs, and jugglers; plus: a ventriloquist, an accordionist duo, and a dance trio. To add to the party atmosphere it was arranged for Stan and Ollie to stay on stage after their sketch, and act as hosts to a free-and-easy of party games, competitions, and a Junior Talent Show. If this sounds like the format for a show that could last all night – it was, as the review from the *Guardian Journal* will verify:

They always say the sign of a good party is the length of time it lasts without anyone realising how late it is getting. 'Laurel & Hardy's Christmas Party' had such a riotous opening that Hardy had to interrupt the fun and games the children were having, because the second-house queue was getting restive, outside.

The famous pair of film comedians act as genial hosts of this grand family entertainment, and provide thirty minutes of slapstick buffoonery in a brand new but traditional sketch. One exasperated sigh from Hardy, or one twitch from Stan's eyebrow – is still enough to send all the youngsters and their parents into hysterics.

The *Evening Post* offered similar observations, except that the twitch in Stan's eyebrow (the one which sent people into hysterics) now belonged to Ollie. Obviously, Stan had swapped it for a couple of blank stares:

Shrieks of delight greeted Laurel & Hardy at the Nottingham Empire. The twitch of an outraged eyebrow from Ollie, or the whites of Stan's eyes raised mournfully to an unkind Heaven, are the signal for every child and adult in the audience to go into that specially delicious brand of hysterics that only clowns of their calibre can conjure up. How splendid it is to recapture that old rapture 'so funny, it hurts'!

The climax of the show, needless to say, is the party on the stage at the end, when Stan & Ollie invite boys and girls to come up and join in a talent contest, with many exciting prizes. Those who are too shy are not forgotten, and each child leaves the theatre clutching a book, a comic or a balloon, thrilled with a wonderful evening.

And when the latter reviewer says: "many exciting prizes " they were indeed "exciting prizes." During the war, new toys, especially imports, would not have been readily available. The children would have been given second-hand toys, or toys made by dad from salvaged materials – the favoured one being wood. But here, amongst the prizes Stan and Ollie were handing out were scooters (metal ones, with metal wheels and rubber tyres), dolls, colouring books; and jig-saw puzzles. There were even bikes – brand-new, shop-bought bikes. And hobby horses – the metal ones made by MoBo Toys.

Mobo Spotted Bronco — The Original All-Steel Walking Horse

[MOBO toys were manufactured by D. Sebel & Co., London, England, from the early 1950s onwards. The rider would apply pressure to the foot-rest (best done by standing up in the saddle), which activated the horse's legs and moved it forwards.

Hopefully, Babe didn't stand up in the saddle to activate his; otherwise, instead of the movement being slowly forwards, it would have been instantly downwards.

[Taken on the 1952 Tour.]

MOSS'
EMPIRE
THEATRE · NOTTINGHAM
Chairman: PRINCE LITTLER Man. Dir.: VAL PARNELL Man.: T. H. TILSON
Commencing MONDAY, DECEMBER 21st
FOR A LIMITED SEASON OF FOUR WEEKS
BERNARD DELFONT PRESENTS
HOLLYWOOD'S GREATEST COMEDY COUPLE!
HERE IN PERSON!
STAN & OLIVER
LAUREL HARDY
AND THEIR
XMAS PARTY
SEASONAL FARE FOR ALL THE FAMILY
A YULETIDE SHOW FULL OF GOOD THINGS!
XMAS ARRANGEMENTS
DECEMBER 21st WEEK
6.15 TWICE NIGHTLY 8.30
Matinee: BOXING DAY at 2.30
NO PERFORMANCES CHRISTMAS DAY
DECEMBER 28th WEEK
3 PERFORMANCES DAILY
2.30, 6.15 & 8.30
JANUARY 4th & 11th WEEKS
6.15 TWICE NIGHTLY 8.30
Matinees: WEDS. & SATS., 2.30
BOX OFFICE OPEN
10 a.m. to 9 p.m.
Telephone: 40361-2

The *Evening News* contained some hitherto unknown facts about the actual sketch:

> The principal scene is in a hospital ward, with Hardy as a patient and Laurel as a visitor who has brought a bunch of lilies with him – just in case! Other comic characters include the nurse, the undertaker, and a physician who is introduced as "Dr. Beserk." **[AUDIO]**

To illustrate one off-stage happening during Laurel and Hardy's stay in Nottingham, it is necessary to reflect on the longevity of their partnership. During their many years together, the Boys had been questioned by tens of thousands of fans and press representatives. The most repeated and, therefore, infuriating question was asked when they **weren't** together. To Stan they would always say, "Where's Ollie?" and to Ollie, "Where's Stan?" To have had this happen continually, day after day, for twenty-seven years, was enough to send them into a fit of screaming, and prompted the following:

Each evening, whilst in Nottingham, Stan and Babe took a taxi from the County Hotel to the theatre, even though the two buildings were less than fifty yards apart. This might seem a strange thing to do, but one must consider that Laurel and Hardy were able to attract a crowd big enough to stop them covering even this short distance. One evening, Babe decided to give the taxi a miss. Before he'd gone two yards a fan stopped him and asked the inevitable question, "Where's Stan?" With total disdain Babe replied, "In my bloody pocket," and marched on. The word "bloody" was a *very* strong expletive back in those days; and so, mouth agape, the offender reeled away feeling thoroughly chastised.

On Christmas Day, Stan chose to give a miss to whatever festivities the County Hotel were laying on, and spent the day with the Healeys at the Bull Inn. Hardy took the opportunity to see how a British family celebrated Christmas, and went with him – as did their wives. All were treated to a traditional turkey dinner, followed by plum pudding. I can just imagine the Hardys saying: "That's the *second* time in a month we've had to eat turkey."

[AJM: Americans always eat turkey on Thanksgiving Day – fourth Thursday in November].

Bill Healey and wife Olga giving Stan and Ollie instructions on how to pull a pint – as if ...

The day after Boxing Day, Laurel wrote to Trixie Wyatt, saying of the show at the Empire:

```
We had a very good week's business here to start off the
run, and expect to have a very Big week commencing tomorrow
- going to do 3 shows a day, so it's going to be pretty
hard, as we do our act & appear in the Xmas Party too -
then the last two weeks we do Two matinees a week - shall
be glad when it's all over & we get back to Twice Nightly
again.
```

> Up and coming ventriloquist 11 year-old Bobby Collins, doing an invited guest spot on the Christmas Show, with his pal – Ginger. I wonder if he knew that Stan's dad's nickname was 'Ginger.' [Most people don't realise that Stan had red hair.]
> Delighted to say I met Bobby in 2017. Sadly Ginger … well we won't go into that!

Two weeks later and Laurel's thoughts were directed away from "twice nightly," towards "television nightly."

```
My Dear Booth [Colman]-                          Jan.12th 1954.
Strange thing, just had a letter from Ben Shipman - Hal
Roach Sr. called him & is very anxious to make a deal with
us for 40. TV. shorts to start releasing next Sept. - wants
us to make some over here & the balance in Hollywood. He
also offers me full charge of Production, so we will think
it over. Weather here has turned warmer - snow & ice dept.
gone. Thank goodness.
```

With interest added by the proliferation of prizes, and the build-up to the Junior Talent Finals, the 'Laurel & Hardy Christmas Show' did tremendous business for the full length of its 4-week run; after which, in the middle of January, the company moved on to Portsmouth, where Stan got his wish for the show to revert to its "twice-nightly" variety format.

During the party's return stay at the Queen's Hotel in Southsea (they had stayed there in 1947), Stan Laurel came across to Dereck Riddell, the night porter, as being, " … a very thin and worried-looking man." Oliver Hardy too, didn't seem at all well. On a visit to take tea to Babe's room, Dereck found him sat in a chair with his feet in a bowl of hot water and a blanket around him, trying to fight off the effects of a cold. Although this scene has comic overtones, reminiscent of a ploy used by Hardy in the film *Sons of the Desert*, this time it wasn't a laughing matter, as it would turn out to be a very serious illness.

Meanwhile, the show went on, but the local press hadn't improved their standards, and, if it hadn't been for the review in the *Evening News*, Laurel and Hardy would have passed in and out of Portsmouth like sheep in the night (as Laurel might have said):

> Laurel & Hardy strolled onto the stage of the Theatre Royal to a delighted roar of welcome. It was as if everyone was thinking: 'Gracious, they haven't changed a bit.' Maybe Oliver has added just a couple of extra chins, and Stan may have a wrinkle or two showing through his greasepaint – but it was the same old imperious heavyweight Hardy and the same nervously plodding Laurel.
>
> Come to that, their style of comedy has hardly changed a bit. With slick patter the usual modern trend, they still rely on their natural visual humour and the beautifully-timed comment. A unique pair, they delighted everybody.

After the show on Monday (18 January 1954) the theatre manager held a surprise party to celebrate Babe's sixty-second birthday, at which all the cast turned out, to watch the ceremony of "the cutting of the cake." [See also page 195].

In the company at that time was a young comedy entertainer named Harry Worth. Harry had played three weeks on the 1952 tour, and was now in the fifth week of the fifteen he would spend on the 1953–54 tour. Harry commented on Laurel and Hardy:

> They were lovely people. They had time for you, and would talk to you. I used to spend a lot of time particularly with Ollie in his dressing room. I used to sit and listen to him telling me about the old days and he didn't mind. He'd sit there, rolling his own cigarettes, with one hand. Stan was busy writing letters.

Harry was billed as a ventriloquist, but he performed the opening part of his act without the doll, 'Fotheringay,' and it was this comedy patter which was earning him good laughs. Harry continued:

> They took an interest in all the acts, and they took an interest in me particularly because they liked my style. By the time I was appearing on those bills, I'd introduce two or three minutes of patter before I brought on my dolls. I used to talk about myself and what I was going to do. It struck them as funny, and Ollie said: "Now you develop that style. The vent is OK, but comedy might get you somewhere."

MOSS'
Empire
THEATRE NOTTINGHAM
Proprietors: MOSS' EMPIRES, Ltd.
Chairman: PRINCE LITTLER
TELEPHONE: 40361/2
Managing Director: VAL PARNELL
Manager: T. H. TILLSON
MONDAY, DECEMBER 21st
FOUR WEEKS ONLY
DEC. 21st WEEK
6.15 TWICE NIGHTLY 8.30
MATINEE SATURDAY 2.30
NO PERFORMANCES CHRISTMAS DAY
DEC. 28th WEEK
3 PERFORMANCES DAILY
2.30 • 6.15 • 8.30
JAN. 4th & 11th WEEKS
6.15 TWICE NIGHTLY 8.30
MATINEES WEDS. & SATS.
AT 2.30
HOLLYWOOD'S GREATEST COMEDY COUPLE!
HERE IN PERSON
BERNARD DELFONT presents
STAN LAUREL AND OLIVER HARDY
AND THEIR
CHRISTMAS PARTY
A YULETIDE SHOW BRIMFUL OF GOOD THINGS FOR ALL THE FAMILY
DERRICK ROSAIRE'S WONDER HORSE TONY
BETTY KAYE'S PEKINESE PETS · BOB BEMAND'S PIGEONS
HARRY WORTH The New Style Ventriloquist · URSULA & GUS Continental Jugglers
ROY & RAY Singing Accordionists
JILL, JILL & JILL Dance Team
Orch. Stalls 5/6 Centre Stalls 5/- Stalls 2/6, 4/- Dress Circle 5/- Boxes 26/- (inc. tax) Balcony 9d. (no tax)

Under Hardy's encouragement and guidance, Harry did just that. The spot at the beginning of the act was lengthened bit by bit, until the routine with the doll became a secondary feature. Come the end of the tour, the vast improvement had been noted by William Willis – manager of the Palace Theatre, Plymouth, who wrote:

Harry Worth earnt and deserved a very good reception. He has developed and improved his act tremendously in the past year or so. While as a ventriloquist he may not be outstanding from a technical point of view, his presentation, material, and personality combine to make an act which is very much to the popular taste.

Later, Harry "lost" the doll altogether, to the effect that for thirty-five years he was one of the most respected character-comedians in Britain – with numerous TV, radio, and stage shows of his own. Here, though, in 1954, how strange that only a couple of months previously it had been Stan Laurel who had given inspiration to a young ventriloquist (Ray Alan) – now, it was Babe Hardy. Sadly Harry died during the writing of the first edition of this book, but not before he had revealed the fascination of observing Stan Laurel as he was about to walk on stage:

> There was this tired old man in the wings. On the first note of 'Cuckoo,' Laurel became visibly ten years younger. He always made his entrance on the same note – he was such a perfectionist.
>
> At the end of the sketch, Laurel would step forward to make a speech, but would be dismissed by Hardy with a hand movement and a facial gesture which indicated, 'As if he could.'

(Extracts from an interview with Harry Worth, conducted by Glenn Mitchell.)

I wish I had heard Harry Worth say: *When I was on the show with Laurel & Hardy, I was so far down the bill, there were some pigeons listed above me. And you know what pigeons do, don't you?* [See box-office card on previous page..]

When playing the Royal Theatre Portsmouth on the previous tour, 1952, it would appear that Laurel (if not both comedians) had stayed at the Royal Beach Hotel, in Southsea; as Stan had written a letter on their headed paper, as follows:

```
                                              Sept. 8 52.
Dear Mrs Willies,
Thanks for your kind invitation to lunch or tea, sorry it
is not possible due to one or two previous engagements,
plus our shows and preparing to leave for the states
Oct.8th. We appreciate your kind thoughts and trust you
will fully understand.
```

Stan may well have wished that he could re-apply two factors in that letter; the first being to stay at the Royal Beach Hotel, and the second to have a meal at Mrs. Willies's – the reason being as follows:

Each night, after finishing at the theatre, the only place our subjects could get something to eat was back at the Queen's Hotel, in nearby Southsea. By one account, the night porter's attempts at preparing a meal would have been frowned upon by the "screen" Laurel & Hardy. After a few days of enduring the bad food, the Boys aired their complaint to a contractor, Perce Champin, who was fixing a window-sash in their room. Stan also moaned about having to put money into a gas-meter, when they were already being charged such high prices for their rooms. He resorted to asking Perce if he knew the address of a local landlady, who would give them a fair deal.

Perce turned the conversation towards local theatres, and thrilled Stan with stories of the acts he had seen: Florrie Ford, Billie Bennet, 'Old Mother Riley,' and Dante – the Magician (who had appeared with Laurel and Hardy in their 1942 film *A-Hauntin' We Will Go*). Feeling considerably cheerier for his chat, Stan invited Perce to be their guest at the theatre. Typically of Laurel, anger had rapidly disappeared and kindness, rather than wrath, had followed.

But it wasn't just food Laurel had a moan about. In this letter he expresses disappointment with numerous other standards:

```
                                            Jan.19th.'54.
My Dear Jacques & Dorathea [Bock Pierre],
Just finished a 4 weeks run in Nottingham which included a
block of matinees - so this is the first chance I've had.
Hope you had a nice Xmas. We spent the day with my Sister.
She has a small Hotel & Pub near Nottingham - which was an
old church back in the days of Oliver Cromwell - I felt
like a bloody Ghost walking around there!
Show Bus. not too good in general here. They are all
blaming the invasion of TV, which I don't think has
anything to do with it. There is a terrific amount of un-
employed plus a lot of labour trouble - strikes, etc. Just
a case of bad conditions in the Country. The TV programs
I've seen, would certainly drive people INTO a Theatre -
even to see a bad show! They are awful! There is no
Sponsorship - consequently - the cheapest thing is offered.
Our new sketch turned out quite successful.
```
It was recorded on tape during our opening week [Northampton]. Think you will get a kick out of it when I get back to run it for you. Of course it has greatly improved since then & may have another recording made later on. Living conditions are good, but very expensive. Weather has been good, so far a very mild Winter but Feb. & March are generally bad here.

We just heard from Hal Roach Sr. He wants us to make 40 TV. shorts. That's a hell of a way to start the New Year! We can stay here till next Sept. but the Australian Tax situation has been settled now & its possible we may go there in May for a six months run. I would like that for a change - am getting tired of wearing a monocle! If our deal for Australia goes through will of course let you know.

I find it unbelievable that Stan was still holding out hope of a deal to tour Australia. For starters, he and his partner weren't physically up to it. Weren't the two of them aware of the high temperatures they would be having to deal with? During the 1941 tour of the Caribbean, Hardy was puffing and blowing constantly, and perspiring freely, to try and combat the heat — and in 1950, when filming near Marseilles, it was the intense heat which had caused him to develop heart fibrillation. Laurel too had been badly affected by the heat at the same location shoot.

Then there was the matter of the Roach TV deal. If Stan was thinking of the Australia option, when was he envisaging the TV shows being made?

The next journey, however, involved just a short trip up the "London Road" to the Chiswick Empire. The Boys had last played there in 1947 as replacements for 'The Inkspots' but, this time, were there in their own right. The *Brentford & Chiswick Times* afforded them the following:

> Laurel & Hardy receive a great ovation. This is a riotous act, in which Oliver Hardy is confined in a mental ward because he thinks he is a bird, and which finally ends with both he and Stan Laurel losing their speech and clucking like hens.

Chiswick Empire

The prize-giving at the children's matinee was again the only point of interest in newspapers and, even then, the concentration was on naming all the children.
[Note that on the scenery there is a printed logo which reads:
"Constructed by Grand OPERA HOUSE, Belfast."]

The Boys were staying at the May Fair Hotel in Berkeley Square, for the duration of this, and their next, booking – Finsbury Park Empire. At the latter they fulfilled the week's engagement they had been unable to do earlier owing to Stan's illness. *The Stage* was there to record the event:

> Laurel & Hardy naturally come to this essentially family theatre for the benefit of the many who wish to see them in person, and are very welcome. The most amusing thing about them turns out to be that they are very like themselves after all. Their comedy is gentle and, it must be confessed, not very funny. But it serves to show two familiar figures in characteristic situations that recall, by inference, the joyous laughter of the films, to which, in fact, their humour is naturally more closely attuned.

And that was it. Laurel's cold back in November had generated more column inches. And, at the beginning of the 1952 tour Babe Hardy had commented: "*We both like the provincial theatres. It is here where our act is best appreciated - especially by the children.*"

His observations can now be seen to have been founded on solid reasoning, as these last two appearances in London venues had gone totally unappreciated. Thankfully, the two old troupers were now off to play the provinces.

o-o-0-o-o

Chapter 14

SUNDERLAND AIN'T NO WONDERLAND

At the conclusion of the London run, the Laurel and Hardy family followed the other "run," and went from London to Brighton by car. However, on this occasion, it wasn't their wives they shared it with, but with a couple of famous music-hall stars. John M. East revealed, in his biography of Max Miller, that Stan Laurel had recounted the following story to him:

> Finally, it was in 1953 when Max invited us to the theatre he was playing. He was using much the same material, but he was as bright as a button.
>
> That lovely artist, Turner Layton, drove Babe and I down to Brighton that Sunday. Dear old Max only cracked one gag: "Which one of us is going to top the bill?"
>
> No doubt about it, Max Miller was the most private and solitary performer I've ever met. I mean on, and off the stage. I got the impression it was almost impossible for him to share anything. He even kept his thoughts to himself.
>
> It was following that predictable talk about the weather, and how the variety theatres were dying on their feet, that he dried up. Babe and I were tired out and it wasn't the time or place for show business backchat. It was rather funny, wasn't it, when Babe said, "Come on Turner, give us a song."
>
> I don't mean this in a nasty way, but I reckon that the Cheeky Chappie only came to life if you went to the theatre where he was appearing, and paid five shillings for a seat in the stalls.
>
> No director could tell Max what to do; his act was faultless. He didn't need actors to feed him lines, or, more important, share the spotlight with him. Moreover, actors would cost him. He wanted to keep all the money from the box-office for himself.
>
> For Max Miller the audience became his prop; his supporting cast; his inspiration. He stood on that stage, responsible to nobody and taking all the risks. He really was "The One-and-Only" – a very unusual 'Cheeky Chappie'."

Once in Brighton, rather than a return stay at the Grand Hotel, the Laurels and the Hardys booked in at the Royal Crescent Hotel, from where Laurel wrote this letter:

```
                                            Feb.10. '54.
My Dear Booth [Colman]-
Yes, having a real cold spell - the last couple of weeks in
London was really bad & of course hit the Theatres all
over, some of the houses had shocking Bus. The coldest in
many years, a bit warmer down here thank goodness - &
reasonable bus. for winter in a summer resort. Just getting
over another lousey cold & the ear dept. again. Nothing
further on the Roach deal - frankly am not too interested
one way or the other.
```

Of the show, the *Sussex Daily News* had this to say:

> It is a sentimental journey for many of us – our visit this week to the Brighton Hippodrome. If we neglected to pay our homage, convey our regards, it would somehow constitute a base betrayal of our youth. For these two ageing zanies were part and parcel of the life we lived in the thirties. They were undisputed sovereigns of Screen Cloud-Cuckoo Land. Above all they were an antidote to the ills we were heir to. And so we just had to go along.

An interesting question was then raised:

How would it all go down with the teenagers of today, reared on a diet of Martin & Lewis? There were remarkably few of them present in a packed house, but there was a generous sprinkling of exuberant kiddies. Could it be that Ollie & Stan have somehow missed a generation?

The *Southern Weekly News*, too, raised some points pertinent to Laurel and Hardy's longevity:

> Two generations have come under the spell of Laurel & Hardy. They occupy a unique place among the comedians of the century. Their greatness lies in the simplicity and cleanness of their humour. The fact that they are no longer at the peak of their fame is due more to radio than to the passing years. Nearly all the modern funny men, both in the United States and in England, are the products of pure radio. There was no place in radio for Laurel & Hardy. Visual humour declined, and only the chosen few appeared on film.
>
> Now comes television, and the trend is already going back to slapstick. The microphone-hugging comic will soon become as passé, as 'steam radio.' All of which goes to suggest that Laurel & Hardy's very welcome return is not so much a glimpse of the past, as of the future. They were as cleanly funny as ever, and went straight to our hearts and freshened many half-forgotten memories.

Ann Redman, with the winners of her competition in the *Evening Argus*.

Douglas Salmon (Ann Redman's husband), the reviewer for the *Evening Argus* wrote:

> Still Masters of Slapstick. They came in with the flapper age, flickered their way through the silent films and on to the talkies. Our grandmas laughed at them; our mums laughed at them; and last night – we laughed at them. So synonymous with fun that we laughed as soon as they walked on. We laughed again at Ollie's disgusted look; we laughed when Stan sat on his hat; and we laughed a rather poignant little laugh when he stood in the corner and cried.
>
> They guyed their way through a simple slapstick farce, but it did not really matter what they did. They were Laurel & Hardy; funny, fantastic Laurel & Hardy – a snatch of our boyhood days back again.

Backstage at the Brighton Hippodrome is John King, who owned the 16mm rights of thirty-six 2- and 3-reel Laurel & Hardy comedies, made in the early thirties.

Stan is holding the 1954 film hire catalogue, listing their films, and Ollie is holding a library print.

[With thanks to David Greeno.]

Sunderland Ain't No Wonderland

Douglas Salmon was to say of his meetings with Stan and Babe:

> During my ten years in journalism – including Fleet Street – and twenty-five years in television, I have met quite a few people, but I can say with all honesty that Stan and Ollie were among the nicest – lovable is not too strong a word – of them all. They were a delight, and being with them was like being in the middle of one of their films. They were kind, really funny – hilarious in fact – and always good humoured.

Following such a fine tribute, the world's favourite comedy duo next travelled by train to Norwich, for their one and only visit to the county of Norfolk. Monday noon, 16 February, a reporter caught them outside the Royal Hotel, about to get into a black Jaguar car to go to rehearsals.

The two of them were wearing heavy overcoats and berets. Even so they were feeling the cold, but not as much as Lucille who was in bed with a chill.

On their way to the theatre the two stars took an interest in the local architecture, and seemed most impressed by the City Hall.

At the theatre Stan jokily informed the driver:

The stage door, please – not the front entrance. That is reserved for ladies and gentlemen.

For the management of the Norwich Hippodrome, booking Laurel and Hardy was a very ambitious project, and the most expensive show they had ever staged. To meet the high cost of the show (£1,750 – of which £1,000 went to Laurel and Hardy) the Hippodrome did what many theatres before them had been forced to do, and raised their seat prices – by sixpence. "Even so," the *Eastern News* defended, "I imagine there are few places where you could see such world famous stars as Stan & Ollie, at such reasonable prices."

Considering the quality and size of the show, the price increase was, of course, totally justified, as one can judge from the review in the *Eastern Evening News*:

> Here they are, just the same as ever. They're still at the top of the tree, and if the tree is shaking it's only with the laughter of their audiences. 'Birds of a Feather' is not a sparkling piece in itself, but to see Laurel & Hardy playing it is sheer joy. It is done with all their consummate skill, so quietly, so effortlessly, so effectively. It's great fun. You'll be sorry if you miss it.

To further strengthen the mystique surrounding seeing Laurel and Hardy 'in person,' he added:

> The pair so resembled their film selves that when the curtain went up the audience took a minute or two to realise they were seeing their childhood comedy favourites in the flesh.

The *Eastern Daily Press* was also enthusiastic about the live appearance of Laurel and Hardy:

> Laurel & Hardy on the stage with their vast experience of perfect timing, quaint gestures, grimaces and unexpected repartee are even funnier than in the more remote entertainment of the screen. The audience were still laughing when the curtain fell and the pair said 'Goodnight.'

As the show business expression goes: "Always leave them laughing," so we'll do just that — but how long will it last? Well "not long" is the answer to that. From warm praise in Norwich, it was "under a cold shower" on Tyneside the following week, when Stan didn't get so much as a mention. Only the review in the *Sunderland Echo* serves as a reminder he was there:

> Although we have seen Laurel & Hardy once before at the Sunderland Empire, their visit this week is another clear example of the tremendous change which has taken place in popular comedy style. I am not suggesting that Laurel & Hardy are not funny, but that their humour, illustrated through specially written sketches, is an anachronism. It belongs to the silent film or the immediate post-silent era and there is a great deal the modern shift comedian can learn from that particular approach to the problem of how to make people laugh. The slapstick is thoughtful, wistful, and broad. Messrs. Laurel & Hardy give us nostalgic reminder of a grace long since discarded and lost.

It would appear Laurel wanted to forget all about his visit to Sunderland, for in a letter three weeks later, he wrote:

```
The bus. [business] was shocking in Sunderland - Worst week
of our tour - The audiences were blasé, - so a miserable week
was had by all.
```

The manager's report echoed Stan's claims:

> Well received. They are working well indeed, and their material is much stronger than on their previous visit here, but, even so, they are not going more than well in any part of the house, and their ability to attract has greatly diminished.

The manager added he would have them back only with very strong support acts. Four years later, Stan was still harbouring the pain of this appearance, as this extract from a letter of 21 February 1958 will show:

```
Note the Empire Sunderland is still doing bad bus. I can't
understand why they keep open & lose money week after week,
it doesn't make sense. Am sorry for the acts playing to empty
houses, I know how I felt the last time we were there, it was
a miserable week, was glad to get out of it.
```

Just prior to their 1952 appearance in Sunderland, Stan had reiterated: *"There's one thing that remains the same – Northern audiences. They're wonderful."* It had taken the events of the last two visits for Laurel to realise how wrong this statement was. When the Wearsiders had been able to bask in his reflected glory, they had claimed him as their own – even though his spiritual home was across both the River Wear and the River Tyne, in Tyneside. Now that Laurel was fallen from his high pedestal, the Wearsiders made no attempt to put him back but, like a broken statue, totally discarded him.

There is no need to pity Stan for this display of irreverence, for he is only one of countless numbers of comedians who have had their pride taken away by the treatment meted out by audiences in this part of England. Wearside has never produced a comedian from inside its boundaries, and has rarely accepted one from outside.

Sunderland Ain't No Wonderland

The only bright point of Stan's stay in Sunderland was in meeting up with Trixie Wyatt, the girl he had played in panto with in 1907 (when she was Trixie Knight), and whom he had been regularly corresponding with in more recent years.

Stan, by now, must have been totally disillusioned with the show's acceptance, but found no cause for self-analysis. In most aspects he was a totally honest person but, when it came to facing up to rejection, he was sometimes very reluctant to admit to any personal failing. In September 1954 (after returning to America) he wrote:

```
I have been reading that the show business has been taking a
turn for the better & sincerely hope it continues & fully
recovers from the slump of last year. We certainly were over
there during the worst of it, the business was just shocking,
very depressing for all concerned.
```

In 1952 the Laurels and the Hardys had stayed at the Grand Hotel Tynemouth, and travelled to Sunderland each evening by ferry and car. This time they stayed at the Royal Station Hotel, in the city of Newcastle. This negated having to use the ferry to cross the Tyne River, as they could now cross by the Tyne Bridge, and cover the fifteen mile journey in around thirty-five minutes. The change of accommodation also eliminated the poor conditions of the Grand Hotel they had previously endured. But again, it was exceptionally cold during their stay in Newcastle. One can only hope that the hotel had stocked up with coal this time around. No-one would want a repeat of the 1947 arctic conditions.

And the cold wasn't the only downside. Conditions were getting gloomier by the day:

```
My Dear Booth [Colman]-                           Feb.26.'54.
Bus. here is not too good - seems to be a slump all over
the Country - however, one of those things that we get once
in a while, we go to Glasgow next (March 1st) then to
Hippo. Wolverhampton, Empire Sheffield, Empire York, Palace
Grimsby, Empire Leeds & Empire Edinburgh. This may be the
finish of our tour here & its possible we may return home
after that, we can stay here till Sept. but Delfont wants
us to reduce our centage & guarantee - which of course is
not agreeable to us. He is not losing any money with us,
but he is not making as much as he was before, so he wants
us to cut so he can make more - (the old story - these guys
are not satisfied to make a little profit - they want the
lot!)
We are expecting Shipman over - so things may get
straightened out, but frankly - I wouldn't mind coming home
for a rest - the trip has been a bit hard on me & I don't
feel like knocking myself out for the sake of a few extra
weeks work.
Weather here is fairly mild for this section of the Country
- usually very bad this time of year.
```

[AJM. I hope Stan wasn't considering staying until September as his 'Permit to Re-enter the United States' was due to expire on 24 August 1954. If so, he might have found himself writing to his old music-hall pal, Charlie, to ask if he had a spare room in his manoir in Switzerland.]

In Glasgow the following week the Boys faced more "cold" treatment on this 1954 leg of their British tour, for the weather there was comparable with the terrible winter of 1947. The city was affected by snow storms, black-outs, and blocked roads; and on the day of their arrival two explosions crippled the power-station. Half of Glasgow was without electricity and, with temperatures below zero, no coal was to be had. Rehearsals at the Empire were able to go ahead with the use of an emergency lighting supply, but in the afternoon the manager announced: "Unless the normal supply is resumed by this evening, there will be no show."

The show did go ahead but, in the reviews which followed, if words were pieces of coal there wouldn't have been enough to toast a marshmallow. The *Daily Record*, which carried the biggest write-up, said only:

> There was nothing anonymous about 'alcoholics' Laurel & Hardy when they appeared on stage, to inject cheer into the hearts of the chilled victims of the power cut. The good old-timers still get the laughs with the simplicity of mime, direct dialogue, and their much loved style of verbal economy.

The snow, ice, and black-outs continued throughout the week but, even though business was badly hit, the Boys were well received.

Remember Benny Barron, one half of 'Graham and Barron,' coming to see Stan at the Sunderland Empire? Well here at the Glasgow Empire is Jackie Graham — the other monkey.

The lack of press coverage must have been a sore disappointment to Stan, especially, as his earlier links with Glasgow had led to his becoming its adopted son. Seeking a shoulder to cry on, he left his winter hole at the Central Hotel to go and look up the man to whom he expressed a great debt for his show business success – A.E. Pickard. This great showman was still able to grab headlines, but the one that week was not one of his best:

> Self-styled millionaire Albert Ernest Pickard (79) of 92 Balshagray Avenue, Glasgow, was charged with careless driving.

There is also evidence to indicate that Stan sought comfort of a more homely kind as, along with the other three members of his travelling party, he stayed at Sir Alex King's residence, *Ta-Na-Righ* (Gaelic for "House-of-Kings") at 2, The Grove, Whitecraigs, Glasgow, for one night or more. Maybe Alex King had a supply of coal. Laurel also sought solace at his beloved Metropole Theatre, obviously working on the author's invented adage:

"If the present is hurtful – revert to the past."

Sunderland Ain't No Wonderland

In reviewing the show at the Wolverhampton Hippodrome, the following week, the *Express & Star* sought to relate Stan and Ollie's heyday in films to their current live appearance:

> For many years before the second world war the names of Laurel & Hardy were synonymous with comedy at the cinema. During the war, a number of new screen comedians came to the fore, and the old team were seen less and less at the cinemas in this country. It is some considerable time since a Laurel & Hardy film has been seen in Wolverhampton or, for that matter, any other town. But the reception given them, on their first joint stage appearance in the town, surpassed any at the Hippodrome for many years. Their sketch was most amusing and entertaining.

The above review of Monday night's first-house could hardly differ more from local boy Ron Mason's version of the second-house:

> It was a farce – and not a comedy one. The last house we went to started, I believe at 8pm, and they gave us all sorts of acts "in support" till about 9.20, and then "they" came on – both drunk if you ask me, and gave us a silly, hard to hear, or grasp, pot pourri of some kind or other of giggly nonsense for about 20 minutes, and then went off. They weren't even there at the final [curtain] call. What a huge disappointment it was to fans who went miles to see them.
>
> I understand it wasn't just my one "off-night," either. People who went on other nights said the same – that the show would have been a flop with, or without, Laurel & Hardy, and they got money for nothing.
>
> I prefer to remember Laurel & Hardy from their films, not their nights in Wolverhampton. As much as my esteem is (still now) for them both, it spoiled our evening, and stunned us both. Sorry if you expected another sort of letter.

Mr. Mason obviously has a very strong affection for the films of Laurel & Hardy, and was obviously disappointed at what was effectively a shadow of their screen characters. I would not like to believe however that their poor performance was marred by drink – and certainly not Stan, who was in abstinence because of his diabetes. Yes! Hardy *was* a known drinker, and was often seen popping out of theatres between shows, to visit backstage bars. And "Yes!" there have been other unsubstantiated reports in this account of Babe being "under the influence." However, in this instance, it is more likely that exhaustion was the factor in their poor mobility. And as for "slurred speech," it is for more likely that the poor microphone set-up was responsible for incoherent dialogue. As for any other failings, one has to bear in mind that Laurel and Hardy were sixty-four and sixty-two years-old respectively, and both were in poor health. Hardy mobility was restricted because of his excess weight and bad knees, and Stan's diabetes caused, among other side-effects, severe fatigue. Travelling the length and breadth of the UK, doing thirteen shows per week, would be enough to drain even the youngest and fittest of show business stars so, for these two, the task was even more gruelling.

George Knox, who was in the theatre orchestra, was a little kinder in his summary. He said only of the two stars:

> They looked really tired, and working against time. Still – they brought the house down.

With all the talk of Stan and Babe "looking tired," and with further such comments to come — including admissions from the Boys themselves — it defies logic that the two of them were still looking to extend the tour:

```
QUEENS HOTEL - Birmingham
                                         MARCH.11th.'54.
My Dear Booth -
Ben Shipman should be here soon now - we have an offer of a
tour in Belgium & Greece in a Big Revue (just to do our
act). It may not be the one that we are doing now, as they
have some pantomime idea for us. It is a splendid offer
financially (in $) so Ben is coming over to look into it.
```

```
They want us to open in May, which is perfect for us. Will
let you know as soon as I know definite. Nothing further on
the Roach deal so far, but he has asked Ben to try & make a
deal with us. We are playing in Wolverhampton this week but
staying in B'ham. (15 mile drive each way, every night).
Weather warm & sunny - a treat after the last few weeks of
cold.
```

On Tuesday, six year-old Pauline Johnson had tea with the lovable buffoons at the Queen's Hotel, Birmingham, as the prize-winner of a competition in the *Wolverhampton Chronicle*. Stan and Babe were for ever giving little children such treats. They loved to see the look of glee on their faces, and were proud that they could impart so much happiness just by letting the children meet them. Babe, especially, loved little girls. Never having had a child of his own, he would always immediately pick them up and give them a big squeeze.

Pauline Johnson having tea at the Queen's Hotel, Birmingham – 12 March 1954
('Lost' photo from *Wolverhampton Chronicle*)

That same week, another little girl was brought backstage, as a treat for winning a music award. Accompanied by her father, nine year-old Barbara Leighton was firstly taken to meet Stan, who said: "Come along Barbara Vicki, and say a big hello to 'Uncle' Ollie." Popping her into Babe's dressing room, Stan returned to join her father Jack, and revealed that Babe was not too well, and was seeing a doctor. Jack expressed his concern at bothering Hardy by bringing Barbara, but Stan told him he had insisted on seeing her.

In his dressing room, Hardy said: "Come along Barbara, climb up on your Uncle Ollie's knee." Due to his size, she managed it with difficulty, whereupon he sat hugging her, and asking questions about her piano playing. With a child's innocence Barbara told Mr. Hardy that he looked tired, to which he replied that he was very tired, and thanked her for her concern. When it came time to go, her father came back to the dressing-room and, as Barbara climbed off his knee, Hardy said: "I'm looking forward to seeing you at your first concert."

When Barbara was gone, the tired old comedian remained sitting there. Something the little girl said may have made him reflect up on his own mortality as, when Jack popped back to say goodbye – Babe Hardy was crying.

o-o-0-o-o

Chapter 15

KEEP RIGHT ON

At Sheffield, next on the tour, a reporter from *The Star* caught the Boys having a pot of tea backstage at the *Empire*. He described them as looking "cold and miserable." Of their trip from Wolverhampton Hardy said: "Not a very good place to have come from." The account continued:

They sipped their teas in silence for a few moments, and then Stan Laurel turned a face, wrinkled by years in the service of comedy, and said: 'Don't expect us to be funny off-stage at this time of day.'

'Yes,' they said, 'it was pleasant to be back in Sheffield. No, it didn't seem like two years since they were last here.'

Oliver Hardy shifted his bulk to a more comfortable position on a small chair. He gave it as his opinion that it was bloody cold. Said Stan: 'He gets more English every day. You'd think it was Ollie who is the British citizen, not me.' Both were wearing blue berets. Why? 'Comfort' said Stan. 'I can't get into a small car with a proper hat on,' said Ollie. THEN they moved off towards the stage for a rehearsal. The pot of tea was empty.

SHEFFIELD EMPIRE

Of the show, the *Sheffield Telegraph* wrote:

> Laurel & Hardy, at the Sheffield Empire, fill a sketch with all their endearing old tricks, which is certainly not to say there is anything stale about them. The phrase: 'they haven't changed a bit' is a great compliment to them. It is their sheer genius for comedy that makes them as good as ever.
>
> When Oliver being lowered out of a window on a knotted sheet, tells Stanley to tie the other end to something, of course he ties it around his own neck. And Oliver remonstrates with him in the way that has made millions of friends for Stanley all over the world – 'You might have killed me'. So there you are. They are very lovable and very funny.

The review in *The Star* betrayed none of the stage action, but was full of compliments:

> Laurel & Hardy attempt one of the hardest things imaginable in the world of entertainment – to transfer their well-loved slapstick from screen to stage. The devices of the films, where anything is possible and anything can be hidden, are tried on the all-revealing stage. With a few reservations, the trick can be said to have come off, and the passing of the years has not impaired their impeccable timing. To watch Laurel as he wrecks his partner's ponderous schemes by a kind of triumphant diffidence is to watch clowning at its very highest. By the contrast of his example, one is made to realise just how much subtlety of facial expression is neglected by modern music-hall artistes.

At the City Hall on Thursday afternoon, the Boys opened the 'Prelude to Spring' hair fashion preview. There, they demonstrated their tonsorial artistry when Stan was seen to draw one model's tresses through his palms, and Ollie stood ready to trim them with garden shears. Fortunately, both handed over to the professionals before the lady became a James Finlayson look-alike. Doh!

The tour was scheduled to end on 17 April but, by now, Stan Laurel and Oliver Hardy had become very dispirited with touring Britain. As we know, both were constantly tired and Babe, especially, had long-found the hours to be too demanding. Stan seemed to be holding himself together health-wise, but was finding the financial rewards of theatre work insufficient, and threatening to become even less. That week he disclosed to Trixie Wyatt, in a letter written at the Grand Hotel, Sheffield:

```
We can stay over here till next Sept. but due to slump in
Theatre Bus. in general, we have been asked to cut our
Guarantee & Percentage - which of course, we are not in
favour with. our running cost & expense would be just the
same as now, so naturally it wouldn't pay us to stay here for
the small amount of profit. However our manager is flying
over from Los Angeles to look into an offer we have for a
tour in Holland. Belgium & Greece with Australia & New
Zealand to follow, which would be more profitable to us than
staying in England, as it is new Territory for us & an
opportunity to make Big money. If nothing happens - we shall
of course return home to the States & make Pictures for TV.
```

While awaiting the elusive cloud with the silver lining, and the go-ahead to travel tens of thousands of miles, Laurel and Hardy didn't even move out of Yorkshire for their next engagement – York.

The manager of the York Empire – J.J. Cullen – gave them a warm welcome, but after that it was mainly downhill.

Keep Right On

The reviewer for the *Yorkshire Evening Press*, too, felt no need to exert himself. Of his backstage encounter, 'Mr. Nobody' (his title – not mine) revealed little:

> 'How do you like working in this country?' I asked Stan. He said he preferred working over here, as for one thing it was less strenuous. 'In America we give four, five, six or maybe seven shows a day, including Sundays,' he told me. 'There, the first show of the day starts at about ten in the morning and the last finishes at about eleven at night.' Among the places which they hope to visit during their week's stay in York, is the Castle Museum.

[AJM: The figures of up to seven shows a day ... between 10am and 11pm bear no credence whatsoever. Laurel and Hardy had played three city-to-city stage tours in America in 1940 and 1941, but the number of performances then was comparable with the ones in British variety theatres.

My guess is that Laurel is more likely to have said something on the grounds of: "The number of shows doesn't bother me. When I was playing in American Vaudeville (between 1910 and 1922), in some theatres you had to do as many as ..." and then quoted the figures. My theory is that the reporter then reconstructed the wording to make bygone Vaudeville sound like present-day American theatre.]

Having squeezed every last ounce of information from the two comedians, Mr. Nobody allowed T.S. Williams, of the same newspaper, to have a go:

> The surprising thing about Laurel & Hardy is that they are so much like themselves. Ollie looks as reposed as a heavy man usually does, but being a comic is not easy. There is much action and a great deal of nervous tension all the time one is on the stage. Apart from his stage work, he generally takes things easy. He has a slight American intonation that one is not conscious of in films.
>
> Stan Laurel does not go sight-seeing much, either. It is a life of hotel and theatre. He shrugged and made a comical face. He laughs suddenly and often offstage, and it occurs to you that you don't remember him laughing very often in films.

The show itself was also summed up in few words:

> Laurel & Hardy, at York Empire this week, are an argument for the real flesh-and-blood stage against mere pictures on celluloid. Funny as they are on films, they delight still more in their sketch, which is laughter from start to finish.

A different view came from Brian Lazarus, a member of the audience at the same show – first house, Monday.

> The theatre was half empty, and the sketch wasn't helped any by a poor amplification arrangement. Ollie, in bed centre stage, and Stan, sitting to the left, both had a microphone on a stand and would attempt to speak directly into it. Often though, when turning aside to deliver certain lines, the sound would fall away and the line be lost.

Another audience member revealed:

> [In the hospital scene] Stan had to help Ollie onto the bed. He did it with great effort and – HE WASN'T KIDDING!

Ronald Nendick, violinist in the orchestra, also had his expectations deflated. On his return home from the theatre, his wife was surprised to see a very sad look in his eyes instead of the ecstasy she had expected upon his having met his boyhood idols. Ronald explained to her that the contrast of looking up adoringly at the two mirth-makers on the big screen, to the sight of Oliver Hardy straddling two chairs, backstage, in a dressing room lit by a single naked bulb, was too great a burden for his mind to accept.

Over at the Royal Station Hotel, York, yet another hidden side was revealed. Billy McCaffrey, a floor-waiter, was assigned to look after the Hardys and the Laurels. First daily task was serving them breakfast in bed, in their separate suites. Then, at 10 o'clock, and at hourly intervals thereafter, Billy had to take a double-whisky to Hardy, for which he was tipped very handsomely.

For dinner, the foursome would dine together in the hotel restaurant and then, after the show, would come back to the hotel bar for a little nightcap. In all that time, Billy never saw the two comedians out of stage costume or make-up. A similar report had come from their stay at the

Central Hotel, in Glasgow, three weeks earlier, which would seem to indicate that the Boys, in not having the energy or patience to remove their make-up and costumes before leaving the theatre, were indeed extremely tired.

Royal Station Hotel, York

From York, our weary foursome travelled seventy miles south-east to the fishing port of Grimsby, in the Humber estuary. Here the big attraction according to the *News Pictorial* was getting a free seat by winning the colouring competition, the advert for which ran:

> Children! Here is your chance to meet Laurel & Hardy themselves – the world-famous funny men you have so often laughed at on the screen – and to be given by them an autographed book you will always treasure. This famous pair are appearing at the Palace, Grimsby, and at the Saturday matinee twelve lucky boys and girls will meet sad little Stan and outsize Oliver. They will get free seats for the show, too.

Just how the "lucky twelve" got on, or whether anyone else turned up for Laurel and Hardy's performance, the *News Pictorial* didn't bother to tell. Hopefully a lot more was gained from the presence of the "world-famous funny men" than the handing-over of twelve books.

Part of the answer, at least, was supplied by the *Evening Telegraph*:

> To see Laurel & Hardy in the flesh, on stage is rather like watching a legend spring to life. Their films have been part of the lives of several generations now, but Hollywood is a long way from Grimsby and its inhabitants a little unreal. But there is nothing unreal about Ollie and Stan. Both look and behave exactly as they do on the screen –

Keep Right On

which is more than can be said for some other film stars. Their sketch is a textbook example of the art of raising laughs without a single blue gag.

It was some twenty-three years later that the *Grimsby Evening Telegraph* chose to print a more in-depth analysis. Labelling Laurel and Hardy's 1954 visit "part of their farewell tour of Britain before retirement," they related:

> Stan & Ollie addicts came from all over the county to see them. Even so, their stay, and indeed their whole tour, was comparatively low-key, as they had no wish for show-boosting publicity. They had become somewhat unfashionable, almost has-beens, in the eyes of even many of their old admirers.
>
> They were ageing, and not in the best of health. Styles were changing, as were tastes. Only their total absence from film-making and indeed their deaths would enable television to create a new cult which has introduced fresh generations to the amazing art of Laurel & Hardy and allowed millions more to wallow in glorious nostalgia.

Latter-day interviews with some of the people who had been around at the time also revealed an, as yet, unseen picture. Hardy was reported as being thoroughly miserable and uncommunicative. Although in the theatre each evening two hours before the start of the show, he totally ignored the backstage staff. When the winners of the children's painting competition went backstage, one noted him blatantly sporting a whisky flask. He would also "top himself up" in the Palace Buffet Bar, across the connecting passage from the theatre. Stan, who was still abstaining, didn't go with him, apart from the one occasion he posed for a photograph, pulling pints behind the bar – [a 'lost' photo].

Above: The Dolphin Hotel, CLEETHORPES.
[Still there, but not in use as a hotel.]
Left: Palace Theatre, GRIMSBY.
[Demolished 1979]

The Boys and their wives stayed at the Dolphin Hotel, in nearby Cleethorpes, where their rooms were kept like incubators to shield them from the cold. There they kept themselves in total privacy, taking all meals in their rooms, and never once going to the dining room. Still dissatisfied with his lot, Hardy, in Laurel's room one evening, whilst awaiting their taxi, was observed looking out of the hotel window exclaiming: "What are we doing in a goddamn place like this?"

Hardy's question was well-founded: What *were* the world's greatest comedy couple doing in places like Grimsby. When the whole of the US had thrown its most well-loved comedy double-act on the scrap heap, the screen legends had been rescued by the British theatre-going public; but now, on this third tour, both Babe and Stan had every reason to bemoan their lot. On the 1947 tour they had worked six of the major theatres in London, whereas on this tour the number was just three London venues — and not major ones at that. In 1952 they had spent two weeks each at both Dublin and Belfast, whereas now – none. Bad timing also meant that they had had to miss out on the summer shows at holiday resorts, where the theatres were guaranteed to be packed with holidaymakers each night – so gone where the likes of Blackpool, Rhyl, Southport, Boscombe, Southsea, Brighton, Margate, Southend, and Butlins Skegness.

To fill the tour schedule, the two living legends had had to put into less salubrious venues – some were actually 'white elephants,' and others were dilapidated and just about staving off the threat of demolition. Most of those bearing the latter description were being run by Fred Butterworth, of the FJB Theatre group, who must have been handed control of these theatres on the proviso that he spend money on doing them up. These were: the Hippodrome theatres at Boscombe; Norwich; Wolverhampton, and Aston (Birmingham); plus the Grand Theatre Southampton; New Theatre Northampton; Palace Theatre Grimsby; and the Empire York – all theatres played by L&H on this 1953-54 tour (except for the Grand Theatre Southampton). History seems to recount that the demise of these theatres happened pretty quickly. Sad to say that only two of the actual buildings now survive.

Stan Laurel felt embittered enough to later write of these theatres:

```
                                        Dec.24th.'55.
My Dear Jeanette & Lawrie:-
It must be going on two years since we saw you last -
doesn't time fly.! Sorry to hear the puppy died, he
probably couldn't stand the lousey Butterworth circuit,
```

Back to Grimsby, where we left Hardy questioning what they doing there. Stan was obviously aware of his partner's lack of tolerance, and his curtness to members of staff, and did all he could to redress the balance. At each town and city they played, he kept a pile of half-crowns both in his hotel room and in his dressing room; and, each and every time someone ran an errand or did a small service, he tipped them one of the coins.

As to the immediate future, Laurel divulged to Booth Colman:

```
                                        March 30th.'54.
Ben Shipman arrived & checked on the Holland - Belgium &
Greece deal. It did'nt look so good as they had pictured
it. First, could'nt guarantee getting Dollars out - so,
that's OUT.
We are not going to continue with Delfont, but may play a
couple of extra weeks for him after Edinburgh (April 12th.)
Have had an offer to play a Twelve weeks run in Blackpool
(Big sea side resort here) starting end of June. Sounds
good, so Ben is now in London, checking on that, also an
offer to make a picture. He may fly to Australia & look
over the situation there, as soon as things are settled
here. Will keep you posted re what happens.
```

Again I have to question what the heck were Stan and Babe thinking, by going along with these plans. It was the equivalent of a man running a marathon, who has "hit the wall" after twenty miles, but is planning to run another marathon as soon as he completes this one. That is — if they *do manage* to complete this one!

o-o-0-o-o

Chapter 16

MARATHON MAN

At the next stop-over, Leeds, the show played its third week out of the last four in Yorkshire. With Laurel and Hardy now having visited Leeds on ALL FOUR tours, one might have expected the local papers to wax lyrical, but the *Yorkshire Evening Post* was short in the extreme:

> That familiar tie-wiggle, that doleful face. What else could these things mean but those two favourites, Laurel & Hardy. With all their old skill, they entertain young and old at Leeds Empire and, judging by their reception from the first night audience, they occupy a warm spot in the heart of Leeds audiences.

The manager of the Empire Theatre went a little further, and wrote in his weekly report:

> Although the novelty of their first appearance 'in person' lost a good bit of support, they still prove themselves popular. The sketch is very well received and got good laughs.

One week after his last letter to Booth, Laurel is still full of plans for his next "marathon," plus a THIRD one after that.

```
                                          April 7.'54.
Think now, we shall stay over here till Oct. The deal for
Blackpool is practically settled for a 3 month engt. with
an option of an extra month - to start in June - will of
course continue with Delfont till that time, with the
exception that we shall take a couple of weeks vacation
before we open in Blackpool. (need a rest bad).
Ben Shipman is looking into the Australian deal to follow,
but if it doesn't materialize we shall of course return
home - have an
idea of taking our
own show for a
tour of Canada -
Have never played
there (as a Team)
should do OK for a
couple of months
run.
P.S. Just recd. a
letter from
Mitchell Gertz -
wants to make a
deal for Colgate
Comedy Hour on
April 25th.
Addressed us - c/o
BERNARD DEL FONTE!
What a Lad!
```

[AJM: *The Colgate Comedy Hour* was a comedy and music variety series, which hosted some of the biggest stars of the day. It aired live on NBC, and ran from 1950 to 1955.]

Laurel and Hardy's accountant-turned-manager, Ben Shipman, hoping to open new doors for his star act. First off is this one at the Queens Hotel, Leeds.

137

THE THREE TENORS

Photo courtesy of Italian author - Camillo Moscati.

One night, world-famous Italian tenor Luigi Infantino — who was in appearing in concert at the recently re-opened St. George's Hall, in Bradford — made the short journey to Leeds, and went backstage to greet his comic heroes. Laurel & Hardy films had a massive fan base in Italy, which the Boys had witnessed on a whistle-stop tour of Italy in 1950. Their popularity had grown thanks mainly to the impact of their 1933 comic opera *Fra Diavolo*, of which Laurel was happy to relate in this letter of 1963:

```
The L&H film version of 'Fra Diavalo' is still shown every year
in Italy, it was showing in Milan when Hardy and I were there
in 1950, the English was 'dubbed' in Italian language, I got a
big kick out of L&H speaking
Italian just like the natives!
```

[AJM: The 1950 screening which Stan and Babe attended was the thirteenth time *Fra Diavolo* (aka: *The Devil's Brother*) had been released in Milan. The fact that *Fra Diavolo* is based in Italy has more than a little to do with its popularity. The equivalent to cinemagoers in England would be an Italian film about *Robin Hood*.]

So, to show his thanks for all the enjoyment Laurel and Hardy had given him, and fellow Italians, Luigi Infantino decided to treat them to a rendition of a famous aria, and invited Babe Hardy to duet with him. The wonderful sounds issuing from the dressing room soon turned to dis-harmony, however, when the voice of one Stanley Laurel was injected into the rendition – which in turn prompted Betty Kaye's Pekinese dogs to lend their vocal contribution.

(Oh! for a tape-recorder).

Another backstage visitor that week was George Wilkinson, an old classmate of Stan's, from the King James I Grammar School, Bishop Auckland, where Stan had boarded between January 1902 and July 1903. Laurel was delighted to see George, but very saddened to learn that several of their fellow classmates had been killed in the First World War. They had happier results recalling the masters and their nicknames, many of which George claimed young Jefferson had invented. Ida was present, and interested to learn of her husband's schooldays from the boy whom Stan described as having "taught me all my bad habits." Stan took George along to see Babe, but found him to be resting, so let him be. Hardy, he told George, was suffering from heart trouble, so the opportunity was missed.

This excerpt from the *Bradford Telegraph & Argus*, date 5 May, gives us a rare revelation into how Hardy spent his daytime while Laurel was writing letters, or meeting with friends.

> Mr. Hardy told the Telegraph & Argus that he and his wife had just visited Harrogate and Knaresborough which he described as "really wonderful" though he couldnt manage the walk to Mother Shiptons cave as it was "a bit too far for me."

[AJM: Harrogate is roughly sixteen miles north of Leeds, with the neighbouring town of Knaresborough being two miles further on. From the website www.mothershipton.co.uk we learn that the park is a remnant of the Royal Forest of Knaresborough. Over the last four centuries, millions of visitors have been enchanted by the park's natural beauty, with the added attractions it offers, such as: Mother Shipton's Cave and the petrifying well; The Worlds End pub; the viaduct; Knaresborough Castle; the mill and weir; and the woodland path that winds alongside the river and through what remains of the Royal Forest of Knaresborough.] Is it any wonder that Hardy found the walk "a bit too far," and needed to rest in his dressing room?

Leeds led to Edinburgh, another city receiving a fourth visit from the screen legends.

While overseeing Laurel and Hardy's forty pieces of luggage, upon arrival at the Caledonian Station, Edinburgh, tour manager JACK WHITMORE stands back to allow the Boys a little playtime for the cameras.

After interviewing the two stars at Monday morning rehearsals, a reporter from the *Edinburgh Pictorial* had this to say:

> The two veteran funsters, Laurel & Hardy, are the nicest star team I've ever met. It's not just that they are pleasant and polite, though as far as these two virtues are concerned they could put many of the alleged big stars to shame, it's something far more than that and I can only put it down to that mysterious endearing quality that has kept them favourites for so long.
>
> Stan said how much he had enjoyed the Queen's Coronation, which he and Hardy had watched on TV before leaving California. Still being shown on American television every night, were Laurel and Hardy's own films. On entering the dressing-room, Babe first begged an excuse to sit down. This accomplished, he promptly began to extol on the beauty of the fair city of Edinburgh:
>
> 'Edinburgh is definitely the nicest part of England,' he said.
>
> 'Scotland,' corrected Stan.
>
> 'No, England,' asserted Hardy, at which an argument ensued.
>
> Coming back to the subject, Babe said,
>
> 'I like Edinburgh. I don't think there is a more restful spot in the world. I just like sitting at the hotel window and looking out at the castle.'

Lucille Hardy reiterated her husband's feelings for Edinburgh. Back in 1952, whilst shopping in R & W Forsyth's she had remarked to an assistant: "We didn't care much for Glasgow, but we love Edinburgh." Laurel, too, was equally complimentary – as noted in this later letter:

```
We visited Edinborough again in later years to play at the
Empire theatre there, but due to working we did'nt get
around to see very much of other sights. Our rooms in the
hotel were directly in front of the Castle - really a
magnificent sight at sunset, quite inspiring.
```

The interview in the *Pictorial* continued with Babe Hardy saying: "We think we will be here all week, but we won't know until they have seen tonight's show." Well, here is what the reviewers said after seeing it. First, the *Evening News*:

> Laurel & Hardy made a welcome return to the Edinburgh Empire last night. Their performance was all too brief, but their unmistakable forms created laughs without a word of support. They are naturally beginning to show their years, but proved that they are just as young in heart as when they began as a comedy team 27 years ago.

Stan and Ollie were wondering how this little girl was so good at doing yo-yo tricks, until it was revealed that her father is former world yo-yo champion – Art Pickles.

And back to the *Edinburgh Pictorial* interview, which concluded:

> Their secret – I would say that they enjoy entertaining as much as the public enjoy being entertained. Couple this with the fact that they have never let success go to their heads, and I'm sure that there lies a substantial part of the answer.

On Tuesday Stan and Babe chose the winners of the 'Lovely Shopgirl' competition in the *Evening Dispatch*, from photographs sent in by the contestants. The three winners were then brought backstage later in the week to receive their prizes from the comedy couple.

Winners of the Dispatch "Lovely Shopgirl" competition, Doreen Culbert, who works in the Berkertex department at Smalls, stands between the judges of the contest, Laurel and Hardy, after receiving her prize. On the right is the runner-up, Helen English, who works in Beveridges, Kirkcaldy. And third prize winner, Margaret McKillon, of Cochrane's, Baxter's Place, Edinburgh, is on the left.

That week, from his room in the *Caledonian Hotel*, with its lovely view of the castle, Stan wrote to Trixie Wyatt:

```
                                                  14-4-54.
We had a nice week in Leeds - Bus. good for a change - We
opened up good here too, but weather has started to get
nice - which is not good for the Theatres as people like to
stay outdoors in the warm weather - Don't blame them.
We have a deal on to play a summer season in Blackpool
starting end of June - but if it doesn't go through - we
shall return to the States. I understand we are now booked
up to June 7th - but we have not been notified yet.
```

At last, Laurel seems to playing down the reality of further tours. All that was needed now was for the comedy couple to complete this one.

o-o-0-o-o

Chapter 17

CUT SHORT

The next booking took the show to Carlisle — England's most northerly city, on the outskirts of the Lake District. Although Stan had wonderful memories of trips to the Lake District, his visits would have been to towns at the southern end, nearer to Ulverston, which was some seventy-plus miles from Carlisle. Why, before now, Laurel and Hardy had not been booked into a venue near Ulverston is a mystery, especially as there was a suitable theatre in nearby Barrow-in-Furness. Be that as it may, on Monday, the Mayor and Mayoress of Carlisle gave a party for Stan and Babe at Her Majesty's Theatre.

[LOST PHOTO] The Town Clerk and the Mayor & Mayoress giving a party, with a gigantic spread of food consisting of a bowl of nuts and an ashtray (or maybe it's just two ashtrays).

Godfrey Gate, from the *Carlisle Journal*, was on hand to assess their characters:

> 'My name is Gate,' I said. 'Mine is Laurel,' said the thin man. 'And I'm Hardy,' added the fat one. As if I didn't know! But this unassuming, almost humble self-introduction is, I have found, typical of the modesty of two characters who have held a unique place in entertainment for going on thirty years. No theatrical affectation – just down-to-earth condescension. Only a kind of humble satisfaction and sense of privilege that during their career, they have performed the important service of making millions laugh. That is Laurel & Hardy. I say sincerely, that meeting this oddly-assorted pair, looking off-stage much as they do before the footlights or the camera, has been an experience I shall always wish to remember.

Having such affection for Laurel and Hardy, Gate obviously wasn't going to miss watching their show:

143

The sketch contains a lot of the slapstick humour of the Laurel & Hardy films. So slickly done and – my! – how easy it all comes. While Stan & Ollie clowned in and out of two bars, vainly searching for each other and, miraculously almost rubbing shoulders without one spotting the other, the lady next to me had hysterics; the two small boys immediately in front jumped in a frenzy of delight; the whole circle seemed to rock with atom-bomb explosions of laughter. Then I knew for certain how worthwhile has been the career of these two funny men who have made so many people so happy.

Two Boy Scouts cleaning Laurel and Hardy's shoes. Let it be said that no other double act were fit to do so.

Dick Allen, of the *Cumberland Evening News*, found that the sketch stood up well to Laurel and Hardy's film reputation:

> The show will be remembered by Theatre patrons for another generation. Laurel & Hardy brought back to us all those crazy pictures which have filled cinemas all over the world for almost thirty years. Their act is not new, spectacular, nor even brilliantly written. But it is the funniest thing I have seen in the live theatre for a long time – because it is Laurel & Hardy.

Having watched the show, Allen met the Boys backstage. He too found it odd that this was the double-act's first visit to Carlisle. Stan added: "As far as I know, I have never been here before."

[AJM: Stan's memory failed him there – he had actually played Carlisle in March 1908, in the Levy & Cardwell pantomime *Sleeping Beauty*].

Between houses, Dick invited the Boys across the road to the Howard Arms for a drink. Stan declined, saying: "I don't want one." Whether Ollie had told him to say this because they only had fifteen cents between them, Mr. Allen did not reveal!!

At the County Station Hotel, Carlisle, Laurel wrote to a fan:

```
We had a lovely week in Edinburgh & really hated to leave
"Bonnie Scotland," but hope we shall have the pleasure of
coming back again in a year or so, & hope then you will pay
us a personal visit!
    We expect to return to U.S.A. end of June & I shall be
pleased to send you a letter from California.
```

Ah good! Laurel has seen sense, and is calling it a day. But — hang on! Just two days later came:

```
Ben Shipman left Paris for home last week end, he was here
for about a month, but only saw him a couple of times. We
are taking a rest next week (26th).
We have a deal for a 12 weeks run in Blackpool commencing
June 28th. at the South Pier, but unless some changes are
made in the contract, we shall probably return home. We are
thinking of making the trip by freighter, which stops at
different foreign ports & through the Panama Canal. It
would be a nice rest & very interesting. However, will let
you know our plans as soon as definite.
```

Well at least the Blackpool booking didn't involve touring.

On completion of their week in Carlisle, and their stay at the County Station Hotel, facing Station Square, the Laurels and the Hardys had a free week — Sunday April 26 to Sunday 2 May. It is believed the Hardys remained in the Lake District for at least part of that week, to do a little sightseeing. Babe loved sightseeing, and made sure to find time to do so on all four British tours. As well as the recent visits to Harrogate and Knaresborough, he is recorded as visiting Gleneagles, Scotland (1932); the Scottish Lakes (1947), touring around Warwickshire (when playing two weeks in Coventry); and visiting the Shakespeare Theatre, Stratford — plus all the other public appearances he had made with Stan, as detailed in these two books. No doubt there were others, but which went unrecorded.

As for Stan, he seems to have been still in the mode he was in when making films. i.e. while Hardy was out playing golf, or spending time at the racetrack, he would stay behind and work on the current film. This letter places him at the Queen's Hotel, in LEEDS, in the middle of the week-off, where one would surmise he had swapped sightseeing for letter writing:

```
My Dear Booth [Colman]:-                        April 29.'54.
I guess our letters crossed, as I gave you details of our
plans up to June 7th. which will be our final date for
Delfont. If nothing happens after that we shall probably be
on our way home. We still can go to Australia - altho' the
Tax situation is clear, the difficulty is, the amount we
can take out in Dollars - so that is mainly the cause which
is holding us up. Had a nice rest this week for a change so
feel fit & ready to tackle the last six weeks.
```

Hardy would have been back in time for a return engagement at the Bradford Alhambra, which they had played in 1952.

The *Telegraph & Argus* logged their sketch as follows:

> Time does not seem to have changed Laurel & Hardy physically (as we saw at the Alhambra, Bradford, last night), nor has it altered their slapstick technique. Together, they are a team, expert at causing confusion without effort.

The manager's report revealed:

> Very well received. These popular film artistes are as laughable as ever but are not proving the box office appeal of previous visits.

The *Telegraph & Argus* article continued with some of Stan's views of comedy, and Hardy's views of television. Stan stated:

> 'There is always room for new comedians; there is room for hundreds of them. I would certainly like to see more good comedians on stage and screen.'

Hardy, on reflecting that few good comedies were being made for the screen today, said: 'People want their comedy a little too arty-crafty, if you know what I mean,' then added, 'The pace of T.V.

Laurel outside the No.1 dressing room – named "The Mother Goose Room" – at the Bradford Alhambra. He has cut out his name off one of the flyers, and stuck it on the door, just to let people know that Mother Goose isn't actually in there.

competition in America is so strong that Hollywood will feel the blast of the wind even more strongly during the next few months. Three-dimension [3-D], wide screens, and other "gimmicks" are no substitute for good films. You have to give the public something really good, whatever tricks of presentation you use.'

But with television sets at 100 guineas – well outside the price range of working-class families – theatres and cinemas were yet to keep going a little longer before attendance figures were hit by patrons becoming "home" viewers.

When asked why Laurel and Hardy had been given so little television exposure on the tours, Bernard Delfont conceded: *"The media thought they were past it, and not worth covering."* Even newspapers and magazines held the same viewpoint of the two Hollywood screen legends. When Chaplin biographer David Robinson (who was writing for the magazine *Sight and Sound* in 1953) asked the editor if he could go and interview Laurel and Hardy at the Brixton Empress, she asked: *"Why would you want to interview them? ... Well, if you insist, we will take a look at it and see if it is worth publishing."*

So in all the entries in this book, where I have questioned why there was no newspaper coverage of Laurel and Hardy, it would seem that the answer lies with this attitude being held by the editors in question. How lucky we are, therefore, that these ninety-plus years later, we can still observe Laurel and Hardy in their classic film comedies.

Still letter-writing at the Queen's Hotel, in Leeds, Stan gave this update:

```
My Dear Trixie [Wyatt]-                        May 6.'54.
I don't think the Blackpool deal is going through, so think
we shall return to the States - middle of June or as soon
as we can arrange a sailing date. We are going to Aston on
Sunday by car, & will stop in & see my sister for a few
hours on the way - it will probably be the last chance I'll
get to see her before I leave.
```

Laurel went to the Bull Inn at Bottesford to see his sister, but it was the barmaid who grabbed this photo opportunity, outside the back door.

Stan also dropped off a load of the luggage and props they had been ferrying up and down the country, some of it from the 1947 tour, for his sister to put into storage in one of the out-houses.

Having made the promised visit to Stan's sister, the party drove on to Aston – a ward of Birmingham. Of their show the following day at the Aston Hippodrome, the *Birmingham Mail* committed itself to only: *"Last night's audience gave a great welcome to Laurel and Hardy,"* which doesn't exactly give us an opinion as to what happened during the twenty minutes *after* they had walked on stage. The *Birmingham Post* reviewer went little-way to inform us:

> If Laurel & Hardy are a little disappointing it is because their style of comedy has been exploited so successfully on the screen and benefits so much from the scope and resources this medium has to offer. Though their dialogue was sometimes an encumbrance, their act is polished and amusing.

Cut Short

> Stan and Babe caught making their way to the stage door, down the side of the Aston Hippodrome. Behind them is the Barton Arms.
>
> When the Boys played in Wolverhampton, they stayed fifteen miles away, at the Queens Hotel, in Birmingham. But here in Aston, no record of where they stayed has been found. Popular belief is that they stayed at the Barton Arms. Until confirmation is received to the contrary, it would seem that wishful thinking will continue to place them there.

Birmingham-based John McCabe took the opportunity to travel the short distance to Aston, to have further interviews, to extend his notes, for inclusion in his biography of the comedy kings. Also between shows, Stan wrote to childhood friend Trixie Wyatt:

```
Well Dear, we have decided to finish our tour in Swansea,
week of May 24th. we were to have finished two weeks later
but did'nt like the dates they offered, so called the whole
thing off.

We expect to sail about June 12th. if we can get
accommodations on one of the Holland-American Line ships,
which goes direct to Los Angeles through the Panama Canal.
they are Cargo ships & stop in for a day or so at different
Foreign ports on the way - it's about a 30 day trip, so would
be an interesting trip & give us a nice rest, & when we
arrive, its only about an hour's drive to our house in Santa
Monica, so it practically takes us to our doorstep. If we
went on the "Queen Mary" we would arrive in New York & then
ride 3 days & nights on the train to Los Angeles. This way
(Cargo Ship) is more convenient besides being a great saving
in fares. Going on the "Mary" to Los Angeles, costs, for all
of us, £1500. this other way £700.

We shall go to London from Swansea & wait there for sailing
date, do'nt know where we shall stay yet, but will let you
know. Eda flew to Paris last Tuesday to see some friends
before we leave. She will be back again tonight.
```

So Plymouth, the place where Sir Francis Drake had finished his game of bowls before going to war with Spain, had now become the penultimate engagement on the tour.

Whether or not Laurel and Hardy were able to bowl over the people of Plymouth can be gauged from local newspaper reviews. The *Western Morning News* saw the match as follows:

> Laurel & Hardy are extremely shrewd and efficient funny men. They like to work out their comic situations and perfect them to the final detail, and displayed such craftsmanship on their first appearance in Plymouth. All fanciers of Hollywood's comedy couple will rejoice at seeing clowning that is real clowning again. Once seen – some will say endured – they were never forgotten; their personality produced a type of comedy which was unique on the screen and is not less so on the stage. And personality makes good entertainment.
>
> Laurel & Hardy know what they are about. Above all they know the difference between a joke that is funny, and a joke that merely ought to be funny. They have always made it their business to know.

The *Evening Herald* had a similar view:

> Laurel & Hardy at the Palace Theatre this week, look a little older, and are not as boisterous as they used to be – perhaps because Oliver Hardy was suffering from a chill and had to have penicillin treatment before the act last night – but all their old cleverness and that delightful craziness is still there.

Little did the critics know when penning these reviews, but the devastating truth was: Laurel and Hardy had played their last-ever performance.

o-o-0-o-o

Chapter 18

THE LAST FAREWELL

On the second day of the Plymouth engagement, Laurel was still completely unaware of the seriousness of Hardy's deteriorating condition; and, from his dressing room in the Palace Theatre, wrote only of their plans for the forthcoming weeks:

```
My Dear Booth:-                                May 18th. '54.
The Blackpool deal is out, so we have decided to close the
tour next week in Swansea & as soon as we can get a sailing
date, we shall be on our way home.
We are trying to come back on a cargo ship by the way of
the Panama Canal, but as they have no definite sailing
dates, it is uncertain when we shall leave here. Anyway we
are going to London & will wait for the first opportunity,
& will advise you as soon as we know. The trip takes around
thirty days & arrives at San Pedro.
Eda flew to Paris for a few days last week, to visit some
friends there & really enjoyed the flight both ways & is
fully SOLD on that medium of travel.
```

The dreadful truth emerged later in the day, as detailed in this *Western Morning News* report of Wednesday 19 May 1954.

> The variety show last night at the Palace Theatre was without the star turn of Laurel & Hardy. Minutes before the curtain was due to go up, Oliver Hardy had to withdraw because of illness. Despite a high temperature, Hardy arrived at the theatre hoping that he would be able to go on, but when his temperature was taken it showed 103.4, and he was sent to bed. He was examined by a specialist, and the partnership's manager said it was hoped that Hardy would be fit enough to appear later in the week.
>
> Stan Laurel did not go on without his partner, but a full programme was given by the support acts.

Later that same day, the position was clear, and the *Evening Herald* made the sad announcement:

> Laurel & Hardy will not be appearing for the rest of the week. Oliver Hardy who became ill shortly before last night's show is confined to bed, and will not be fit enough to re-join the company.

By an unbelievable coincidence, on the very evening on which Laurel and Hardy made their last stage appearance, another world-famous double-act came to an even more tragic ending. Arthur Lucan, of the man-and-wife comedy duo 'Lucan & McShane' (aka: 'Old Mother Riley & Kitty') actually died in the wings of the Tivoli Theatre, Hull.

On Thursday, the *Herald's* latest report on Babe was:

> Mr. Hardy was confined to his bed in the Grand Hotel today. A specialist who saw him diagnosed a virus infection. Mrs. Hardy said her husband was 'slightly better, but still feeling terrible.' He will remain in the hotel until he has recovered.

The following day Hardy's temperature was lower but, as well as a severe bout of flu, he was diagnosed as having suffered a mild heart attack.

With only one more week of the tour to run, the remaining shows were cancelled. Joe Church completed the week at Plymouth, and Gladys Morgan & Co. stood in the following week, at Swansea Empire.

Although Laurel didn't go on stage at all, he did go to the theatre each night to give moral support to the acts. In an interview with the *Western Independent*, Stan spoke of his regrets for the people of Plymouth:

> I am like a lost soul without Hardy. It has been very unfortunate, especially as this is the first time we have been here. Hardy went on, on Monday, but he should not have done so. The audience were very pleasant and nice. We had a wonderful reception. It has been very disappointing to us that we could not go on. We are sorry the people have been disappointed.

For the benefit of people who might be wondering why Stan didn't go on alone, he said:

> I would not attempt it. I know it would have been disappointing. I am completely lost without Hardy. We do comedy sketches – situations. I am not a gag-man.

Of Laurel and Hardy's on-stage relationship, in general, Harry Worth made the following general observation:

> When Stan wanted to, he could make Ollie laugh any time. And when Ollie started laughing, there was a lot of him to go. Trying to control himself was awful. But, some way or other, Stan conveyed this warmth, this love, this appreciation of his friend to the audience. Once you can join in something going on, on the stage – something that is fun – it goes round. It's a wonderful thing to see.
>
> Oliver Hardy thought Stan Laurel was the greatest comedian that ever was, and I think Stan had the same regard for Ollie.

On 24 May, after days spent dealing with correspondence, Laurel went off to the Washington Hotel, London, to make travel arrangements. Statements were made to the press that Hardy would follow him when well enough. The two would then return to the States where, after a rest period, they would be involved in making a television series.

Just over one week after the cancelled engagement at the Plymouth Palace, Laurel wrote to the manager, expressing his regrets:

> My Dear Mr. [William] Willis:-   May 26th.'54.
> Mr Hardy is feeling better, but of course still very weak. However, we are sailing for the States June 2nd. so think the voyage & rest will do him a lot of good.
>
> We too were very disappointed, not being able to fulfil our Engt. with you. Unfortunate for all concerned, could have been a profitable & happy week. Anyway, we hope to have the opportunity & pleasure of meeting & playing for you again in the near future.
>
> Mrs Laurel & Mr & Mrs Hardy join in kindest regards & every good wish always, & remember us kindly to Mr Heath, The staff & regular Patrons.

On the same day, Stan wrote to his good friend Booth Colman, from his new location at the Washington Hotel, London:

> Babe is feeling better, but [we] decided to cancel last few weeks & return home.
>
> We sail from Hull, June 2nd. on the MS "MANCHURIA" & due to arrive Los Angeles (San Pedro) June 27th. via the Panama Canal. Having nothing to rush back for so thought it would be a change to come back on a cargo ship. Think I mentioned the idea to you in my previous letters.
>
> The Line we are coming on is THE EAST ASIATIC CO.LTD. a Danish concern, should be an interesting trip & also a nice rest after this hard tour since last September.
>
> Busy as hell getting ready, so excuse short letter.

The Last Farewell

Poster for the show that never was.

Four days later and the Laurels *and* the Hardys had relocated to Hull, as explained here in this letter — written by Laurel in the Royal Station Hotel, to his cousin Nellie:

```
Hardy is feeling better, but still very weak.
We sail from Hull - Wednesday June 2nd on the M.S.
"MANCHURIA." Beatrice is coming tomorrow (Monday) to stay
till we leave. We stopped in at her place on our way to
Birmingham about three weeks ago.

We didn't expect to come to Hull till Tuesday June 1st. but
when we read about the threatened East Coast Railway strike
we got out of London as quick as we could - didn't want to
chance missing our ship.
```

MV Manchuria

The Danish cargo ship, MV *Manchuria*, with only ten passengers aboard, was bound on a twenty-three-day trip for Vancouver – stopping off en route at St. Thomas (14 June), Curacao, and then through the Panama Canal – after which, the captain was charged to drop off the Laurels and the Hardys at Long Beach, California (26 June).

Of the reasoning behind taken this ship, and not one of the Cunard liners, Stan opined:

```
I really prefer traveling this way as you do'nt have to
dress up for meals etc. as you do on the big passenger
ships. There was only 10 passengers on this trip (12 is the
limit they carry) so its practically like being on a
private yacht.
```

On all four of their British Tours, the two former Hollywood film legends had been welcomed by enthusiastic crowds at every town and city. They had been given hospitality by the Mayors and Mayoresses, and invited to every major function, event, banquet, and dinner. They had played to packed houses, and been visited backstage by top showbusiness celebrities, all desperate to meet them, and pour out their love and admiration. They had even played to the Royal Family. And, when crossing the Atlantic, they had sailed on the world's greatest passenger liners, and been mobbed each time on embarkation and disembarkation.

Now, they were leaving totally unnoticed, on a cargo ship — a freight-carrying motor vessel.

The whole circumstance could be viewed as a sad ending to the comedy duo's long illustrious partnership, but let us not forget that they were leaving behind them a vast comic legacy, and a wealth of happy memories for the people who had seen 'live on stage' the greatest comedy duo of all time:

STAN LAUREL & OLIVER HARDY

The Last Farewell
SHIP SHAPES

Ida and Stan caught during life-boat drill — or is that Mae West?.

Looks like they couldn't find a big enough life-jacket for Babe

Ida has had enough of wearing her life-jacket. Now, if only they had done one in fur …

After-dinner drinks at the Captain's table – Z.W.A. Pedersen

Stan gets a surprise birthday cake from the stewards – John and Arnold.

Tral-la-la, lal la la, lal la … Pom, Pom.

On 3 June 1954 two ageing comedians went unnoticed as they waved goodbye to England from the stern of a ship bound for America. The skinny, red-haired one had first made a similar journey over forty years earlier; and, watching the shoreline fast disappearing, could not help but reflect on the intervening years – years that had seen him rise from a struggling music-hall artiste, to one of the world's best-loved film comedians. This accolade was shared by the huge man standing at his side – his inseparable business partner for the last twenty-eight years.

THE END

ACKNOWLEDGEMENTS

[N.B. The majority of those acknowledged here gave their assistance during research for the First Edition, between 1987 and 1993. Sad to say that a number of them will have since passed on since, but I have no way of checking just who. Only those I have personal knowledge of are marked with an asterisk to signify "deceased."]

[KEY: "*" indicates "deceased"]

-----0-----

My sincere thanks to all those whose valued contributions made the story of "The British Tours" as near to definitive as one could hope it to be.

A Special Mention to:

Roy Sims – whose assistance with the book, from birth to maturity, was invaluable; to Bruce Crowther – for guiding me on my first, faltering steps; to Billy Marsh* – who gave me credibility, and whose memory is astounding; Jean Darling*; Jeffrey Simmons; and Eric and Joy Dalton – for their encouragement and guidance; to Norman Wisdom* – who realised my life-times ambition; to Olga Varona* and Archie Collins – who put aside illness to write a loving documentation; John and Jean Cooper; Jefferson Woods*; and Nancy E. Wardell* – who so kindly allowed me family insights; taxi driver John Jones – for the heart-touching story; Shirley Davies – who painted such poetic pictures; and Eric Nicholson; Ray Alan*; Peter Goodwright; Billy Barron*; Dorothea Birch*; Bill Butler MBE; George Cockayne; John Eddolls; Sybil C. Henderson; Audrey Jenkins; Robert F. Kennedy*; Francis J. Mavin OBE; Nancy Jane Reid; and Ronald Thomson* – for their personal eye-witness accounts.

Many thanks also to:

Dr. Kathleen Barker*; Mrs V. Bolton; Estelle Bond; Allen Bromley; Charlie Brooks; Rod Byrne; Frank Carson*; Nora Chadwick; Perce Champin; B.D. Cook; L. Crane; Mary Crettol; Mike Davie; Freddie Davies; Norma Devitt; Kim Drinkwater; Joe Ellis; Peg Francis; Alec Frutin*; R.R. Fry; John Galloway; Elizabeth M. Gammage; Malcolm Gilbert; Chris Hawes; Kevin Henriques; Mrs. S.M. Hess; Emily Hopper; Terry Johnson; Liddell Johnston; Ron Kerr; George Knox; Edward J. Laker; Brian Lazarus; Jack Leighton; Jimmy Logan*; Billy McCaffrey; Veron McGinley; Ron Mason; John Mullinder; J.S. Myers; Mrs. R.J. Nendrick; Mrs. V. Osmond; Dick Pearce; Ron Pearson; Les Pudney; Dereck Riddell; Johnnie Riscoe; Billy "Uke" Scott*; Arthur E. Shorter; Giles Squire; George Strzodka; Valerie Sturges; Mrs. L. Swindells; Carole Thomas; Herbert D.G. Tinkler; Patrick J. Trainer; Jack Twells; Peggy Valentine; Max Wall*; Gerald H.A. Warr JP; Ben Warriss*; Elsie Waters*; Jock M. Whitehouse; George Wilkinson; Mrs. Willis; Bea Winterburn; Ken Woodward; Mrs. Wotherspoon*; David Guy-Johnson; Hazy Paul; Leo Roberts; Derek Sculthorpe; Leslie Melville; Penny Corner; Gordon Bailey; Patrick Vasey; and Jason Allin. And to Ethel Challands* for her extreme generosity.

The "Sons of the Desert" — UK

Rob Lewis; Stephen Bolton; Laurence Reardon; Mike Jones; Graham McKenna; Dave Walker; Derek Ward; Philip Martin Williams; and David Wyatt; who unselfishly shared what they had. And to Peter Brownlow; for his valued assistance.

The "Sons of the Desert" — Europe

Chris James (Sweden); Michael Ehret (Germany); Bram Reijnhoudt (Netherlands); Gunther Mathias; Siep Bousma (Netherlands); Peter Mikklesen (Denmark) Marc de Coninck (Belgium)

To the Societies:

Concert Artistes Association – Jimmy Perry*; Entertainment Artistes Benevolent Fund – Reg Swinson; Grand Order of Water Rats – John Adrian* and Charlie Chester*; Northamptonshire Police – Tom Paintain and Jack Spiller; Scotland Yard (Black Museum); West Mercia Constabulary – A. W. Sykes.

ACKNOWLEDGEMENTS

To the Libraries who were helpful in the extreme:

BELFAST – Jennifer Grant; BIRMINGHAM – Patrick Baird; BLACKPOOL – James K. Burkitt; BOLTON Department of Education – Brian Hughes; BOURNEMOUTH Local Studies – Mrs. R.M. Popham; BRADFORD District Archives – Gina L. Szekely; BRIGHTON – Stephanie Green; BRISTOL – Miss D. Dyer; BURY – Mrs. R. Hirst; CARLISLE – Stephen White; COVENTRY – A.J. Mealey; DUDLEY Archives – Mrs. K.H. Atkins; DUMFRIES – John Preston; DUNDEE – J.B. Ramage; DUNFERMLINE – John Jamieson; DURHAM County Library – J. Main; EALING – Miss A. Terre; EDINBURGH – Norma Armstrong; GLASGOW Mitchell Library – Elizabeth Carmichael and Anne Escott; GLASGOW University – Miss E.M. Watson and Claire McKendrick; GREENOCK Watt Library – Mrs. L.E. Couperwhite; HARTLEPOOL – Miss M.E. Hoban; HULL – Peter J. Ainscough; KENILWORTH – L. Alexander; LEAMINGTON SPA – Gary Archer; LEEDS – Mrs. A. Heap and Mrs. J.H. Horne; LEWISHAM Local History Centre – Richard A. Martin; LIVERPOOL Brown, Picton and Hornby – Janet Smith; LONGSIGHT – Hilary Pate; NEWPORT – Mrs. S. Pugh; MANCHESTER – Helen Foster and David Taylor; NEWCASTLE – F.W. Manders and Patricia Sheldon; NEWCASTLE Blandford House – Bruce Jackson; NEWCASTLE James Joicey Museum – Joe Ging*; NORTH SHIELDS Local Studies – Eric Hollerton; NORWICH – C. Wilkins-Jones; NOTTINGHAM – Dorothy Ritchie; OLDHAM – Deidre L. Heywood; PETERBOROUGH – R.W.E. Hillier; PLYMOUTH – J.R. Elliott; PORTSMOUTH – John Thorn; RHYL – Rona Aldrich; ST. ANNES – P. Shuttleworth; SALFORD Local History – Royston Futter and Tony Frankland; SHEFFIELD – J.M. Olive; SHREWSBURY Local Studies – Anthony M. Carr; SOUTH SHIELDS – Rod Hill and T. Graham; SOUTHAMPTON – H.A. Richards; SOUTHPORT Atkinson Library – J. Hilton; STAFFORD William Salt Library – Ms. P. Davies; STALYBRIDGE Tameside Local Studies – Alice Lock; STOCKPORT – Mrs. M.J. Myerscough; STOKE on TRENT – N. Emery and Miss A. Ormsby; SUNDERLAND – D. Hinds and Jeffrey Devine; SUTTON – Mary Batchelor; SWANSEA – Brian Thomas; SWINDON – D.M. Allen and Roger Trayhurn; SWISS COTTAGE – Malcolm Holmes; WAKEFIELD – John Goodchild; WALSALL Local History – Cath Yates; WIGAN Record Office – N. Webb; WOLVERHAMPTON – Elizabeth A. Rees; YORK Archives – Mrs. R.J. Freedman; YORK – Elizabeth A. Meline; and LONDON – Abbey Road Studios.

[Unless otherwise stated, all the above are "Central Libraries."]

PLUS: British Film Institute – Tony Widdows and Sue Wilson; Cinema Theatre Association – David Jones; Leslie Bull; R. Benton; Donald Hickling; Bill Flockney; Fred T.P. Windsor; Barry R. Stevenson; Huntley Archives – John Huntley*; Scottish Film Council – Janet McBain; Stoll Moss Archives – George Hoare*; Theatre Museum – Jonathan Gray; The Theatres Trust – D.F. Cheshire; Writer's Guild of Great Britain – Nick Dalziel.

The Public Records Department, Kew; and the Cunard Archives, Liverpool University – for the shipping data; and Scott T. Rivers (for the Australia news clips).

And a massive thank you:

To the staff of the British Newspaper Library, Colindale, who, with unquestioning service, supplied me with literally thousands of newspapers during one hundred and fifty-five visits.

Sincere Thanks Also:

To the Newspaper Companies – who printed my appeal and supplied photographs:

Accrington Observer; Bir*mingham Post & Mail* – Richard Edmonds and Carol Evans; *Bolton Evening News*; *Bournemouth Daily Echo*; *Bradford Telegraph & Argus* – Mike Priestley; Bristol *Evening Post*; *Cumberland News* – Dick Allen; *Daily Mail* – Nigel Davies; *Eastern Evening News* – Derek James; T. Bailey Forman – Ralph D. Gee; *Glasgow Evening Times*; *Grimsby Evening Telegraph*; *Edinburgh Evening News*; *Irish News Ltd* – Martina Stewart; *Isle of Thanet Gazette*; *Newcastle Evening Chronicle*; *Northampton Chronicle & Echo*; *Portsmouth News* – Keith Ridley and Alan Montgomery; *South Wales Evening Post*; *Southern Evening Echo* –

ACKNOWLEDGEMENTS

Alison Tilley; *Shrewsbury Chronicle* – Alan Godding; Solo Agency – Danny Howell; Staffordshire *Evening Sentinel*; *The Stage* – Graham Ireland and Peter Hepple; *Sunday Sun* – Robin Etherington; *Sunderland Echo* – Chris Storey; *Blackpool Gazette* – Robin Duke and R.P. Officer; *Wolverhampton Express & Star*; *Yorkshire Evening Post* – John Thorpe; *Yorkshire Express*; *Doncaster Free Press* – Chris Page; *Left Lion* – Gav Squires; *Grantham Journal* – Graham Newton.

And to the Hotels:

LONDON, Savoy – Peter Crome and Rosemary Ashbee; TYNEMOUTH, Grand – Mrs. J. Richardson; EDINBURGH, Caledonian – Allan G. Blest; RHYL, Westminster – Mrs. A.M. Qureshi; SOUTHPORT, Prince of Wales – John Barrington-Fortune; CARDIFF, Park – Doris McIntyre and Frank Bois; SOUTHAMPTON, Polygon – Anne Midgely; BRISTOL, Grand – Christopher Skidmore; SCOTLAND, Gleneagles – Ian Wilson; DUDLEY, Station – Mrs. E. Stephenson.

For the kind use of photographs – from their personal collections:

Roy Sims; Rob Lewis; Paul E. Geruicki; Randy Skretvedt; Tyler St. Mark; Siep Bousma; Bernie Hogya; Cliff Sawyer; Scott MacGillivray; Bill Cubin*; John Ullah; Marc de Coninck; Bram Reijnhoudt; Harry Hoppe; Willie McIntyre; Tony Traynor; Huntley Jefferson Woods*; Nancy E. Wardell*; David Tomlinson; Stephen Neale; David Crump; Ronald Thomson*; Phillippe Petit; and Camillo Moscati.

Colin Greenwell; Cliff Temple*; Olga Varona* and Archie Collins; John and Jean Cooper; Billy Barron*; Charlie Cairoli Jnr. & Claudine; Ron Kerr; George Cockayne; John Eddolls; Sybil C. Henderson; Audrey Jenkins; Francis J. Mavin OBE; Mike Davie; A. Nesbitt; Nancy Jane Reid; Lt. Cdr. Richard Swift (R.N.Rtd.); Mrs. Willis; Norman Wisdom*; Kenny Baker*; Richard Townend; Gordon Bailey; Lynda Gocher; Carole Anne Williams; Alan Parsons; John Pinchbeck; Ron Roper; and Roy Baines.

IMAGE SOURCES

Back Cover Colour Photo – The British Tours part 1 — Nick Wall

Back Cover Colour Photo – The British Tours part 2 — Aimee Spinks

Getty Images – Morgana Gooding; Alamy; Cine-Variety (Mike Lang); Carl M. Cole; Autographs Inc.; Blackpool Gazette; Madame Tussauds; London – Undine Concannon; Google images; Author's Collection.

> [Every effort was made to trace the present copyright holders of the photographs and illustrations contained within these pages. Anyone who has claim to the copyright of any of those featured; please make representation to the publisher, who will be only too pleased to give appropriate acknowledgement in any subsequent edition(s).]

It isn't that long ago when the only way to receive photographs was by negatives or prints being sent by post. Nowadays, with email, and especially with tens of thousands of related images available to download from the Internet, keeping tabs on the source is nigh on impossible. My sincerest apologies, therefore, to anyone I may have omitted to acknowledge as source.

And with much Gratitude to:

John McCabe* – for his encouragement, appraisal of the manuscript, and loan of photographs.

And to Bob Spiller, and Alison Grimmer – by whose brilliant perceptions, and much appreciated suggestions, the text of the First Edition was greatly enhanced.

And lastly to Lord Delfont* and Billy Marsh* – who revived the career of two neglected comedians, and without whom there would be no story.

o-o-o-0-o-o-o

ACKNOWLEDGEMENTS
BIBLIOGRAPHY

John McCabe — The Comedy World of STAN LAUREL (Robson)

John McCabe — Mr. LAUREL & Mr. HARDY (Signet USA)

John McCabe — BABE – The Life of Oliver Hardy (Robson)

Pawson/Mouland — LAUREL BEFORE HARDY (Westmorland Gazette)

Jack Read — EMPIRES HIPPODROMES & PALACES (Alderman Press)

Randy Skretvedt — LAUREL and HARDY – The Magic Behind the Movies (Moonstone)

Ken Owst — LAUREL & HARDY in HULL

Scott MacGillivray — LAUREL & HARDY – From the Forties Forward (iUniverse Inc.)

Simon Louvish — The Roots of Comedy

And to the Authors and writers:

Dave Bradshaw* – Press Officer Butlins, Skegness, and ex-journalist.

Bill Ellis – Seaside Entertainers: 100 years of Nostalgia.

Bill Evans – Ex-Journalist – East Kent Times.

Leslie Frost – Thanks for the Memories.

John Montgomery – Comedy Films; and others.

Douglas Salmon – Ex-Journalist and Ex-BBC Television producer.

Tony Wheatley – TV and Radio Scriptwriter.

David Robinson – Chaplin biographer.

Reference works:

CURTAINS!!! — (John Offord)

London Theatres and Music Halls — Diana Howard

Writers & Artists' Yearbook — (A & C Black)

-----0-----

ARTICLES

LAUREL & HARDY MAGAZINE – Rob Lewis

Glenn Mitchell — HARRY WORTH (Laurel & Hardy Magazine)

BOWLER DESSERT – Willie McIntyre

John Land — The Jeffersons in Bishop Auckland (Bowler Dessert)

-----0-----

WEBSITES

Laurel & Hardy Magazine (Rob Lewis, Howard Parker) – www.laurelandhardy.org

Letters From Stan [Laurel] – www.lettersfromstan.com – hosted by Bernie Hogya

Queen Street Arms, Keighley – www.valendale.myby.co.uk/pubs

Ellis Island Foundation – www.ellisisland.org

o-o-0-o-o

FILM FOOTAGE

1932 Jul 27   LONDON – Screen Artistes Federation Social Club   (book 1 page 16)
Laurel and Hardy make an appeal for the "Cinema Trade Benevolent Fund."
[They *are* talking, but the sound is considered lost.]
It was screened in British cinemas on 3rd November. The footage is undated, but the author has placed it here as that is when L&H were at the Screen Artists Federation Dinner.

Universal Talking News

1932 Jul 28   TYNEMOUTH – Grand Hotel, and Tynemouth Plaza   (book 1 page 22)
After leaving the Grand Hotel, Tynemouth, the Boys relocate to the veranda of the Plaza Cinema, overlooking the beach. There they sign autographs, make speeches, clown for the crowd of thousands, and give out presents to 600 children.
Filmed silent, but with title cards. Amateur footage.   (J. G. Ratcliffe)

1932 Jul 29   EDINBURGH – Edinburgh Castle, and Playhouse Theatre   (book 1 page 26)
L&H shown disembarking at Waverley Station, and being escorted along the platform. Second scene is a walk around the Castle grounds; and third is a lengthy sequence at the Playhouse showing the cinema and its large number of pageboys, the huge projection room, and then Stan and Babe on stage.   (Alan J. Harper)

A second version contains a longer sequence of the Edinburgh Castle walkabout, along with the arrival and departure, by car, at the North British Station Hotel.

1932 Aug 8   EALING – Stan Visits His Father   (book 1 page 49)
Stan filmed with his father Arthur Jefferson and stepmother, Venetia, outside their home at 49 Colebrook Avenue, Ealing. London W13. Most of the footage is shot in the doorway, with both father and son mugging to the camera.

1932 Aug 10   PARIS – Champs Élysées   (book 1 page 52)
Gaumont's "CAR OF THE COMEDY STARS." – Stan and Ollie board a chauffeur-driven Renault; the car crosses Paris with the Boys waving to the camera; they arrive at Claridges, in the Champs Élysées; do some business with a policeman checking their passports; and finally enter the hotel.

1932 Aug 31   NEW YORK CITY, Broadway   (book 1 page 60)
Considering this was done on location, in ONE-TAKE, it emerges as a delightful piece of footage.
Hardy is engaging throughout, staying within character and seemingly ad-libbing.
At one point, when the cop says he wants to speak to the driver, Hardy utters the killer line: "I don't think the driver can talk. In fact, I don't think the driver can see."

Hearst Metrotone News

1947 Feb 10   SOUTHAMPTON – On board the Queen Elizabeth   (book 1 page 67)
(Monday)   Interviewed by John Parasols on arrival. They talk about the forthcoming tour and
              the proposed film *Robin Hood*, then do the "You're standing on my foot" routine.
              Robert Taylor and Barbara Stanwyck are also interviewed.
                                                                            (Pathé Newsreels)

1947 Mar 14   LONDON – Daily Mail Ideal Home Exhibition, Olympia   (book 1 page 84)
(Friday)   Entertainer Tessie OShea and actress Vera Pearce sitting on Hardys knee, at the
              Stak-a-Bye tubular tables and chairs stand. Stan grins, and is kissed by Tessie.
                                                                            (Pathé Newsreels)

1947 Mar 21   KENT – Romney Hythe & Dymchurch Railway   (book 1 page 92)
(Friday)   Laurel and Hardy are welcomed at New Romney Railway Station by Mr. & Mrs.
              Howey – owners of the line. They do business of opening the tunnel doors with a
              huge key; fool about on the engine; then get into a Pullman Car and set-off for
              Dungeness along the section of line they have just re-opened.
                                                            (Gaumont, Movietone, and Paramount)

1947 Apr 28   LONDON – Daily Mail Film Awards, Dorchester Hotel   (book 1 page 99)
(Monday)   Laurel and Hardy arrive late and interrupt Lady Rothermere presenting an award
              to film actress Margaret Lockwood. There is then some improvised comic
              business, instigated by Hardy, with flowers plucked from a nearby vase.
                                                      (Pathé Newsreels, and Gaumont British News)

1947 May 6   LONDON – Comedians at the Apollo   (book 1 page 101)
(Tuesday)   Laurel and Hardy, Sid Field, The Crazy Gang, Tommy Trinder, and George
              Robey, dressed in farmer's smocks, selling programmes outside the Apollo
              Theatre, prior to a matinee benefit performance for the "Farmer's Disaster Fund."
                                                                            (Pathé Newsreels)

1947 May 27   ULVERSTON – Coronation Hall, and 3 Argyle Street   (book 1 page 110)
(Tuesday)   L&H appear on the balcony of the Coronation Hall, overlooking a packed crowd
              in the square below. Laurel is presented with a copy of his birth certificate, which
              Hardy snatches away from him. Next they visit the house where Stan was born,
              and then are seen in the grounds of the Golf Hotel, before being driven away.

1947 Jul 17   WESTON-SUPER-MARE – Outdoor Swimming Pool   (book 1 page 134)
(Thursday)   Stan and Babe are seen entering the open air swimming pool. Inside, they and
              their wives judge the 'Modern Venus' beauty competition in front of 6,000 people.

[continued]

Footage and Audio Recordings

1947 Nov 2   "Aboard the French Boat train bound for London"   (book 1 page 153)
(Tuesday*)   "The Laurels and the Hardys en route from Paris to London to attend the *Royal Variety Show*," is on the catalogue notes, and also on the soundtrack, for this footage — but this is incorrect. It was actually shot during the train journey from Jeumont to Paris on **28 October 1947***, wherein they are seated at a dining table, and attempt some comedy business with the cutlery and menu. The end sequence shows the comedy couple disembarking at the Gare du Nord station.

(Pathé Newsreels)

1952 Jan 28   SOUTHAMPTON – Arrival Aboard the 'Queen Mary'   (book 2 page 4)
(Thursday)   Laurel and Hardy are interviewed on the quayside, as they come off the gangplank at Southampton. They interact with two local girls dressed as hula-dancers. Hardy quickly excuses himself, and Laurel is left to try to ad-lib some comedy business. Unable to do so, he 'kills' time by treating the girls to lollipops.

(Movietone, and Gaumont)

1952 Jan 31   LONDON – Variety Club Luncheon, Empress Club   (book 2 page 7)
(Thursday)   L&H are first seen seated at a charity dinner, at which boxer Freddie Mills, comedian Charlie Chester, and CoCo the clown are also present. Later, Eamonn Andrews interviews them, and then they do the, "You're standing on my foot" routine with CoCo.

(Pathé Newsreels)

1952 Mar 14   GLASGOW – Opening of the Stage and Screen Memorial Club (book 2 page 26)
(Friday)   Present is Albert Pickard – former owner of the Britannia Theatre. Hardy does a quick gag with Pickard's customised car. [colour]   (Colonel A.E. Pickard)

1952 Jul 28   BRADFORD – Alhambra Theatre   (book 2 page 60)
(Monday)   Stan's second-cousin, Nancy Wardell, and her mother are seen visiting Stan and Ida, in his dressing-room at the Alhambra Theatre, Bradford. Stan, in costume, chats with his visitors, kisses Nancy, and mugs for the camera.

(Shot by Nancy's sister-in-law on 9.5mm. Lasts only a few seconds.)

1953 Oct 22   NORTHAMPTON – New Theatre   (book 2 page 97)

(Wednesday) Laurel and Hardy's taxi is shown arriving at the stage door. They do business of getting in and out on the wrong side. Once in their dressing room, Laurel brushes Hardy's coat and catches his chin with the brush, then traps Hardy's coat in a trunk. The latter sequence is almost certainly what the Boys did on the *Face the Music* television show, five days earlier.   (Pathé Newsreels)

-----0-----

RADIO

1932 Jul 26   NATIONAL – on air broadcast from the BBC London Studio.   (book 1 page 15)

1947 May 29   NORTH – *Morecambe Night Out* – live on air BBC interview by Reg Smythe in the dressing room of the Victorian Pavilion, Morecambe.   (book 1 page 113)

1952 Jun 17   BBC BELFAST – broadcast from the Grand Opera House, Belfast – link up with an "on air" Talent Show at the Tonic Cinema Bangor, for which Laurel and Hardy acted as judges.   (book 2 page 51)

1953 Oct 10   DUBLIN – interviewed for radio by a Mr. Boden regarding the debut performance of their stage sketch *Birds of a Feather* the following day at the Olympia Theatre. [No recording was made, but the script is extant.] (book 2 page 94)

1953 Oct 23   MIDLAND – *What Goes On* – interview by Philip Garston-Jones, backstage at the New Theatre, Northampton.   (book 2 page 102)

TELEVISION

1950 Jun 10   SHIP'S REPORTER SERIES – Oliver Hardy Interview.   (book 1 page 160)
Babe Hardy is interviewed aboard the RMS. *Caronia*, bound for France, prior to the shooting of *Atoll K*.   National Television Guild

1952 Feb 20   BBC – *Picture Page* – interview by Leslie Mitchell   (uconfirmed* [page 8])

1953 Oct 17   LONDON – BBC Studios: *Face the Music*, hosted by band leader Henry Hall, and featuring music mixed with Variety entertainers. Laurel and Hardy did a short scripted sketch, which involved Henry Hall introducing them to the "audience at home," followed by a short slapstick routine in which Stan traps Ollie's tie while he is packing a suitcase, and Stan struggles to free him.
[No recording was made, but the script is extant.] (book 2 page 95)

RADIO TIMES   October 9, 1953

Television Programmes
OCTOBER
17 SATURDAY

FACE THE MUSIC
Among those present at 9.30

LAUREL AND HARDY   REG DIXON

9.30   Henry Hall invites you to
FACE THE MUSIC
with melodies and songs, old and new, famous artists and interesting personalities including
Reg Dixon
Joyce Grenfell
Line Renaud
Sally Barnes
Benny Lee
Don Saunders
Peter Glover
Sheila Mathews
The Keynotes
Bobby Beaumont
David Miller
and the Happy Hoe-Downers
and an interview with
Stan Laurel and Oliver Hardy
Settings by Frederick Knapman
Dance Director, Peter Glover
Musical associate, Albert Marland
Orchestra directed by Henry Hall and Eric Robinson
Produced by Graeme Muir

GRAMOPHONE

1932 Aug 18   *Laurel & Hardy in London* (Columbia CAX 6488 DX370)   (book 1 page 53)
Recorded at the Columbia Studios, Abbey Road, London.

o-o-0-o-o

Page 1 of Laurel's script for the taped radio interview
DUBLIN – 10 October 1953

```
TAPE INTERVIEW....BODEN - LAUREL & HARDY.

BODEN.      WELL MR. HARDY, I'D LIKE TO ASK YOURSELF AND
            YOUR PARTNER MR. LAUREL ABOUT YOUR CAREERS.

HARDY.      WE'LL BE HAPPY TO ANSWER ANY QUESTIONS,
            WHAT WOULD YOU LIKE TO TALK ABOUT?

BODEN.      WELL, COULD I TALK TO YOU BOTH....IS MR. LAUREL
            AROUND?

HARDY.      YES, HE'S OVER THERE TALKING TO THE STAGE MANAGER.
            YOU SEE WE'RE DOING A BENEFIT MATINEE HERE AT THE
            OLYMPIA THEATRE TOMORROW AFTERNOON, FOR THE IRISH
            RED CROSS AND DONNYBROOK PARISH.
            [handwritten: The new Catholic church in]

BODEN.      YES, SO I UNDERSTAND. THAT'S A VERY WORTHY CAUSE.
            BUT DO YOU THINK WE COULD TALK TO MR. LAUREL FOR
            JUST A MOMENT?

HARDY.      CERTAINLY. I'LL CALL HIM. STAN.....STANLEY!

LAUREL.     (off mike) YES....YES.... WHAT IS IT?

HARDY.      THIS GENTLEMAN HERE WANTS A RADIO INTERVIEW.

LAUREL.     HE DOES?

HARDY.      YES, AND I THINK WE OUGHT TO HELP HIM.

LAUREL.     SURE, WHY NOT..... WHAT'S YOUR NAME?

BODEN.      BODEN.

LAUREL.     WELL, MR. BODEN, WHERE WERE YOU BORN?

BODEN.      WELL, MR. LAUREL, THAT'S NOT EXACTLY.....

HARDY.      NO, NO, STANLEY, THAT'S NOT THE IDEA.

LAUREL.     IT ISN'T?

HARDY.      NO. CERTAINLY NOT.

LAUREL.     ALRIGHT, WHAT ARE YOUR HOBBIES, MR. BODEN?
```

Footage and Audio Recordings

AUDIO TAPE

1947 Jun   BLACKPOOL, Palace – tin plate recording   [Extant] (book 1 page 116)

1952 Apr   NOTTINGHAM, Empire – *A Spot of Trouble* sketch   [Extant] (book 2 page 40)

1952   WARRINGTON, Ritz Cinema – message to ABC MINORS.   (book 2 page 46)
[No known copy of the recording]

1953 Oct 19   NORTHAMPTON, New Theatre – *Birds of a Feather* [Extant] (book 2 page 102)

1954 Dec   NOTTINGHAM, Empire – *Birds of a Feather* sketch   (book 2 page 116)
[Location of recording not known]

EUROPEAN RECORDINGS

1947 Oct 1   COPENHAGEN, Radio interview   (book 1 page 153)

1947 Oct 04   COPENHAGEN, K.B. Hallen   (book 1 page 153)
Short amateur recording of the opener to Laurel and Hardy's act, before launching into *The Driver's Licence* sketch. Hardy makes reference to Esbjerg. Stan corrects him and Ollie says "Odense," but then goes on to mention Copenhagen.
(So which is it?).   [Recorded on the 4 or 5 October] (2 mins 10 secs)

1947 Nov 2   PARIS, Gare du Nord Station.   (book 1 page 153)
The Laurel and Hardy party leaving Paris by train, from the Gare du Nord, to attend the Royal Variety Performance, the following day.

1947 Dec 10   BELGIUM,   (2 mins 59 secs) (book 1 page 152)
Recorded at a press reception, the day after their arrival.

1947 Dec 19   BELGIUM, Alhambra Theatre   (2 mins 20 secs) (book 1 page 157)
Short extract of *The Driver's Licence*, recorded sometime between 19 December 1947 and 1 January 1948.

o-o-0-o-o

THE BRITISH LOCATIONS

KEY:

The theatres which Laurel and Hardy played, and the hotels at which they stayed are listed on the left. In brackets is the capacity of each theatre, followed by the address.

Their current state, or whatever now occupies their former sites, is on the right-hand side.

The date in brackets is the year the venue was demolished, where applicable.

-----0-----

CUMBRIA

ULVERSTON, 3 Argyle Street.	occupied house
County Station Hotel, Court Square, CARLISLE.	Hallmark Hotel

Demolished:

CARLISLE, Her Majestys (1,300) Lowther Street.	(1970s) Iceland

SCOTLAND

GLASGOW, Britannia Music Hall, 115 Trongate.	[Grade A listed] working theatre
GLASGOW, La Scala (1,300) 155 Sauchiehall Street.	gutted – clothes shop
Central Hotel, Gordon Street, GLASGOW.	Grand Central Hotel
EDINBURGH, Playhouse (3,131) 18-22 Greenside Place/Leith Walk.	musicals and concerts
North British Station Hotel, Princes Street, EDINBURGH.	Balmoral Hotel
EDINBURGH, Empire Palace (2,016) Nicholson Street.	[refurb' 1992] Festival Theatre
Caledonian Hotel, Princes Street, EDINBURGH.	Waldorf Astoria Caledonian

Demolished:

GLASGOW, Metropole (2,000) Stockwell Street.	(1961) offices
GLASGOW, Empire (2,500) 31-35 Sauchiehall Street/West Nile Street.	(1963) shops

THE BRITISH LOCATIONS

NORTH EAST

NEWCASTLE, Stoll Picture House (1,389) Westgate Road.	Tyne Theatre & Opera House
Royal Station Hotel, Neville Street, NEWCASTLE.	working hotel
Grand Hotel, Percy Gardens, TYNEMOUTH.	working hotel
NORTH SHIELDS, Gaumont Cinema (1,790) Russell Street.	bingo
Town Hall, Saville Street, NORTH SHIELDS.	Grade II listed
SUNDERLAND, Empire (1,550) High Street.	working theatre

Demolished:

TYNEMOUTH, Plaza (713) Grand Parade.	(1996) restaurant and shops
NEWCASTLE, Queens Hall (1,400) Northumberland Street.	(1983) shopping arcade
NEWCASTLE, Empire Palace (1,849) Newgate Street.	(1963) Swallow Hotel
Albion Assembly Rooms, 19 Norfolk Street, NORTH SHIELDS.	(1985) wasteland
Ayton House, Ayres Terrace, NORTH SHIELDS.	new houses
Gordon House, 8 Dockway Square, NORTH SHIELDS.	new houses

TYNEMOUTH Grand Hotel

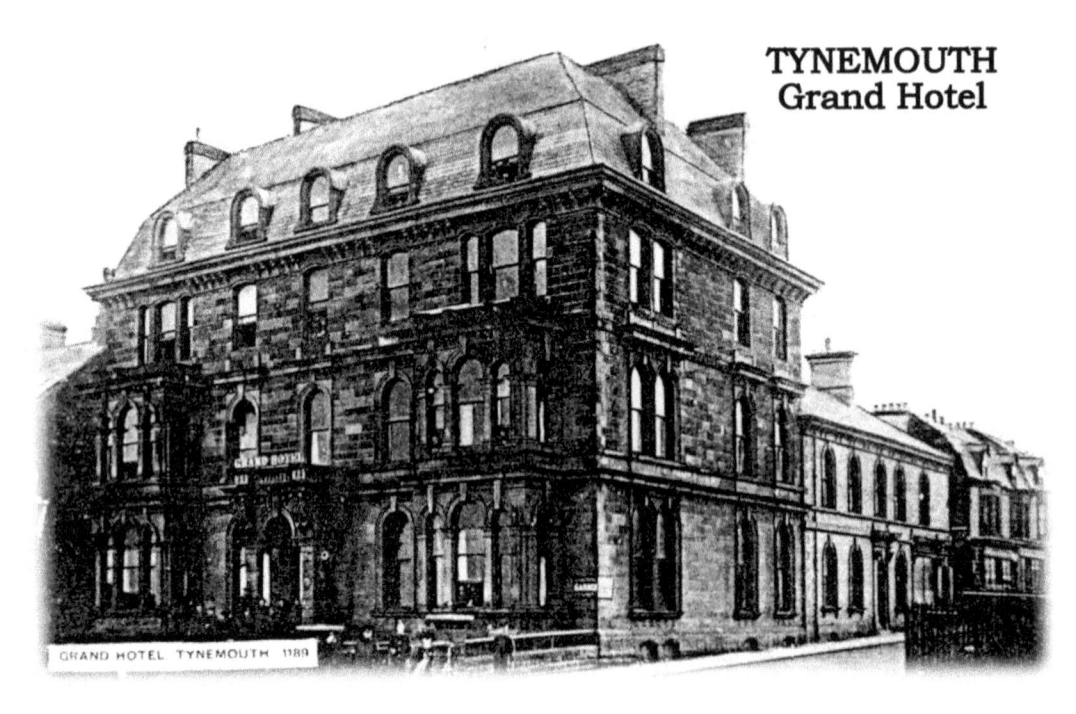

YORKSHIRE

YORK, Empire (1,000) Clifford Street.	Grand Opera House
Royal Station Hotel, Station Road, YORK.	Principal Hotel
HULL, New, Kingston Square.	working theatre
Royal Station Hotel, Ferensway, HULL.	Royal Hotel
Dolphin Hotel, Alexandra Road, CLEETHORPES.	Smoke Shack
LEEDS, Majestic Cinema (2,392) City Square.	2018 – £40 million refurb into office spaces
Queens Hotel, City Square, LEEDS.	working hotel [built on site of old one – 1937]
Midland Hotel, Cheapside, BRADFORD.	working hotel
BRADFORD Alhambra, (1,480) Morley Street.	working theatre
BRADFORD, Exchange Station Hotel, Bridge Street.	Great Victoria Hotel

THE BRITISH LOCATIONS

Demolished:
HULL, Palace (1,800) Anlaby Road.	(1965) flats
GRIMSBY, Palace (1,509) Victoria Street.	(1979) Palace Court and car park
LEEDS, Empire Palace (1,750) 108 Briggate.	(1962) Harvey Nicols – Empire Arcade
Queens Hotel, City Square, LEEDS.	[1935 - see earlier entry]
SHEFFIELD, Cinema House (763) Fargate.	(1961) Fountain Precinct - shops
SHEFFIELD, Empire Palace (3,000) Charles Street.	(1959) shops
Grand Hotel, Church Street, SHEFFIELD.	(1974) Fountain Precinct – shops

SHEFFIELD Grand Hotel

MANCHESTER

Midland Hotel, Peter Street.	working hotel
MANCHESTER, Palace (2,000) Oxford Street.	working theatre
Grand Hotel, 8 Aytoun Street.	working hotel
SALFORD, Opera House (2,070) Quay Street.	Grade II listed

Demolished:
ARDWICK GREEN, New Hippodrome (2,100) [former Empire].	(1964) roadway
New Oxford Picture Theatre (1,150) Oxford Street.	(2017) office block

LANCASHIRE

BOLTON, Lido (1,800) Bradshawgate.	(2005) (façade only) converted to flats
MORECAMBE, Victoria Pavilion (2,960) Winter Gardens, Marine Road.	renovated 1992
BLACKPOOL, Tower Ballroom, Promenade.	restored 1956
BLACKPOOL, Empress Ballroom (3,000) Winter Gardens.	restored 2017
BLACKPOOL, Baronial Hall, Winter Gardens.	preserved
Metropole Hotel, Princess Parade, BLACKPOOL.	working hotel
Clifton Arms Hotel, St. Annes Road West, St. ANNES.	working hotel
SOUTHPORT, Garrick (1,600) Lord Street.	bingo
Prince of Wales, Lord Street, SOUTHPORT.	working hotel

Demolished:
Elms Hotel, Princes Crescent, BARE.	(2012) luxury flats
BLACKPOOL Palace (2,012) Central Beach.	[ground] Poundland and Harry Ramsden's
BLACKPOOL, Picture Palace (1,972) Central Beach.	(1961) [above] Viva Cabaret

THE BRITISH LOCATIONS

LIVERPOOL

LIVERPOOL, Empire (2,293) Lime Street.	working theatre
Adelphi Hotel, Lime Street.	Britannia Adelphi Hotel

IRELAND

DUBLIN, Olympia (1,750) 72 Dame Street.	restored 1974
Gresham Hotel, OConnell Street, DUBLIN 1.	working hotel
Royal Marine Hotel, DUN LAOGHAIRE.	working hotel
BELFAST, Grand Opera House (1,050) Great Victoria Street, B12.	restored 1980
Midland Hotel, Whitla Street, BELFAST, BT15.	Midland Building - offices

NORTH WALES

RHYL, Queens, Promenade.	Amusement arcade
Westminster Hotel, East Parade, RHYL.	working hotel

SHROPSHIRE

SHREWSBURY, Granada (1,456) Castle Gates.	bingo
Demolished:	
Raven Hotel, Castle Gates, SHREWSBURY.	(1960) Marks & Spencer

STAFFORDSHIRE

HANLEY, Royal (1,800) Pall Mall.	(gutted) nightclub
North Stafford Hotel, Station Road, STOKE.	working hotel

WEST MIDLANDS

Demolished:	
WOLVERHAMPTON, Hippodrome (1,960) 34 Queen Square.	(1956) Yate's Beer Garden

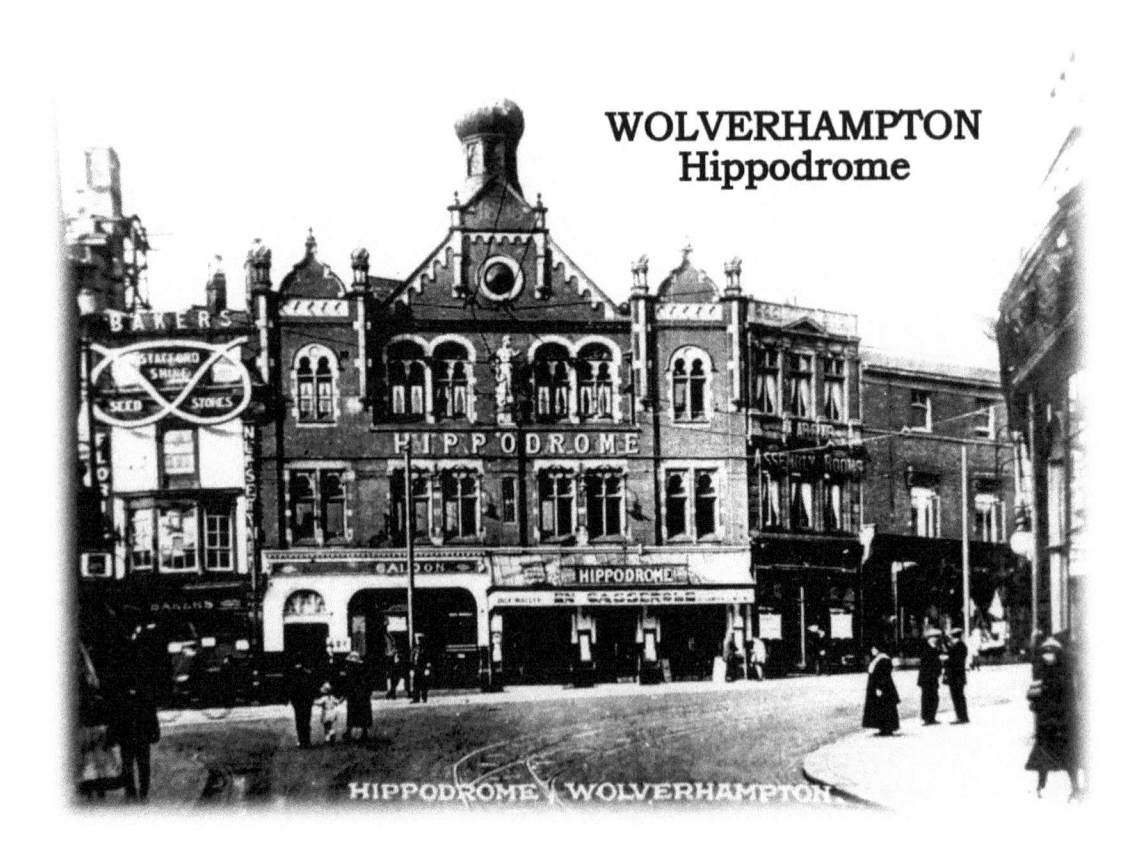

WOLVERHAMPTON Hippodrome

THE BRITISH LOCATIONS

NOTTINGHAM/LINCOLNSHIRE

Plough Inn, West Street, BARKSTON.	converted to flats
Bull Inn, 5 Market Street, BOTTESFORD.	working pub
GRANTHAM, Guildhall, St. Peter's Hill.	working theatre

Demolished:

NOTTINGHAM, Empire (2,200) South Sherwood Street.	(1969) Royal Centre
County Hotel, Theatre Square, NOTTINGHAM.	(1975) Royal Centre
Red Lion Hotel, GRANTHAM, 22-23 High Street.	(1963) Nationwide
SKEGNESS, Butlin Theatre (1,800) Butlins Funcoast World.	(1998) go-kart trak

CAMBRIDGESHIRE

PETERBOROUGH, Embassy (1,500) Broadway.	Edwards Nightclub
Great Northern Hotel, Station Road, PETERBOROUGH.	working hotel

NORFOLK

Royal Hotel, Prince of Wales Road, NORWICH.	(Grade II) offices

Demolished:

NORWICH, Hippodrome (1,836) St. Giles Street.	(1966) car park

MIDLANDS

Clarendon Hotel, The Parade, LEAMINGTON SPA.	Clarendon Court – flats
Abbey Hotel, Priory Road, KENILWORTH.	[converted 1982] flats
Chesford Grange Hotel, Chesford Bridge, KENILWORTH.	working hotel
BIRMINGHAM, Hippodrome (2,000) Hurst Street.	working theatre
Midland Hotel, New Street, BIRMINGHAM, B5.	Burlington Hotel
DUDLEY, Hippodrome (1,500) Castle Hill.	derelict
Station Hotel, Castle Hill, DUDLEY.	working hotel

Demolished:

COVENTRY, Hippodrome, Trinity Street.	(2002) Millennium Place

COVENTRY New Hippodrome

THE BRITISH LOCATIONS

BIRMINGHAM, Gaumont Cinema (2,200) Steelhouse Lane.	(1983) Wesleyan
Queens Hotel, New Street, BIRMINGHAM.	(1966) Pallasades – part of Grand Central
ASTON, Hippodrome (1,800) Potters Lane.	(1981) Drum Art Centre (closed)

NORTHAMPTONSHIRE

Plough Hotel, Bridge Street, NORTHAMPTON.	working hotel

Demolished:

NORTHAMPTON, New Theatre (2,000) Abington Street.	(1960) Primark Store

NORTHAMPTON New Theatre

SOUTH WALES

CARDIFF, New (1,600) Park Place.	working theatre
Park Hotel, Park Place, CARDIFF.	Park Plaza Hotel

Demolished:

SWANSEA, Empire (963) Lower Oxford Street.	(1960) Primark Store
Mackworth Hotel, High Street, SWANSEA.	(c.1971) Oldway House Arcade

AVON/WILTSHIRE/BERKSHIRE

BRISTOL, Hippodrome (2,000) St. Augustines Parade, BS 1.	working theatre
Royal Hotel, College Green, BRISTOL.	Marriott Royal Hotel
Grand Hotel, Broad Street, BRISTOL.	working hotel
Bear Hotel, Charnham Street, HUNGERFORD.	working hotel

Demolished:

SWINDON, Empire (1,470) Clarence Street.	(1959) Lloyds Chemists

THE BRITISH LOCATIONS

LONDON

"Drayton House", 49 Colebrook Avenue, EALING, W13.	occupied house
WIMBLEDON, Wimbledon (1,700) The Broadway, SW19.	working theatre
Burford Bridge Hotel, Box-Hill, DORKING.	Mercure Hotel
Victoria Palace (1,600) 126 Victoria Street, SW1.	working theatre
LEICESTER SQUARE, Empire (3,226) WC2.	[facade, only, is original] cinema
Drury Lane (2,283) Catherine Street, WC2.	refurbished 2019
Coliseum (2,400) St. Martins Lane, WC2.	London Coliseum
Savoy Hotel, 189 The Strand, W1.	working hotel
London Palladium (2,300) Argyll Street, W1.	working theatre
Washington Hotel, Curzon Street, W1.	Washington Mayfair Hotel
Dorchester Hotel, Park Lane, W1.	working hotel
Apollo (893) Shaftesbury Avenue, W1.	working theatre
May Fair Hotel, Stratton Street, W1J.	working hotel

Demolished:

EALING, Walpole Cinema, Bond Street, W5.	(1981) office block
CHISWICK, Empire (2,154) Chiswick High Road, W4.	(1959) Empire House
SUTTON, Granada (2,000) Carshalton Road.	(1979) Sutton Park House
LEWISHAM, Hippodrome (3,492) 153 Rushey Green, CATFORD SE6.	(1960) Eros House

LEWISHAM Hippodrome

FINSBURY PARK, Empire (2,000) St. Thomas Road, N4.	(1965) Vaudeville Court – flats
BRIXTON, Empress (1,900) Brighton Terrace, SW9.	(1992) housing

ESSEX

SOUTHEND, Odeon (2,750) Elmer Approach.	(dem. 2004) University of Essex
Palace Hotel, Pier Hill, SOUTHEND.	Park Inn Palace

THE BRITISH LOCATIONS

SOUTH COAST

MARGATE, Winter Gardens (1,533) Fort Crescent.	working theatre
St. Georges Hotel, CLIFTONVILLE.	(dem. 2006) awaiting development
Romney, Hythe & Dymchurch Railway, KENT.	fully operational
BRIGHTON, Hippodrome (1,850) Middle Street.	Grade II - closed
Grand Hotel, Kings Road, BRIGHTON.	refurbished hotel
Royal Crescent Hotel, BRIGHTON, King's Cliff	(converted) Royal Crescent Mansions
PORTSMOUTH, Royal (1,050) Guildhall Walk, PO1.	restored 2015
SOUTHSEA, Kings (1,780) Albert Road, PO5.	working theatre
Queens Hotel, Clarence Parade, SOUTHSEA.	working hotel
Royal Beach Hotel, St. Helens Parade, SOUTHSEA.	Western Royal Beach Hotel
SOUTHAMPTON, Gaumont (2,251) Commercial Road.	Mayflower Theatre
Polygon Hotel, Cumberland Place, SOUTHAMPTON.	(dem. 1999) flats
BOSCOMBE, Hippodrome (1,350) Christchurch Road.	Academy Nightclub
Chine Hotel, Boscombe Spa Road, BOURNEMOUTH.	working hotel
PLYMOUTH, Palace (1,200) Union Street.	derelict
Grand Hotel, Elliott Street, The Hoe, PLYMOUTH.	(converted) luxury duplexes

PLYMOUTH Palace

(AJM: It was impracticable to list every theatre, public house, company, civic venue, hotel, etc. to which Laurel and Hardy paid a casual visit, but most are referred to in the text).

We hope you will use these Location pages as a guide to your own British Tours.

Note that they start with Stan Laurel's birthplace, and end at the theatre where Laurel & Hardy played their last ever performance. Can you beat that!!

Happy Hunting!

o-o-0-o-o

PROGRAMME BILLS – 1952

Feb 25   (2 weeks)   PETERBOROUGH, Embassy
Ray & Madge Lamar; Lorraine; Cynthia & Gladys; Saveen & "Daisy May";
Ted & George Durante; Jimmie Elliott; Roy & Ray.
[Assistants in Laurel & Hardy's sketch were Leslie Spurling and George Pugh]

Mar 10   GLASGOW, Empire
Lonsdale Sisters; Lorraine; Walthon & Dorraine; The Great Cingalee;
Saveen & "Daisy May"; Jimmie Elliott; MacKenzie Reid & Dorothy.

Mar 16   (1 night)   NORTH SHIELDS, Gaumont Cinema
Eric Nicholson; Northumbrian Seranaders; Frankie Burns; Betty Hart;
Tony Rowley; James Metcalf; Dick Urwin; Billy "Uke" Scott.

Mar 17   NEWCASTLE, Empire
Skating Sayers; Lorraine; Medlock & Marlowe; Saveen & "Daisy May";
Aerial Kenways; Jimmie Elliott; MacKenzie Reid & Dorothy.

Mar 24   SUNDERLAND, Empire
The Three Adairs; Lorraine; Saveen & "Daisy May"; Voltaire; The Kenways;
Jimmie Elliott; MacKenzie Reid & Dorothy.

Mar 31   HANLEY, Royal
Shane Sisters; Jackley & Jee; Aerial Kenways; Saveen & "Daisy May";
Jackley & Jee; Jimmie Elliott; Reggie Redcliffe.

Apr 7   LEEDS, Empire
Clayton & Ward; Lorraine; Aerial Kenways; Saveen & "Daisy May"; Voltaire;
Jimmie Elliott; Irving & Girdwood.
[Kenneth Henry replaced George Pugh as assistant in Laurel & Hardy's sketch.]

Apr 14   NOTTINGHAM, Empire
Avril & Irene; Lorraine; Lou Folds; Saveen & "Daisy May"; Aerial Kenways;
Skating Websters; Jimmie Elliott; MacKenzie Reid & Dorothy.

Apr 21   SHREWSBURY, Granada
The Three Adairs; Lorraine; Aerial Kenways; Saveen & "Daisy May";
Newman Twins; Jimmie Elliott; MacKenzie Reid & Dorothy.

Apr 28   EDINBURGH, Empire
Merle & Marie; Lorraine; Aerial Kenways; Saveen & "Daisy May";
Newman Twins; Skating Sayers; Jimmie Elliott; MacKenzie Reid & Dorothy.

PROGRAMME BILLS – 1952

ROUTES — 1952 Tour – part 1

1) SOUTHAMPTON
2) LONDON
3) PETERBOROUGH
3a) Grantham
4) GLASGOW
5) NEWCASTLE
5a) Tynemouth
5b) North Shields
6) SUNDERLAND
5a) Tynemouth
7) HANLEY
8) LEEDS
9) NOTTINGHAM
9a) Bottesford
10) SHREWSBURY
11) EDINBURGH

PROGRAMME BILLS – 1952

May 5   BIRMINGHAM, Hippodrome
Clayton & Ward; Lorraine; Aerial Kenways; Saveen & "Daisy May";
Newman Twins; Jack Melville; Jimmie Elliott; MacKenzie Reid & Dorothy.

May 12   SOUTHAMPTON, Gaumont
Lonsdale Sisters; Lorraine; Aerial Kenways; Saveen & "Daisy May";
The Great Cingalee; Newman Twins; MacKenzie Reid & Dorothy.

May 19   LIVERPOOL, Empire
Lonsdale Sisters; Lorraine; Aerial Kenways; Saveen & "Daisy May";
The Great Cingalee; Jimmie Elliott; MacKenzie Reid & Dorothy.
(George Pugh replaced Kenneth Henry in Laurel & Hardy's sketch).

May 27   (2 weeks)   DUBLIN, Olympia
Lonsdale Sisters; Lorraine; Aerial Kenways; Archie Elray & Co;
The Great Cingalee; Jimmie Elliott; MacKenzie Reid & Dorothy.

Jun 9   (2 weeks)   BELFAST, Grand Opera House
Lonsdale Sisters; Lorraine; Archie Elray & Co; Aerial Kenways;
The Great Cingalee; Jimmie Elliott; MacKenzie Reid & Dorothy.

Jun 30   SHEFFIELD, Empire
Lonsdale Sisters; Lorraine; Aerial Kenways; Archie Elray & Co;
The Great Cingalee; Jimmie Elliott; MacKenzie Reid & Dorothy.

Jul 7   BRIGHTON, Hippodrome
Les Valettos; Lorraine; Aerial Kenways; Joan Turner; Voltaire; Jimmie Elliott;
MacKenzie Reid & Dorothy.

Jul 14   MANCHESTER, Palace
Ray & Madge Lamar; Lorraine; Aerial Kenways; Archie Elray & Co; The Four
Fredianis; Pepino's Miniature Circus; Jimmie Elliott; MacKenzie Reid & Dorothy.

Jul 21   RHYL, Queens
Lonsdale Sisters; Lorraine; Aerial Kenways; Archie Elray & Co;
The Great Cingalee; Jimmie Elliott; MacKenzie Reid & Dorothy.

Jul 28   BRADFORD, Alhambra
Lonsdale Sisters; Lorraine; Aerial Kenways; Harry Worth; The Great Cingalee;
Jimmie Elliott; MacKenzie Reid & Dorothy.

PROGRAMME BILLS – 1952

ROUTES — 1952 Tour – part 2

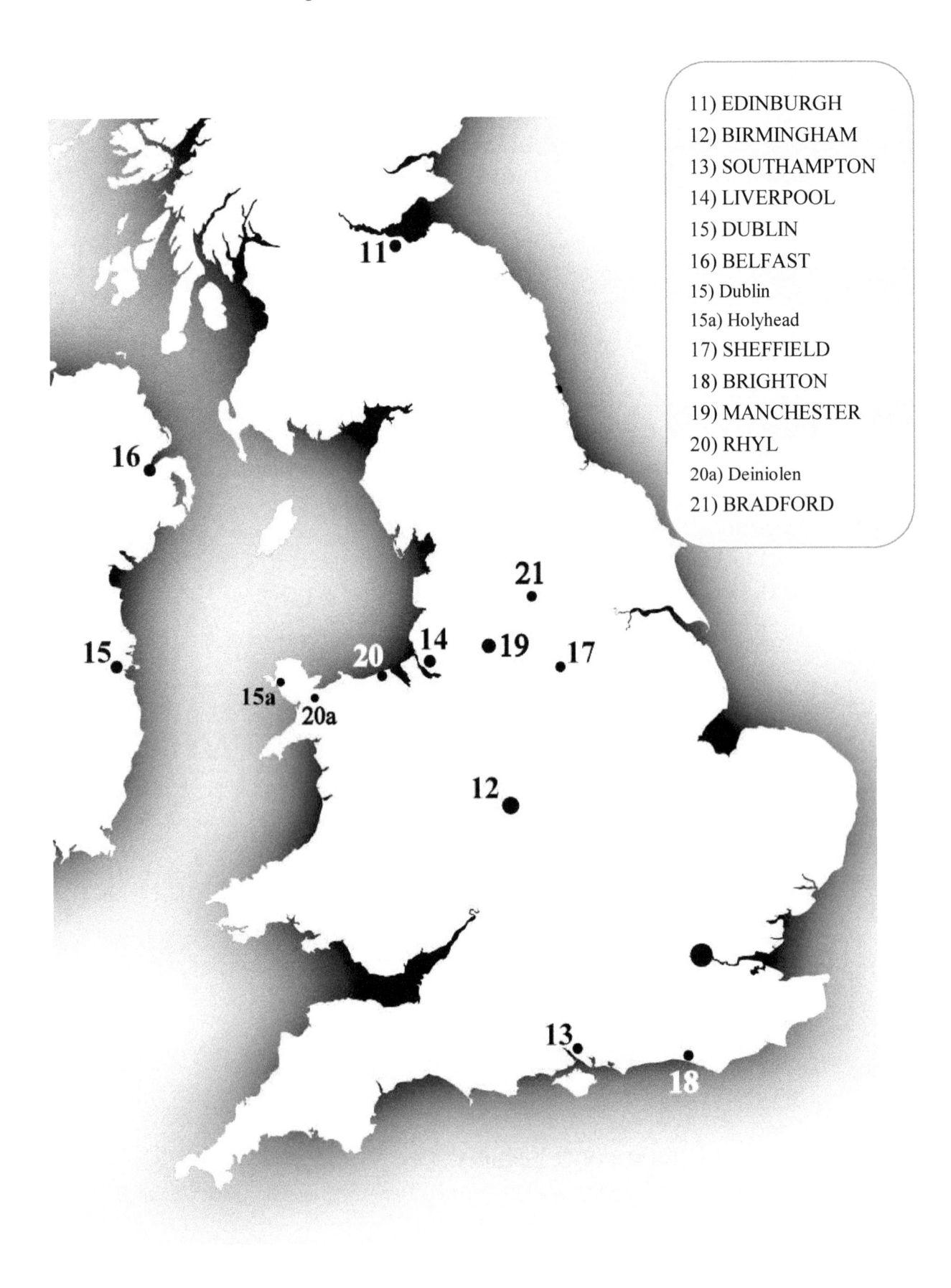

11) EDINBURGH
12) BIRMINGHAM
13) SOUTHAMPTON
14) LIVERPOOL
15) DUBLIN
16) BELFAST
15) Dublin
15a) Holyhead
17) SHEFFIELD
18) BRIGHTON
19) MANCHESTER
20) RHYL
20a) Deiniolen
21) BRADFORD

PROGRAMME BILLS – 1952

ROUTES — 1952 Tour – part 3

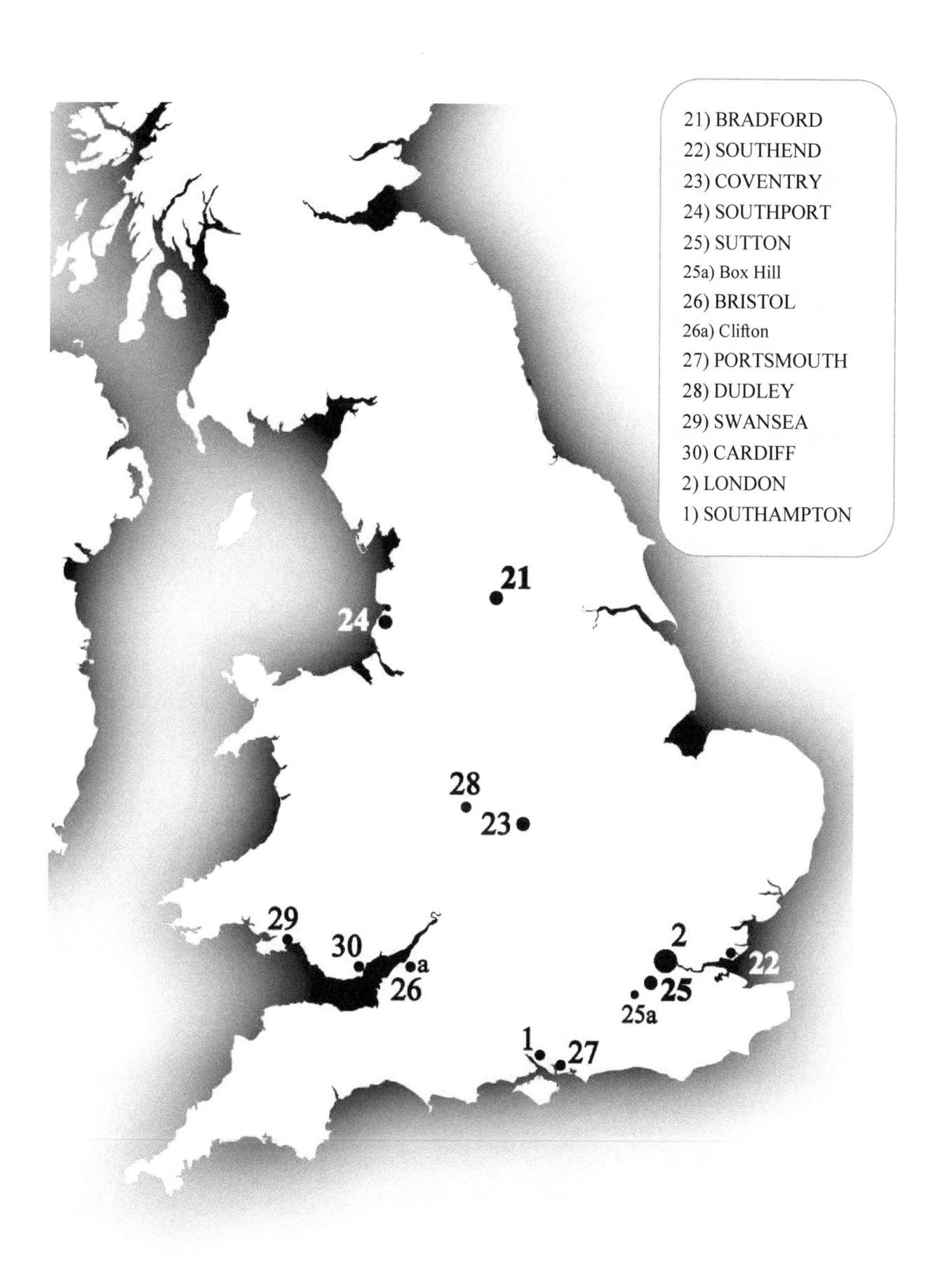

21) BRADFORD
22) SOUTHEND
23) COVENTRY
24) SOUTHPORT
25) SUTTON
25a) Box Hill
26) BRISTOL
26a) Clifton
27) PORTSMOUTH
28) DUDLEY
29) SWANSEA
30) CARDIFF
2) LONDON
1) SOUTHAMPTON

PROGRAMME BILLS – 1952

Aug 4 SOUTHEND, Odeon
Lonsdale Sisters; Lorraine; Aerial Kenways; Archie Elray & Co;
The Great Cingalee; Jimmie Elliott; MacKenzie Reid & Dorothy.

Aug 11 COVENTRY, Hippodrome
Lonsdale Sisters; Lorraine; Aerial Kenways; Harry Worth; The Great Cingalee;
Jimmie Elliott; MacKenzie Reid & Dorothy.

Aug 18 SOUTHPORT, Garrick
Lonsdale Sisters; Lorraine; Aerial Kenways; Archie Elray & Co;
The Great Cingalee; Jimmie Elliott; MacKenzie Reid & Dorothy.

Aug 25 SUTTON, Granada
Lonsdale Sisters; Lorraine; Aerial Kenways; Archie Elray & Co;
The Great Cingalee; Jimmie Elliott; MacKenzie Reid & Dorothy.

Sep 1 BRISTOL, Hippodrome
Lonsdale Sisters; Lorraine; Aerial Kenways; Archie Elray & Co;
The Great Cingalee; Jimmie Elliott; MacKenzie Reid & Dorothy.

Sep 5 (1 night) BRISTOL, Grand Spa Hotel (charity show)
Western Brothers; Fayne & Evans; Len Marten; Fred Ferrari; Ken Morris.

Sep 8 PORTSMOUTH, Theatre Royal
Lonsdale Sisters; Lorraine; Aerial Kenways; Harry Worth; The Great Cingalee;
Jimmie Elliott; MacKenzie Reid & Dorothy.

Sep 15 DUDLEY, Hippodrome
Lonsdale Sisters; Lorraine; Archie Elray & Co; The Great Cingalee;
Jimmie Elliott; MacKenzie Reid & Dorothy.

Sep 22 SWANSEA, Empire
Lonsdale Sisters; Lorraine; Aerial Kenways; Archie Elray & Co;
The Great Cingalee; Jimmie Elliott; MacKenzie Reid & Dorothy.

Sep 29 CARDIFF, New Theatre
Lonsdale Sisters; Lorraine; Aerial Kenways; Archie Elray & Co;
The Great Cingalee; Jimmie Elliott; MacKenzie Reid & Dorothy.

o-o-0-o-o

Assistants in Laurel & Hardy's sketch were Leslie Spurling and Kenneth Henry.
(Unless otherwise stated).
Laurel & Hardy's act was last on the bill.

o-o-0-o-o

PROGRAMME BILLS – 1953-54

1953

Oct 11   (1 night)   DUBLIN, Olympia [Charity performance]

Billy Banks; Anne Jamison; Paddie Crosbie; Freddie Doyle; Elizabeth Carroll; Neil Phelan; Eddie Lambert; Capitol Theatre Dancers.

Oct 19   NORTHAMPTON, New Theatre

Jill, Jill & Jill; Freddie Harris & Christine; Ursula & Gus; Fred Lovelle; Krista & Kristel; Keefe Bros. and Annette; Roy & Ray.

(Laurel & Hardy assisted by: Gordon Craig; Gerald Lennan; Bernard Newson)

Oct 26   LIVERPOOL, Empire

Jill, Jill & Jill; Derek Rosaire & Tony - the Wonder Horse; Mundy & Earle; Ursula & Gus; Ronnie Leslie; Seaton & O'Dell; Roy & Ray; Betty Kaye's Pekinese.

(Laurel & Hardy assisted by: Gordon Craig; Gerald Lennan; Reginald Newson)

Nov 2   ARDWICK GREEN (Manchester), Hippodrome

Jill, Jill and Jill; Ronnie Leslie; Ursula & Gus; Fred Lovelle; Derek Rosaire & Tony - the Wonder Horse; Betty Kaye's Pekinese; Roy & Ray; Laurel & Hardy closed the show. (Assisted by: Gordon Craig; Gerald Lennan; Bernard Newson).

Nov 9   FINSBURY PARK (London), Empire

Jill, Jill & Jill; Seaton & O'Dell; Ronnie Leslie; Ursula & Gus; Bobbie Kimber; Derek Rosaire & Tony - the Wonder Horse; Betty Kaye's Pekinese; Roy & Ray; [Jewel & Warriss replaced Laurel & Hardy.]

Nov 16   BRIXTON (London), Empress

Jill Jill & Jill; Bobbie Kimber; Newman Twins; Ursula & Gus; Keefe Bros & Annette; Freddie Harris & Christine; Roy & Ray.

(Assisted by: Gordon Craig; Gerald Lennan; Bernard Newson).

Nov 23   NEWCASTLE, Empire

Jill, Jill & Jill; Fe Jover and Jack; Freddie Harris & Christine; Ursula & Gus; Ray Alan & 'Steve'; Derek Rosaire and Tony - the Wonder Horse; Roy & Ray; Betty Kaye's Pekinese.

(Laurel & Hardy assisted by: Gordon Craig; Leslie Spurling; Reginald Newson).

Nov 30   BIRMINGHAM, Hippodrome

Jill, Jill & Jill; Fe Jover & Jack; Freddie Harris & Christine; Ursula & Gus; Paul & Peta Page; Derek Rosaire & Tony - the Wonder Horse; Roy & Ray; Betty Kaye's Pekinese.

(Laurel & Hardy assisted by: Gordon Craig; Leslie Spurling; John Sullivan).

PROGRAMME BILLS – 1953-54

ROUTES — 1953-54 – part 1

1) COBH
1a) CORK
2) DUBLIN
2a) Dun Laoghaire
2b) Holyhead
3) LONDON
4) NORTHAMPTON
5) LIVERPOOL
6) ARDWICK GREEN
[3] FINSBURY PARK]
3a) BRIXTON

PROGRAMME BILLS – 1953-54

ROUTES — 1953-54 – part 2

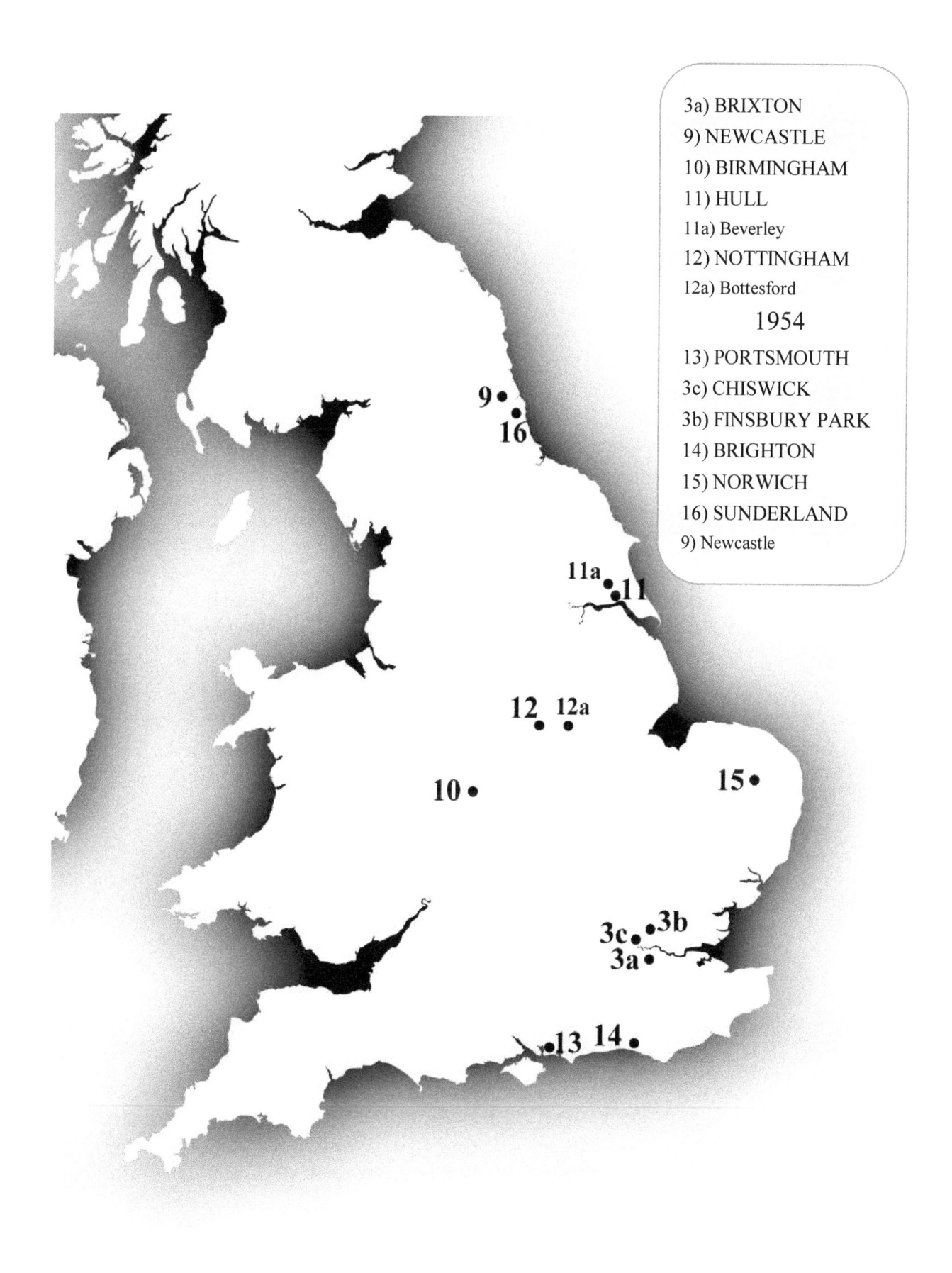

3a) BRIXTON
9) NEWCASTLE
10) BIRMINGHAM
11) HULL
11a) Beverley
12) NOTTINGHAM
12a) Bottesford

1954

13) PORTSMOUTH
3c) CHISWICK
3b) FINSBURY PARK
14) BRIGHTON
15) NORWICH
16) SUNDERLAND
9) Newcastle

PROGRAMME BILLS – 1953-54

Dec 7   HULL, Palace
Candy Sisters & Eddie; Freddie Harris & Christine; Nicol & Kemble;
Fred Lovelle; Ursula & Gus; Roy & Ray; Betty Kaye's Pekinese.
(Laurel & Hardy assisted by: Gordon Craig; Leslie Spurling; John Sullivan).

Dec 14   week off (rehearsals)

Dec 21   (4 weeks)   NOTTINGHAM, Empire
Jill, Jill & Jill; Bob Bemand's Pigeons; Ursula & Gus; Roy & Ray;
Laurel & Hardy – Birds of a Feather; Betty Kaye's Pekinese,
Derek Rosaire & Tony the Wonder Horse; Harry Worth; Roy & Ray.
Stan & Ollie's Christmas Party.

1954

Jan 18   PORTSMOUTH, Royal
Jill, Jill & Jill; Alan Rowe; Ursula & Gus; Harry Worth; Derek Rosaire & Tony -
the Wonder Horse; Paul Arland; Roy & Ray; Betty Kaye's Pekinese.
(Laurel & Hardy assisted by Gordon Craig; Leslie Spurling; John Sullivan).

Jan 25   CHISWICK (London), Empire
Jill, Jill & Jill; Alan Rowe; Ursula & Gus; Harry Worth; Derek Rosaire & Tony -
the Wonder Horse; Paul Arland; Roy & Ray; Betty Kaye's Pekinese.
(Laurel & Hardy assisted by: Gordon Craig; Leslie Spurling; John Sullivan).

Feb 1   FINSBURY PARK (London), Empire
Charmony Three; Alan Rowe; Newman Twins; Arthur Worsley;
Victor Julian & Pets; Nick & Pat Lundon; Paul Arland; Krandon & Karna.
(Laurel & Hardy assisted by: Gordon Craig; Leslie Spurling; John Sullivan).

Feb 8   BRIGHTON, Hippodrome
Lorraine; Ursula & Gus; Harry Worth; Derek Rosaire & Tony - the Wonder
Horse; Paul Arland; Roy & Ray; Betty Kaye's Pekinese.

Feb 15   NORWICH, Hippodrome
Jill, Jill & Jill; Lorraine; Ursula & Gus; Harry Worth; Derek Rosaire & Tony - the
Wonder Horse; Paul Arland; Roy & Ray; Betty Kaye's Pekinese.
(Laurel & Hardy assisted by: Gordon Craig; Leslie Spurling; John Sullivan).

Feb 22   SUNDERLAND, Empire
Jill, Jill & Jill; Alan Rowe; Ursula & Gus; Harry Worth; Derek Rosaire & Tony -
the Wonder Horse; Paul Arland; Roy & Ray; Betty Kaye's Pekinese.

PROGRAMME BILLS – 1953-54

FINSBURY PARK MOSS' Empire THEATRE

Proprietors: MOSS' EMPIRES, Ltd.
Chairman: PRINCE LITTLER
Managing Director: VAL PARNELL
Telephone: CANONBURY 2248
Manager: DAVID W. WILMOT

6.25 ★ MONDAY, FEBRUARY 1st ★ 8.40
TWICE NIGHTLY

HOLLYWOOD'S GREATEST COMEDY COUPLE!

HERE IN PERSON

STAN **LAUREL AND HARDY** OLIVER

BERNARD DELFONT presents

IN A NEW COMEDY "BIRDS OF A FEATHER"

| ARTHUR WORSLEY — IT'S IN THE BAG | ALAN ROWE — BORN TO IMPRESS / NEWMAN TWINS — Feats of Strength | KRANDON & KARNA — ART IN THE BALANCE / PAUL ARLAND AND HIS WONDER FISH — THE MERRY ANGLER | NICK & PAT LUNDON — DANCE TEAM / CHARMONY THREE — Glamour in Harmony | VICTOR JULIAN AND HIS PETS |

Note that the support acts are not the regular ones from the Laurel and Hardy show, as they had played the Finsbury Park Empire back in November 1953, when Laurel and Hardy cancelled owing to Stan having the flu.

PROGRAMME BILLS – 1953-54

PROGRAMME BILLS – 1953-54

PROGRAMME BILLS – 1953-54

Mar 1   GLASGOW, Empire

Jill Jill & Jill; Alan Rowe; Ursula & Gus; Harry Worth; Derek Rosaire & Tony - the Wonder Horse; Paul Arland; Roy & Ray; Betty Kaye's Pekinese.

(Laurel & Hardy assisted by: Gordon Craig; Leslie Spurling; John Sullivan).

Mar 8   WOLVERHAMPTON, Hippodrome

Jill, Jill & Jill; Alan Rowe; Audrey Jeans; Harry Worth; Derek Rosaire & Tony - the Wonder Horse; Paul Arland; Roy & Ray; Betty Kaye's Pekinese.

Mar 15   SHEFFIELD, Empire

Jill Jill & Jill; Alan Rowe; Ursula & Gus; Harry Worth; Derek Rosaire & Tony - the Wonder Horse; Keefe Bros & Annette; Roy & Ray; Betty Kaye's Pekinese.

Mar 22   YORK, Empire

Jill, Jill & Jill; Alan Rowe; Ursula & Gus; Peter Raynor; Derek Rosaire & Tony - the Wonder Horse; Keefe Bros & Annette; Roy & Ray; Betty Kaye's Pekinese.

Mar 29   GRIMSBY, Palace

Jill, Jill & Jill; Alan Rowe; Ursula & Gus; Nicol & Kemble; Derek Rosaire & Tony - the Wonder Horse; Keefe Bros & Annette; Roy & Ray; Betty Kaye's Pekinese.

(Laurel & Hardy assisted by: Gordon Craig; Leslie Spurling; John Sullivan).

Apr 5   LEEDS, Empire

Jill, Jill & Jill; Alan Rowe; Ursula & Gus; Bobbie Kimber; Derek Rosaire & Tony - the Wonder Horse; Peggy Cavell; Roy & Ray; Betty Kaye's Pekinese.

Apr 12   EDINBURGH, Empire

Jill, Jill & Jill; Alan Rowe; Ursula & Gus; Bobbie Kimber; Derek Rosaire & Tony - the Wonder Horse; Dunn & Grant; Dorothy Reid & Mack; Betty Kaye's Pekinese.

(Laurel & Hardy assisted by: Gordon Craig; Leslie Spurling; John Sullivan).

Apr 19   CARLISLE, Her Majesty's

Jill, Jill & Jill; Jimmie Elliot; Ursula & Gus; Bobbie Kimber; Derek Rosaire & Tony - the Wonder Horse; Lorraine; Dorothy Reid & Mack; Betty Kaye's Pekinese.

Apr 26   (week off)

PROGRAMME BILLS – 1953-54

ROUTES — 1953-54 – part 3

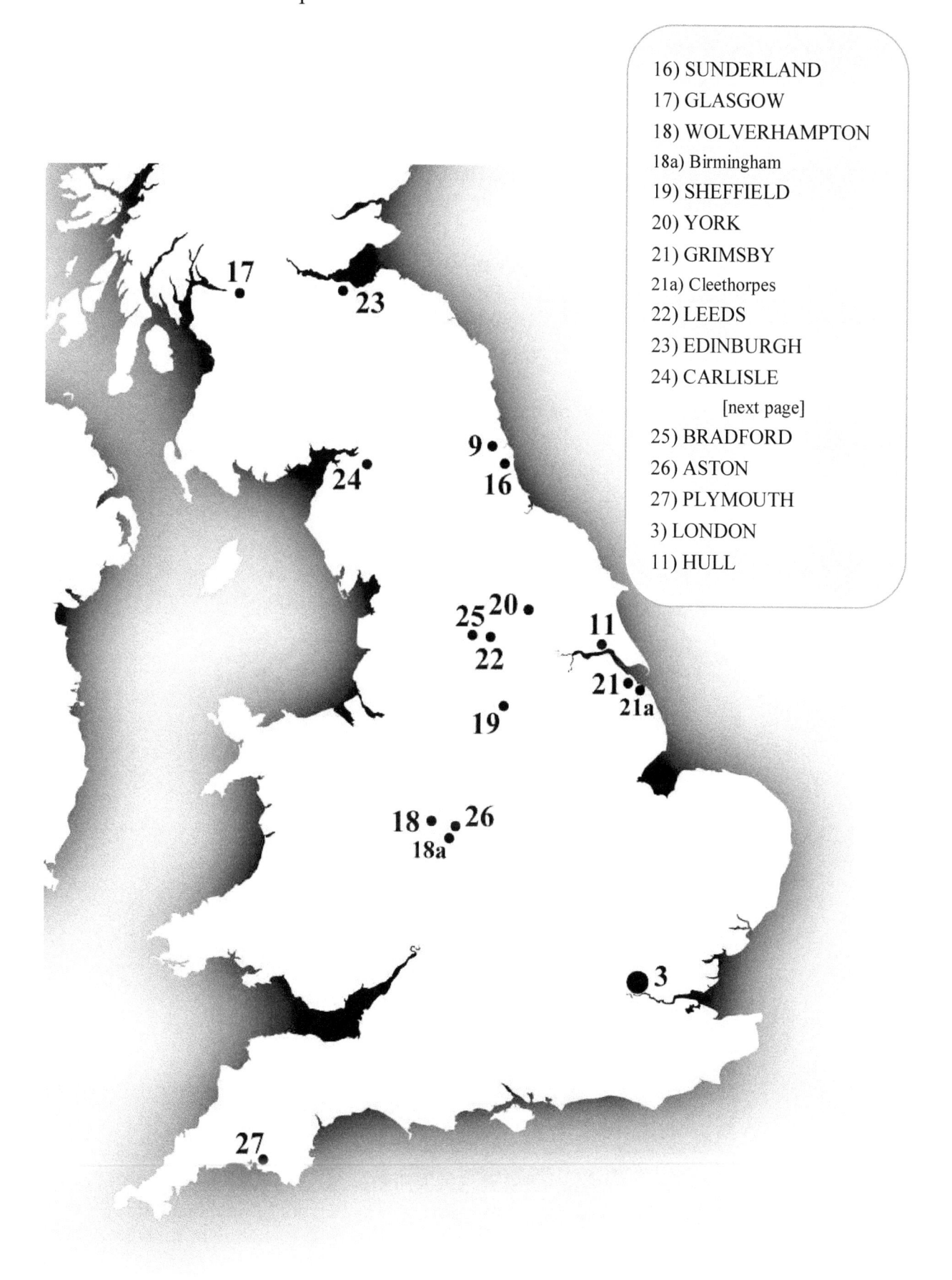

16) SUNDERLAND
17) GLASGOW
18) WOLVERHAMPTON
18a) Birmingham
19) SHEFFIELD
20) YORK
21) GRIMSBY
21a) Cleethorpes
22) LEEDS
23) EDINBURGH
24) CARLISLE
   [next page]
25) BRADFORD
26) ASTON
27) PLYMOUTH
3) LONDON
11) HULL

PROGRAMME BILLS – 1953-54

May 3   BRADFORD, Alhambra

Conway & Day; Alan Rowe; The Skylons; Harry Worth; Derek Rosaire & Tony - the Wonder Horse; Peggy Cavell; Dorothy Reid & Mack; Betty Kaye's Pekinese.

(Laurel & Hardy assisted by: Gordon Craig; Leslie Spurling; John Sullivan).

May 10   ASTON (Birmingham), Hippodrome

Mary & Michael Mills; Alan Rowe; Harry Worth; Derek Rosaire & Tony - the Wonder Horse; Trio Botando; Dorothy Reid & Mack; Betty Kaye's Pekinese.

May 17   PLYMOUTH, Palace

Shane & Lamar; Alan Rowe; Trio Botando; Harry Worth; Derek Rosaire & Tony - the Wonder Horse; Lorraine; Dorothy Reid & Mack; Betty Kaye's Pekinese.

[Mary & Michael Mills were replaced by Shane & Lamar. Peggy Cavell was billed, but did not appear.]

(Laurel & Hardy appeared on the first night only. Joe Church finished the week.)

May 24   Empire, SWANSEA — cancelled.

o-o-0-o-o

"Birds of a Feather" was the penultimate act - unless otherwise stated.
Manager and Stage Director — JACK WHITMORE
Stage Manager and Property Manager — JOHN BARON

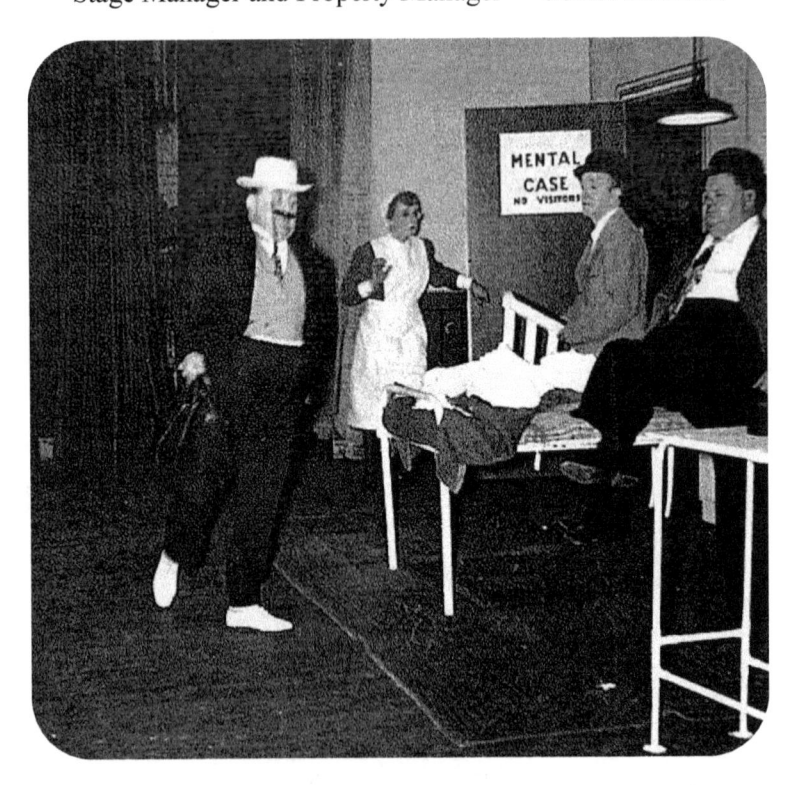

Beginning week 6 (Newcastle Empire) LESLIE SPURLING – who had appeared as the 'cop' in the 1952 tour sketch – joined the Company, in the role of 'Dr. Berserk.' It is thought that he also took over the position of Stage Manager and Property Manager, at the expense of John Baron.

o-o-0-o-o

GALLERY

A FUR CATCH —Lucille and Ida in their best fur stoles, and the Boys suited and booted, waiting to be seated in the dining room of the *Queen Mary*. [New York – 23 January 1952]

Porters were employed to keep fans at bay, when Laurel and Hardy got off the boat train at Waterloo Station, London, which left the way clear for them to get their autographs.
(28 January 1952) [see page 6]

Gallery 1952-54

Hardy tries to make Laurel laugh by doing his trademark tie-wiggle, but Stan has seen it all too many times before. (Central Hotel, Glasgow – 10 March 1952) [see page 25]

You can lead a horse to water, but this picture must be Leeds.
(7 April 1952) [see page 36].

Gallery 1952-54

Prize-giving at the Saturday Children's Matinee, showing the obvious love that both Hardy and Laurel had for children. Dudley Hippodrome (20 September 1952) [see page 74]
(With thanks to Jock M. Whitehouse – pictured back, left)

Comedian Roy Lester gets to meet his idols, during a visit to his fiancée, Pauline Banks — one of the Lonsdale Sisters. (1952 tour) [see page 77]
[With thanks to Syd Francis].

Gallery 1952-54

Signed by Norman Wisdom, to the author: "I was proud to meet them both."
(Backstage Prince of Wales Theatre – 6 October 1952) [see page 78]

Bolton Town Hall Theatre, with my comedy hero, Norman Wisdom: and the late, great Ray 'Ollie' Saunders.' "I was proud to be friends with both." (Author's collection)

Gallery 1952-54

The Lord Mayor of Cork – Patrick McGrath, takes the visiting VIPs to Cobh City Hall, to sign the visitors book. (I just hope there wasn't an inkwell next to it). [see page 89]

IT TICKLES

Selling beer by the bucket
Bull Inn, Bottesford — Christmas Day 1953 [see page 116]

Gallery 1952-54

Mystery Photo: Thought to have been taken on New Year's Eve 1953 (not confirmed).
This would most likely place it at the County Hotel, Nottingham. [Courtesy of Ron Roper]

URSULA & GUS – Continental Jugglers
who appeared on all but four shows during the 1952 tour.
[No! they didn't juggle with the little boy.]

Gallery 1952-54

Hardy's 62nd birthday party, attended by all the Company. 18 January 1954 [see page 118]

1 Roy 2 Ray 3 John Sullivan (?) 4 Gus 5 Leslie Spurling 6 Alan Rowe 7 Harry Worth
8 unknown 9 Paul Arland 10 Jill 11 Betty Kaye 12 Gordon Craig 13 Derek Rosaire
14 Jack Whitmore (Tour Manager) 15 Mrs. Spurling 16 Ida Laurel 17 Ursula 18 Jill 19. Jill
20 21 22 Derek & Betty Rosaire's girls 23 Stan Laurel 24 Lucille Hardy 25 Oliver Hardy.

N.B: 3) John Sullivan 5) Leslie Spurling, and 12 Gordon Craig – played the undertaker, the doctor, and the nurse, respectively in the *Birds of a Feather* sketch. The lady at 8) may be Paul Arland's assistant in his act.

AUTOGRAPHS

Top left: Classic 'Double Derby' pose – by Roach photographer STAX – 1927.
Top right: photo taken circa 1932, but used at the start 1947 tour.
Left and right: Taken at the start of the 1947 tour. Also used in 1952. Reprinted a few times – once with role reversal.
Below: *Air Raid Wardens* portrait. The most-commonly used on the 1947 Tour.

196

AUTOGRAPHS

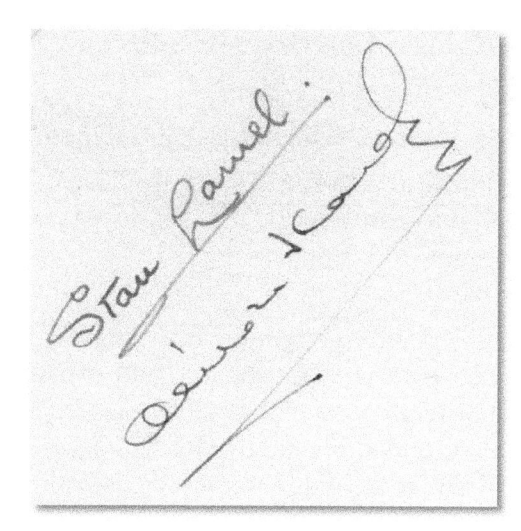

Top left: a typical autograph book signed page.
Top right: signed page with the addition of a sticker, from an original cartoon by Harry Langdon.
Left: Handout from the 1952 Tour. (See story on page 26).
Also used on the 53-4 tour

To demonstrate just how dedicated Stan and Babe were, when it came to catering for their fans, here they are licking, sticking, and filling HUNDREDS of envelopes containing signed photos.

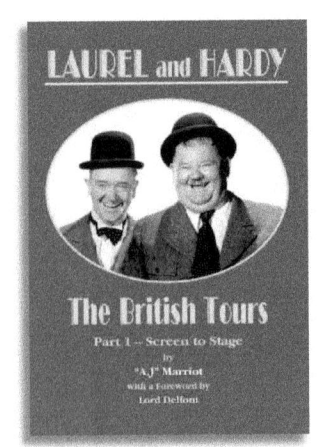

The Author

LAUREL & HARDY – The British Tours
Part 1 – Screen to Stage [1926 to 1951]

Second Edition – Extensively revised, reformatted and expanded

The story starts where our comedy heros meet up at the Hal Roach Studios, and become an inseparable partnership. We then fast forward to the promotional tour of major cities in England and Scotland, which they undertook in the summer of 1932.

Fast forward again to their 1947 British stage tour, for which readers are given a full account of every theatre engagement and every act they worked with; their travel arrangements; the hotels they stayed in; the people they met; previously undocumented public appearances. and descriptions of the crowds of thousands who mobbed them and left them reeling from the onslaught.

Second Edition. 210 pages. Lavishly illustrated — Softback — A4 [297mm x 210mm]
(ISBN 978-0-9521308-8-8) — Available via lulu.com

-----0-----

LAUREL and HARDY – The U.S. Tours

Second Edition – Extensively revised, reformatted. and expanded

After the two comedians meet at the Hal Roach Studios, the story takes an unexpected route. Instead of following them through the making of their films, we are led into a parallel world of public appearances, show business events, theatre tours, wartime fund raising tours, and troop shows. Revealed for the first time ever are details of three major U.S. city-to-city stage tours; numerous trips from the West to the East coast; three junkets to Mexico; and even a tour of Caribbean islands. On their travels, Laurel and Hardy meet a whole constellation of Hollywood stars; befriend a future President; and are invited to the White House. Stan and Babe emerge as warm and lovable, but vulnerable, men – and the reader will experience their every highlight and emotion throughout their long partnership.

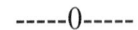

Second Edition. 334 pages. Lavishly illustrated. Softback – A4 [297mm x 210mm]
(ISBN 978-0-9521308-6-4) — Available via lulu.com

-----0-----

LAUREL and HARDY – The European Tours

"The European Tours" details not only the 1947-48 stage tours Laurel and Hardy played around Denmark, Sweden, France, and Belgium, but the year the two Hollywood comedians spent in France, during the making of their 1950-51 film *Atoll K*. Included in this is a promotional visit to Italy; plus details of two earlier visits to France — one by Laurel in 1927, and one by both comedians in 1932.

Readers will get to see the real men behind the screen characters of "Stan and Ollie" — how they coped with being mobbed everywhere they went; the exhaustion of a life of touring; and how they both worked on through serious illness to complete their last film.

From it all, Stan Laurel and Oliver Hardy emerge as lovable, but vulnerable, men – and readers will experience their every emotion throughout these previously undocumented tours.

Second Print. 128 pages – 200 illustrations. Softback – A4 [297mm x 210mm]
(ISBN 978-0-9521308-4-0) — Available via lulu.com

The Author

LAUREL – Stage by Stage

"LAUREL - Stage by Stage" is the prequel to Marriots previous Laurel and Hardy's "Tours" books; and is a companion to "CHAPLIN – Stage by Stage."

It narrates for the first-time-ever all of Stan Laurel's stage shows, from his earliest appearances in British pantomime (as the teenage Stanley Jefferson), right up to his last-ever stage show before entering films.

Along the way he spends over three years touring with Charlie Chaplin, in the most-famous of all comedy troupes – the Fred Karno Company.

The next eight years are spent touring in U.S. vaudeville, playing in song-dance-and-comedy sketch acts with various partners.

Readers will experience every low and high as this comic genius tries to unshackle himself from the hardship and tedium of vaudeville, during a number of attempts to get into the world of film comedy. The amount of detail revealed about these "lost" tours is astounding.

272 pages – 200 illustrations. Softback – A4 [297mm x 210mm]

Second print (ISBN 978-1-78972-555-1) — Available via lulu.com

-----0-----

CHAPLIN – Stage by Stage

Contains every known stage appearance Chaplin made in the UK and, for the first time ever, the ones he made in Vaudeville, touring America with the Fred Karno Company of Comedians.

Along the way, many myths and mistakes from other works on Chaplin will be corrected, and many lies and legends exposed. But, in destroying the negative, a positive picture is built up of the very medium which created the man and the screen character "Chaplin."

Includes extracts from the scripts of the plays and sketches in which Chaplin appeared, complemented by reviews and plot descriptions, all of which help to complete the picture of the influences which affected Chaplin's later film work. Read and be Amazed!

[Although it is a companion to "LAUREL – Stage by Stage" it contains far more text relating to Chaplin, plus numerous different and previously unpublished photos of him.]

Chaplin Stage by Stage *provides a unique and indispensable record of Chaplin's career on the British stage and music hall and in American vaudeville in the formative fifteen years before he entered films. Marriot's phenomenal research gives us an exhaustive chronicle of Charlie's stage appearances – in addition to those of his father and his brother Sydney.* — [DAVID ROBINSON – Chaplin biographer.]

258 pages – 130 illustrations. Paperback – A4 [297mm x 210mm]

Second print (ISBN 978-1-78972-556-8) — Available via lulu.com

-----0-----

Have you bought your copies yet?

A sincere "Thank You" to those who have.

"A.J" Marriot

For information on the First Editions, and how to purchase, go to the author's website:

www.laurelandhardybooks.com

OR e-mail: ajmarriot@aol.com for any enquiries.

o-o-0-o-o

The Author

"A.J" MARRIOT

In 1993, after twenty years as a stand-up comedian, including twelve seasons as a Holiday Camp entertainer, "A.J" Marriot turned his hand to writing. His first book, *LAUREL & HARDY – The British Tours*, has sold in over forty-five countries, and is still much sought after. His second, *CHAPLIN – Stage by Stage*, was acclaimed by biographers and critics alike as being the definitive account of Chaplin's pre-film days. Next came *The Lighter Side of LAUREL & HARDY*, which sold out seven print runs. In December 2011 readers were thrilled to receive the companion to "The British Tours" – namely: *LAUREL and HARDY – The U.S. Tours*, which again bears Marriot's hallmarks of unparalleled research, wit, and warmth towards his subjects.

Between 2001 and 2016 "A.J" was Editor and Features Writer of the *Laurel & Hardy Magazine*, which has the largest circulation of the many Laurel & Hardy fanzines, worldwide.

2014 brought us a second companion to "The British Tours" – *LAUREL and HARDY – The European Tours*. And then in 2017 he gave us the complete history of Stan Laurel's stage, music hall, and vaudeville appearances — before meeting up with screen and stage partner Oliver Hardy — in the book *"LAUREL – Stage by Stage."*

And so his quest to record every aspect of Laurel and Hardy's stage careers is complete, and readers can learn hundreds of previously unknown facts about their lives; and discover hundreds of previously unpublished photos. Best of all readers can do what Stan and Babe did, which is to get closer to the real Laurel and Hardy while they are engaged on these tours.

o-o-0-o-o

LAUREL & HARDY – The British Tours [1st Edition]

What they said:

This book is a must for theatregoers weaned on the music halls, as they will revel in the wealth of theatrical detail recorded. (WORDS & MUSIC)

The author's research is staggering, but from it Laurel and Hardy emerge as kind, sensitive men, always ready to spend time with their fans. (GRANTHAM JOURNAL)

Mr Marriot has produced an awesomely researched book which is absolutely unmissable for any Laurel and Hardy devotee. (MOVIE COLLECTOR)

I think you get more of a sense of them as people than from any other of the Laurel and Hardy books. (PEPPER BOOKS – California)

o-o-0-o-o

Lightning Source UK Ltd.
Milton Keynes UK
UKHW051828030120
356281UK00003B/70/P